Communications in Computer and Information Science   797

Commenced Publication in 2007
Founding and Former Series Editors:
Alfredo Cuzzocrea, Xiaoyong Du, Orhun Kara, Ting Liu, Dominik Ślęzak,
and Xiaokang Yang

More information about this series at http://www.springer.com/series/7899

Ilsun You · Fang-Yie Leu
Hsing-Chung Chen · Igor Kotenko (Eds.)

Mobile Internet Security

First International Symposium, MobiSec 2016
Taichung, Taiwan, July 14–15, 2016
Revised Selected Papers

 Springer

Editors
Ilsun You
Department of Information Security
  Engineering
Soonchunhyang University
Chungcheongnam-do
Korea (Republic of)

Fang-Yie Leu
Tunghai University
Taichung
Taiwan

Hsing-Chung Chen
Asia University
Taichung
Taiwan

Igor Kotenko
SPIRAS
St. Petersburg
Russia

ISSN 1865-0929   ISSN 1865-0937 (electronic)
Communications in Computer and Information Science
ISBN 978-981-10-7849-1   ISBN 978-981-10-7850-7   (eBook)
https://doi.org/10.1007/978-981-10-7850-7

Library of Congress Control Number: 2017962911

Printed on acid-free paper

This Springer imprint is published by Springer Nature
The registered company is Springer Nature Singapore Pte Ltd.
The registered company address is: 152 Beach Road, #21-01/04 Gateway East, Singapore 189721, Singapore

Preface

During the past two decades, mobile Internet technologies have been dramatically growing while leading to a paradigm shift in our life. Despite their revolution, mobile Internet technologies have opened the door to various security threats, which should be addressed to keep mobile Internet environments secure and trustworthy. Moreover, the latest technologies (e.g., distributed mobility management, mobile Internet of Things, 5G networks, and so forth) continuously introduce new security challenges. Therefore, it is of paramount importance to study mobile Internet security.

This volume contains revised and selected papers presented at the 2016 International Symposium on Mobile Internet Security held in Taichung, Taiwan, during July 14–15, 2016. The purpose of MobeSec 2016 was to bring together academic and industry professionals working on different aspects to exchange ideas and explore new research directions for addressing the challenges in mobile Internet security. MobeSec also aims to publish high-quality papers that are closely related to various theories and practical applications in mobility management highlighting the state-of-the-art research. In spite of focusing on security aspects, this symposium welcomes papers that are related to mobile Internet technologies. We believe that MobeSec 2016 was a trigger for further research and technology improvements related to this important subject.

MobeSec 2016 provided an international forum for sharing original research results among specialists in fundamental and applied problems of mobile Internet security. The symposium was organized by the SCH Laboratory of Mobile Internet Security and KISM SIGSMC (Smart Media Convergence), and technically supported by KISM SIGSMC in cooperation with Asia University, Tunghai University, and Soonchunhyang University.

A total of 45 papers related to significant aspects of the theory and applications of mobile security were accepted for presentation at MobeSec 2016. Moreover, this symposium was further enriched by the invited talks of Prof. Shain-Shyong Tseng (Vice President of Asia University, Taiwan) and Dr. Joonsang Baek (KUSTAR, UAE). From all the papers, only 15 were selected for publication in this CCIS volume.

The success of the symposium was assured by the team effort of the sponsors, organizers, reviewers, and participants. We would like to acknowledge the contribution of the individual Program Committee members and thank the reviewers. Our sincere gratitude goes to the participants of the conference and all authors of the submitted papers.

We wish to express our gratitude to Springer and in particular Alfred Hofmann and his team for their help and cooperation.

August 2017

Ilsun You
Fang-Yie Leu
Hsing-Chung Chen
Igor Kotenko

Organization

General Co-chairs

Ilsun You   Soonchunhyang University, South Korea
Fang-Yie Leu   Tunghai University, Taiwan

Program Co-chair

Hsing-Chung Chen   Asia University, Taiwan

Publication Chair

Igor Kotenko   SPIRAS, Russia

International Advisory Committee

Pankoo Kim   Chosun University, South Korea
Karl Andersson   Lulea University of Technology, Sweden

Program Committee

Hyobum Ahn   Kongju National University, South Korea
Benjamin Aziz   University of Portsmouth, UK
Cui Baojiang   Beijing University of Posts and Telecommunications,
                          China
Mala Chelliah   National Institute of Technology, India
Andrey Chechulin   Bonch-Bruevich State University of Telecommications,
                          Russia
Chin-Ling Chen   Chaoyang University of Technology, Taiwan
Justin Chen   National Ilan University, Taiwan
Seong-je Cho   Dankook University, South Korea
Junho Choi   Chosun University, South Korea
Chang Choi   Chosun University, South Korea
Yao-Hsin Chou   National Chi-Nan University, Taiwan
Luigi Coppolino   Epsilon Srl., Italy
Salvatore D'Antonio   Università degli Studi di Napoli Parthenope, Italy
Tianhan Gao   Northeastern University, China
Jianfeng Guan   Beijing University of Posts and Telecommunications,
                          China
Nan Guo   Northeastern University, China
Yi-Li Huang   Tunghai University, Taiwan
Yung-Fa Huang   Chaoyang University of Technology, Taiwan

Shinsaku Kiyomoto	KDDI, Japan
Seng-Tarng Lai	Shih-Chien University, Taiwan
Yong-Hwan Lee	Far East University, South Korea
Jae Deok Lim	ETRI, South Korea
Fabio Martinelli	The Institute of Informatics and Telematics, Italy
Alessio Merlo	University of Genoa, Italy
Mauro Migliardi	University of Padua, Italy
Evgenia Novikova	Electrotechnical University LETI, Russia
Vladimir A. Oleshchuk	University of Agder, Norway
Kyung-hyune Rhee	Pukyong National University, South Korea
Roland Rieke	Fraunhofer SIT, Germany
Igor Saenko	Signal Academy, Russia
Kunwar Singh	National Institute of Technology, India
Fei Song	Beijing Jiaotong University, China
Hui-Kai Su	National Formosa University, Taiwan
Kun-Ling Tsai	Tunghai University, Taiwan
Shian-Shyong Tsenga	Asia University, Taiwan
Chien-Erh Weng	National Kaohsiung Marine University, Taiwan
Isaac Woungang	Ryerson University, Canada
Akihiro Yamamura	Akita University, Japan
Cheng-Ying Yang	University of Taipei, Taiwan
Jeong Hyun Yi	Soongsil University, South Korea
Chia-Mu Yu	Yuan Ze University, Taiwan
Baokang Zhao	National University of Defense Technology, China

Contents

Performance on Clustering Routing for Naturally Deployed Wireless Sensor Networks

Yung-Fa Huang[1(✉)], Jyu-Wei Wang[2], John Jenq[3], Hsing-Chung Chen[4(✉)], and Chung-Hsin Hsu[1]

[1] Department of Information and Communication Engineering,
Chaoyang University of Technology, Taichung 41349, Taiwan (R.O.C.)
yfahuang@mail.cyut.edu.tw
[2] Department of Photonics and Communication Engineering, Asia University, Taichung, Taiwan
jwwang@asia.edu.tw
[3] Montclair State University, Montclair, NJ, USA
jenqj@mail.montclair.edu
[4] Department of Computer Science and Information Engineering,
Asia University, Taichung, Taiwan
cdma2000@asia.edu.tw

Abstract. This paper investigates the optimization on the energy efficiency for naturally scattering deployed cluster-based wireless sensor networks (WSNs). The energy efficiency depends on the number of clusters in WSNs where the cluster head (HD) transmitting sensing data received from each sensor in the cluster and dissipate large energy due to the long distance to the sink. Moreover, the nodes deployment would be Gaussian distributed in large area for naturally scattering senior nodes. Thus, in this paper we based on the numerical results in previous works and further simulated the optimization the number of cluster for a large area WSNs.

Keywords: Wireless sensor networks · Energy efficiency · Clustering

1 Introduction

Recently, the rapidly developed technologies of microelectro-mechanical systems and telecommunication battery make the small sensors comprise the capabilities of wireless communication and data processing [1]. These small sensors could be used as the surveillance and the control capability under a certain environment. Specially, the location of wireless sensor network (WSN) could be a region where people could not easily reach and there is a difficulty to recharge the device energy. Therefore, the energy efficiency of the sensor networks is an important research topic and the lifetime of WSNs could be considered as the most significant performance in the WSN [2].

The energy in WSN is mainly consuming on the direct data transmission [2]. Then, to enable communication between sensors not within each other's communication range, the common multi-hop routing protocol is applied in the ad hoc wireless sensors communication networks [3]. However, due the highly complexity in routing protocols

© Springer Nature Singapore Pte Ltd. 2018
I. You et al. (Eds.): MobiSec 2016, CCIS 797, pp. 1–9, 2018.
https://doi.org/10.1007/978-981-10-7850-7_1

and the most likely heavy load on the relaying nodes, this scheme is not suitable for the highly densely WSNs [4, 5].

The cluster-based one is that those closer sensors belong to their own clusters. One of sensors, called cluster head (CH), in each cluster is responsible for delivering data back to the base station. In this scheme, the CH performs data compressing and sending back to the base station. Thus, the lifetime of CH may be shorter than that of other sensors [6, 7] due to the large energy dissipation in performing the long distance data transmission to the sink. Therefore, for WSNs with a large number of energy-constrained sensors, it is very important to design an algorithm to organize sensors in clusters to minimize the energy used to communicate information from all nodes to the base station [8, 9].

The structure of low-energy adaptive clustering hierarchy (LEACH) proposed by [10] is one of the initiate algorithm to balance the energy issues for cluster based WSNs. The optimal number of clusters in a square area for sensor network with a uniform distributed nodes has been analysis in previous works [11]. However, when the sensor networks are outspread a wide area and are naturally scattering deployed. The distribution of nodes would be Gaussian distributed. Then the optimal number of clusters would depend on the different area. Therefore, in this paper we further investigate the energy efficiency for the naturally scattering deployed clustering sensor networks.

2   Network Models

In practical, the geometry of the WSN is non-regular. However, the square is a basic area to be consisted of non-regular area. Thus, for simplification, in this paper we adopt a square area with the length $M = 300$ m. The network parameters are described in Table 1. The sensing area is with Gaussian distributed sensor nodes as shown in Fig. 1. In Fig. 1, the symbol "×" is represented as a location of the sensing node. When the cluster area is of random distributed, the energy efficiency of sensor nodes on data transmitting is terrible [3]. Therefore, the FCA in previous work [11, 12] is proposed to divide the sensor area into clusters and to deploy CHs uniformly over the network area. However, when the sensor networks are outspread a wide area and are naturally scattering deployed. The distribution of nodes would be Gaussian distributed. Then we divide the area to nine sub-areas. An example for nine sub-area clustering network is shown in Fig. 1. Based on the configuration of square area in a sub-area, the sensors are supposed to be spread out uniformly to the whole area. The data from each cluster will be collected by the CH and these data will be sent back to the base station.

Table 1. The network parameter descriptions for cluster based WSNs

Parameters	Descriptions
q	Number of clusters
M	Length of the sensing square area
Q	Number of sensor nodes
α	Radio exponential exponent
Bn	ID of sub-area

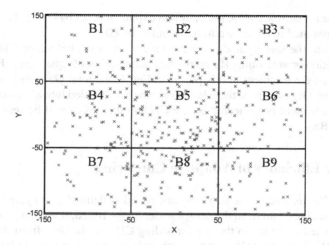

Fig. 1. The sensing area is with Gaussian distributed sensor nodes.

In cluster based WSNs, how to select the CH and further to clustering the sensing area are the most procedures. In a data collection procedure, it is called a round. After the setup state, the LEACH finished two steps of CH election and clustering the area as shown in Fig. 1. In CH election procedure for the rth round, the nodes with a random number, U[0, 1], lower than the threshold,

$$T_n(r) = \frac{p}{1 - p \times \left(r \ \mathrm{mod} \ \dfrac{1}{p}\right)} \qquad n \in G$$
$$T_n(r) = 0 \qquad\qquad n \notin G \tag{1}$$

will be elected as one of the CHs, where p is the expected probability for the CH election, $p = q/Q$ and G is the set of having yet not been elected CH in recent (r mod $1/p$) rounds, $n = 1, 2, ..., Q, Q$ is the total number of nodes in WSN. After the CHs are selected, the clustering is performed by broadcasting the advertisement message in which the CH ID in included. Then, the nodes communicate with the nearest CH by CSMA/CA protocol and send the sensing data to CH. Thus, the clustering procedure is finished.

After clustering procedure, the network is in steady state in which all nodes are in sleep state excepting the communicating nodes. Then, after the data aggregation in CH, the CHs send aggregated data to the base station [13]. Then a round is performed. In wireless communication, the channel models are modeled by

$$P_r = c\frac{P_t}{d^\alpha}, \tag{2}$$

where P_r and P_t are the received power at receiver and the transmitted power at transmitter respectively, c is the propagation coefficient, and α is the path loss exponent,

$2 \leq \alpha < 6$. For a free space area, the path loss exponent is set by $\alpha = 2$. The location of the nodes is assumed to be known to base station by GPS.

In Mac layer, the sensing nodes are assumed to know the belonging CH by centralized based station broadcasting. Based on the configuration of square area, Fig. 1 shows the investigated environment in this paper. In Fig. 1, the total Q sensors are supposed to be spread out Gaussionly to the whole area where is divided into q clusters. The data from each cluster will be collected by the CH and these data will be sent back to the base station (BS).

3   Energy Efficiency of Adaptive Clustering

To evaluate the lifetime of the network, one round is defined as a cycle in which the base station receives data from the sensor node. In one round, it contains the time from the data collected at sensor to the corresponding CH and the time from the CH to the base station. We assume that in each round there is one frame consisted l-bit transmitted by each sensor node. In [8], the energy dissipated in the cluster head node during a single frame can be expressed by

$$E_{CH} = lE_{elec}\left(\frac{Q}{q} - 1\right) + l \cdot E_{DA} \cdot \frac{Q}{q} + lE_{elec} + l\varepsilon_{mp}d_{toBS}^4, \tag{3}$$

where E_{elec} and E_{DA} are the electrical dissipation energy of receiving or transmitting and data aggregation for one bit, respectively. The energy used in each non-cluster head node is expressed by

$$E_{non\text{-}CH} = lE_{elec} + l\varepsilon_{fs}d_{toCH}^2. \tag{4}$$

Because the analysis is based on a sub-area, the density of nodes is assumed to be uniformly throughout the cluster area, then the node density is obtained by

$$\rho = \frac{1}{\frac{M^2}{q}}, \tag{5}$$

where M is the length of the square sensing field. Thus, the distance between the CH and sensor nodes can be obtained by

$$E\left[d_{toCH}^2\right] = \frac{1}{2\pi}\frac{M^2}{q}. \tag{6}$$

Therefore, in this case

$$E_{non\text{-}CH} = lE_{elec} + l\varepsilon_{fs}\frac{1}{2\pi}\frac{M^2}{q}. \tag{7}$$

The energy dissipated in a cluster during the frame

$$E_{\text{cluster}} = E_{\text{CH}} + \left(\frac{Q}{q} - 1\right)E_{\text{non-CH}} \approx E_{\text{CH}} + \frac{Q}{q}E_{\text{non-CH}}. \tag{8}$$

Total consumption energy in one frame in one round for WSNs can be obtained by

$$E_{\text{total}} = qE_{\text{cluster}} = l\left(2E_{elec}Q + E_{DA}Q + q\varepsilon_{mp}d_{toBS}^4 + \varepsilon_{fs}\frac{1}{2\pi}\frac{M^2}{q}Q\right). \tag{9}$$

Therefore, in a sub-area the optimal number of clusters by setting the derivative of E_{total} with respect to q to zero is obtained by

$$q_{\text{opt}} = \frac{\sqrt{Q}}{\sqrt{2\pi}}\sqrt{\frac{\varepsilon_{fs}}{\varepsilon_{mp}}}\frac{M}{d_{toBS}^2}. \tag{10}$$

In this paper, to match the assumption of that the sensor nodes are randomly distributed in the clustering area, the sensor networks are divided to nine sub-areas. That is we assumed that the standard deviation of Gaussian distribution for nodes deploying is known. Then we can estimated the number of nodes in each sub-area. The optimal number of clusters for each sub-area can be obtained by (10). By (10), the optimal number of cluster for different areas and different number of nodes can be depicted in Fig. 2.

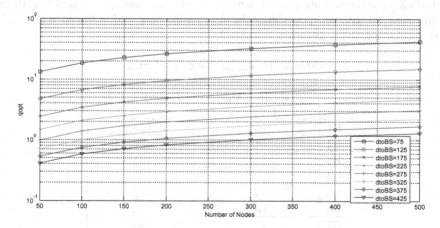

Fig. 2. The optimal number of cluster for different areas and different number of nodes.

4   Simulation Results

In order to verify and compare the optimal energy efficiency for the energy model described in Sect. 3, computer simulation is performed in MATLAB programming. In our simulation, the total number of sensors nodes is one hundred, $Q = 500$. Then, the normal sensor nodes are 500-q. The length of sensing square area is set $M = 300$ m. To be generalized, we assume that the data aggregation is perfect, i.e. each CH sends out one frame in each round. The simulation parameters are depicted in Table 2.

Table 2. The simulation parameters

Simulation parameters	
Electrical energy	$E_{elec} = 50$ nJ/bit
Energy for data aggregation	$E_{DA} = 5$ nJ/bit/signal
Initial energy in each node	1.2 J
Bits per packets	2000 bits
Sensing square area	(−150, −150)–(150, 150)
Number of nodes	$Q = 500$ nodes
Number of clusters	q
BS position	(0, 175) or (50, 175)
Sensing area	$M = 300$ m ($M \times M$)
Networking block area	100 m × 100 m
Path loss exponents	free space $\alpha = 2$
	multipath fading $\alpha = 4$
Amplifier energy	$\varepsilon_{fs} = 10$ pJ/bit/m^2
	$\varepsilon_{mp} = 0.0013$ pJ/bit/m^4

To find the numerical results for optimal number of clusters q_{opt} is found by (10) for all sub-areas, B1–B9, we approximate the d_{toBS} for the base station placed at (50, 175) or (0, 175), respectively as shown in Table 3.

Table 3. The d_{toBS}(m) for each sub-area

	$d_{toBS}(m)(50, 175)$	$d_{toBS}(m)(0, 175)$
B1	168	125
B2	90	75
B3	90	125
B4	230	202
B5	182	175
B6	182	202
B7	313	293
B8	280	275
B9	280	293

After we simulate the deployed for the standard deviation of $\sigma = 50,\ 60,\ 70,\ 80,\ 90$ and zero mean for the Gaussion distributed in the sensing area, we obtain an example for the number of nodes on the nine sub-area B1–B9 as shown in Table 4. Then the optimal number of clusters q_{opt} can be obtained by (10) as shown in Table 4 for BS = (50, 175).

Table 4. The number of nodes and q_{opt} in each sub-area.

	Q	q_{opt}	Q	q_{opt}	Q	q_{opt}	Q	q_{opt}	Q	q_{opt}
σ	50		60		70		80		90	
B	497		483		462		437		418	
B1	9	1	18	1	28	1	29	1	30	1
B2	52	4	51	4	67	4	61	4	44	3
B3	12	2	22	3	10	2	20	2	33	3
B4	55	1	48	1	54	1	58	1	48	1
B5	233	2	181	2	145	2	97	2	92	2
B6	65	1	62	1	53	1	72	1	47	1
B7	15	1	18	1	21	1	22	1	33	1
B8	47	1	63	1	57	1	53	1	63	1
B9	9	1	20	1	27	1	25	1	28	1

From the simulation results in Fig. 3, the minimal energy consumption of one round are with the number of cluster of 9, 10, 10, 10 and 11 for $\sigma = 50, 60, 70, 80, 90$ respectively in LEACH. However, when we select the number of clusters by Table 4, the total number of clusters should be 14, 15, 14, 14, 14 for $\sigma = 50, 60, 70, 80, 90$ respectively. Then, the energy efficiency of total energy consumption in one round are compared for proposed adaptive clustering scheme and LEACH as shown in Table 5. From Table 5, it is observed that the proposed adaptive scheme largely outperform

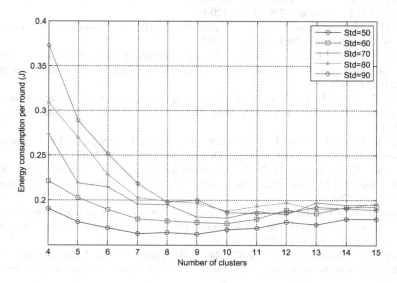

Fig. 3. One round energy consumption for LEACH.

LEACH Fig. 2. The optimal number of cluster for different areas and different number of nodes.

Table 5. Comparisons of energy efficiency between the proposed adaptive clustering scheme and LEACH.

		$\sigma = 50$	$\sigma = 60$	$\sigma = 70$	$\sigma = 80$	$\sigma = 90$
LEACH	q_{opt}	9	10	10	10	11
	E_{total}	0.162	0.174	0.180	0.188	0.184
ACS	q_{opt}	14	15	14	14	14
	E_{total}	0.116	0.113	0.109	0.103	0.099

5   Conclusion

In this paper, we investigate the clustering optimization for naturally scattering WSNs. We propose an adaptive clustering scheme to divide a large area to nine small sub-area for efficiently clustering WSNs. Then, the energy efficiency are compared for proposed adaptive clustering scheme and LEACH. Simulation results show that the proposed adaptive scheme largely outperform LEACH for total energy consumption in one round.

Acknowledgment. This work was funded in part by Ministry of Science and Technology of Taiwan under Grant MOST 105-2221-E-324-019.

References

1. Culler, D., Estrin, D., Srivastava, M.: Guest editors' introduction: overview of sensor networks. IEEE Comput. **37**(8), 41–49 (2004)
2. Akyildiz, I.F., Sankarasubramaniam, Y., Su, W., Cayirci, E.: Wireless sensor network a survey. Comput. Netw. **38**(1), 393–422 (2002)
3. Duarte-Melo, E.J., Liu, M.: Analysis of energy consumption and lifetime of heterogeneous wireless sensor networks. In: Proceedings of IEEE Global Telecommunication Conference, pp. 21–25 (2002)
4. Leu, F.-Y., Chen, H.-L., Cheng, C.-C.: Improving multi-path congestion control for event-driven wireless sensor networks by using TDMA. J. Internet Serv. Inf. Secur. **5**(4), 1–19 (2015)
5. Aram, S., Khosa, I., Pasero, E.: Conserving energy through neural prediction of sensed data. J. Wirel. Mob. Netw. Ubiquit. Comput. Dependable Appl. **6**(1), 74–97 (2015)
6. Schurgers, C., Srivastava, M. B.: Energy efficient routing in wireless sensor networks. In: Proceedings of IEEE Military Communications Conference for Network-Centric Operations, pp. 357–361 (2001)
7. Huang, B., Hao, F., Zhu, H., Tanabe, Y., Baba, T.: Low-energy static clustering scheme for wireless sensor network. In: Proceedings of International Conference on Wireless Communications, pp. 1–4 (2006)
8. Weng, C.-E., Sharma, V., Chen, H.-C., Mao, C.-H.: PEER: proximity-based energy-efficient routing algorithm for wireless sensor networks. J. Internet Serv. Inf. Secur. **6**(1), 47–56 (2016)

9. Thombre, S., Islam, R.U., Andersson, K., Hossain, M.S.: IP based wireless sensor networks: performance analysis using simulations and experiments. J. Wirel. Mob. Netw. Ubiquit. Comput. Dependable Appl. **7**(3), 53–76 (2016)

10. Muruganathan, S.D., Ma, D.C.F., Bhasin, R.I., Fapojuwo, A.O.: A centralized energy-efficient routing protocol for wireless sensor networks. IEEE Commun. Mag. **43**(3), 8–13 (2005)

11. Huang, Y.-F., Luo, W.-H., Sum, J., Chang, L.-H., Chang, C.-W., Chen, R.-C.: Lifetime performance of an energy efficient clustering algorithm for cluster-based wireless sensor networks. In: Thulasiraman, P., He, X., Xu, T.L., Denko, M.K., Thulasiram, R.K., Yang, L.T. (eds.) ISPA 2007. LNCS, vol. 4743, pp. 455–464. Springer, Heidelberg (2007). https://doi.org/10.1007/978-3-540-74767-3_47

12. Huang, Y.-F., Chan, T.-J., Chen, T.-R., Chen, M.-C.: Energy efficiency optimization for hierarchical cluster-based wireless sensor network. Far East J. Exp. Theor. Artif. Intell. **2**(2), 97–107 (2008)

13. Sohrabi, K., Gao, J., Ailawadhi, V., Pottie, G.J.: Protocols for self-organization of a wireless sensor networks. IEEE Pers. Commun. **7**(10), 16–27 (2000)

Mobile Security Assurance for Automotive Software Through ArchiMate

Nobuhide Kobayashi[✉], Shuji Morisaki, and Shuichiro Yamamoto

Nagoya University, Furo-cho, Chikusa-ku, Nagoya, Aichi 464-8601, Japan
nobuhide@dcinc.co.jp, S.Morisaki.JP@ieee.org, syamamoto@acm.org

Abstract. ArchiMate is used to describe Business, Application and Technology Architectures models for Enterprise Architecture. Although the effectiveness of creating security case method in ArchiMate has been shown for mobile services, the applicability of the method was not discussed for the automotive mobile software development. In this paper, the method of creating security cases for mobile architecture models in ArchiMate is applied to an automotive mobile service and evaluated. The result shows the applicability of the method for various mobile security architecture domains.

Keywords: Mobile security · Mobile architecture
Enterprise architecture · ArchiMate · Automotive

1 Introduction

Modern mobile systems, such as automotive systems, especially where the boundaries of operation or ownership are unclear, are often subject to change: new devices, new infrastructures are connected, new technologies such as artificial intelligence are introduced, and so on. As a result, the vulnerabilities of the automotive mobile system have a significant impact on security.

Therefore, it is critical to clarify the process to identify threats due to the vulnerabilities of automotive mobile systems, to update the automotive mobile architecture by using security cases, and to build consensus on accountability. It is also necessary to detect vulnerabilities or threats, to understand the causes, and to prevent them from impacting the mobile system in the future.

In this paper, the proposed security case creation method [1] is applied to argue the mobile security for automotive mobile architecture models. The architecture models can be described by ArchiMate [2] which is standardized to develop architecture models in TOGAF (The Open Grope Architecture Framework) [3]. Security case is an assurance case to show the assuredness on security. Security case can be used to assure the security of automotive mobile architecture models. Section 2 describes related work on approaches for mobile security cases. Section 3 describes the security case creation approach which is based on the structure of automotive mobile architecture model in ArchiMate. In Sect. 4, an example case study is presented. Discussions on the effectiveness of the proposed approach are shown in Sect. 5. Our conclusions are presented in Sect. 6.

© Springer Nature Singapore Pte Ltd. 2018
I. You et al. (Eds.): MobiSec 2016, CCIS 797, pp. 10–20, 2018.
https://doi.org/10.1007/978-981-10-7850-7_2

2   Related Work

The Open Group Real Time & Embedded Systems Forum focuses on standards for high assurance, secure dependable and complete systems. The Open Group announced the publication of the Dependability through Assuredness™Standard (O-DA) published by The Open Group Real-Time & Embedded Systems Forum [4]. At the heart of this O-DA (Open Dependability through Assuredness) standard, there is the concept of modeling dependencies, building assurance cases, and achieving agreement on accountability in the event of actual or potential failures. Dependability cases are necessary to assure dependable systems [5]. The DEOS (Dependability Engineering for Open Systems) process was proposed to manage dependability of complex systems by using dependability cases [6–8].

O-DA brings together and builds on The Open Group vision of Boundaryless Information Flow. The vision includes O-DM (Open Dependency Modeling) and Risk Taxonomy of The Open Group Security Forum, and Architecture models of The Open Group ArchiMate®Forum [2,3]. However, the relationship between O-DA and ArchiMate concepts has not yet been clear. The safety case, the assurance case, and the dependability case are currently the focus of considerable attention for the purpose of providing assurance and confidence that systems are safe. Methods have thus been proposed for representing these using Goal Structuring Notation (GSN) [9–13]. GSN patterns were originally proposed by Kelly [11]. In the absence of any clearly organized guidelines concerning the approach to be taken in decomposing claims using strategies and the decomposition sequence, engineers have often not known how to develop their arguments. It is against this backdrop that the aforementioned approaches to argument decomposition patterns –architecture, functional, attribute, infinite set, complete (set of risks and requirements), monotonic, and concretion– were identified by Bloomfield and Bishop [14]. An experimental result of argument patterns was reported by Yamamoto and Matsuno [15].

Howard, and Leblanc proposed the STRIDE model for analyzing security [16]. The acronym STRIDE was derived from the six threat categories, Spoofing identity, Tampering with data, Repudiation, Information disclosure, Denial of services, and Elevation of privilege. Although the STRIDE model is useful, the relationship among human operations and system components is unclear. It is necessary to analyze security over business, application, and technology architectures in a systematic way. Preschern et al. proposed an approach to analyze security based on safety case [17]. Yamamoto et al. [18] proposed a security case pattern based on Common Criteria for the security domain. Patu and Yamamoto examines several case studies to create security cases [19–21]. Kaneko et al. [22–24] proposed the CC-case, which means Common Criteria case, to integrate security analysis over the life-cycle process.

The methods in [25–27] clarified threats and countermeasures for the mobile security domain. The information can be used for constructing security cases for the domain. However, these proposals can not be applied to analyze risks from the view of business services, even for mobile services, The reason is because they only have focused on analyzing risks and countermeasures from mobile OS architecture such as Android. Moreover, automotive service applications have not been discussed in their approaches.

Yamamoto recently proposed the method to create assurance cases based on ArchiMate models [28], the method to create security cases from ArchiMate was also mentioned [1]. Yamamoto also discussed an approach to resolve conflict between safety and security by using attribute GSN [29]. Although the effectiveness of the security case development method was shown through a typical content navigation service [1], it was not applied to automotive software with the characteristics of AUTOSAR. Nowadays, many automotive software development projects have introduced AUTOSAR [30]. EAST-ADL, SysML were proposed as the description language of AUTOSAR system development [31,32], but the relationship between ArchiMate and AUTOSAR has not been known. If the application method of ArchiMate to AUTOSAR system development would be clear, the former method [1] will be easily applied to create security cases for automotive mobile systems based on the ArchiMate models.

3   Security Case Creation Approach for Automotive Mobile Services

The approach uses ArchiMate to show automotive mobile services in the three layered enterprise architecture, that is business, application and technology. After defining the automotive mobile service architecture, the vulnerability analysis is conducted based on the architecture. Then, security measures are considered for the identified vulnerability. To validate the service security, security cases are described by integrating above artifacts such as identified vulnerability for architecture components, and measures.

3.1   Pattern of Created Security Case

The created security case has a common structure as shown in Table 1. The security case is the application of the assurance case for the security domain.

The first level sub-goal claims state that concept elements and relationships of the model satisfy dependability principles. The second level sub-goal claim states that category of elements and their relationships among the model satisfy dependability principles.

The third level goals are decomposed by instances of concepts and relationships of the models.

The fourth level goals are decomposed by risks for the corresponding instances and are supported by the evidence to mitigate risks. Therefore, the fifth level of the assurance case consists of evidences for the fourth level goals.

In the course of the assurance case decompositions, XML definitions for the model, quality properties, and risk measures are used.

Table 1. Mobile security case pattern with ArchiMate

Hierarchy	Description
Root goal	The root goal states that the model shall satisfy security principle
Architecture layers and relationships	Root goal is decomposed by architecture layers and relationship of the ArchiMate model
Instances of layers and relationships	Third level goals are decomposed by instances of nodes and relationships of the ArchiMate model
Measures for instance vulnerability	Fourth level goals are decomposed by risks for the corresponding instances in the ArchiMate model
Evidence	Evidence supports to mitigate vulnerability of instances

4 Case Study

The example study was conducted to evaluate the effectiveness of the proposed mobile security case creation method for assuring the security of a remote door lock service.

4.1 Target Automotive Mobile Service

The target system of the case study is one of the typical remote control services for the automotive system through smartphones. The configuration of the service is shown in Fig. 1 by using ArchiMate. The model describes BA (Business architecture), AA (Application architecture), and TA (Technology architecture). It also adopts the rules shown in Sect. 4.2 to describe automotive systems.

In BA, a remote door lock control service process is described by triggering the control request through a smartphone. AA is described using AUTOSAR Virtual Functional Bus (VFB) concept [30] which has been adopted in the automotive software development. In this concept, the Virtual Functional Bus provides location transparency for Software Components which realize automotive services defined as the corresponding processes in BA. As a result, a system designer can focus on a realization of BA without considering the mapping of Software Components and hardware nodes called ECU (Electronic Control Unit). According to this concept, in AA, two layers are described as Software Component layer and Virtual Functional Bus layer. The upper layer describes software components and their functionality. There are four Software Components. These are Door control client component, Authorization manager component, Door control server component, and Door controller component. In addition, Registered authorization information as the information related to security is allocated to Authorization manager component. On the other hand, the lower layer describes read/write/control functionality provided by Virtual Functional Bus, and Data Elements which support the information exchange among Software Components are allocated to Virtual Functional Bus. In TA, there are four

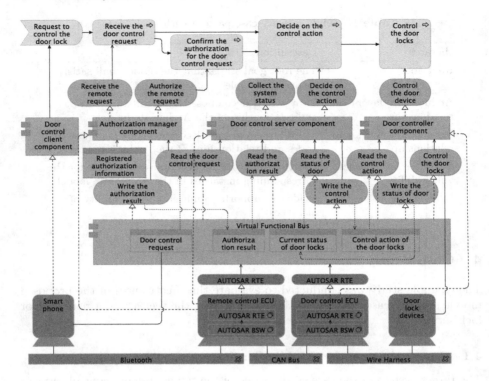

Fig. 1. Example of an automotive mobile service architecture in ArchiMate

nodes, i.e., Smartphone, Remote control ECU, Door Control ECU, and Door lock devices. Smartphone and Remote control ECU are connected via Bluetooth. Remote control ECU and Door control ECU are connected via CAN (Controller Area Network) bus. Door control ECU and Door lock devices are connected via wire harness. In addition, AUTOSAR RTE (RunTime Environment) and AUTOSAR BSW (Basic SoftWare) are allocated to each ECU. AUTOSAR RTE realizes Virtual Functional Bus. AUTOSAR BSW provides real-time operating system and communication functionality to control ECU.

4.2　ArchiMate Description Rule for AUTOSAR System Development

This case study adopted the following rules to AUTOSAR system development using ArchiMate. *Italic words* mean ArchiMate nodes in the rules.

- BA defines automotive services using *Business Process* and *Business Event*.
- AA includes two layer as Software Component layer and VFB layer.
- Software Component layer defines Software Component using *Application Component* and functionalities of Software Components using *Application Service*.

- VFB layer defines VFB as only one element in AA.
- VFB provides Read, Write, and Control interfaces as *Application Service* to Software Components.
- VFB includes data elements as *Data Object* which is accessed via Read, Write interfaces by Software Components
- TA defines a hardware system, and it includes ECUs and other devices as *Device*, and they are connected using *Network*.
- ECU includes AUTOSAR RTE and BSW defined as *System Software*.
- The mapping of Software Component and ECU is shown using *Realisation relation*.
- AUTOSAR RTE provides AUTOSAR RTE Service.

4.3 Security Case

After defining the mobile architecture model in ArchiMate, the vulnerability of the architecture is analyzed by checking each architecture elements based on the model. Then security case is created based on the vulnerability analysis.

Figure 2 shows the top level view of the security case. The security case is generic to all mobile services in ArchiMate, because it is independent of the detail architecture.

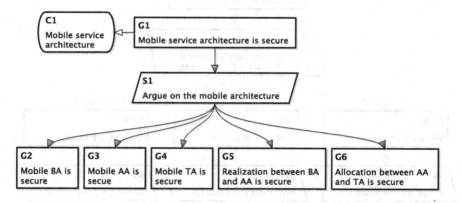

Fig. 2. Example of the top level security case

An example of the next level security case for AA is shown in Fig. 3. It shows the detail of G3 in Fig. 2. And Fig. 4 shows the detail of G9 in Fig. 3. Figure 5 shows the detail of G7 in Fig. 3. The security case is hierarchically decomposed by the Application architecture described in AA.

These claims are then decomposed into sub claims by analyzing vulnerability of each process. For example, in case of "Authorization manager component is secure" claim, there are two sub claims that are corresponding to the vulnerability of fraud AUTOSAR RTE and unsecure communication as shown in Fig. 6. The validness of these two sub claims can be confirmed by measures, i.e., AUTOSAR RTE rating and checking AUTOSAR RTE settings.

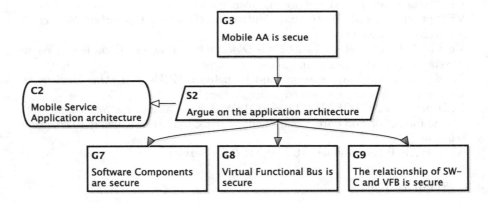

Fig. 3. Example of the security case for Mobile AA

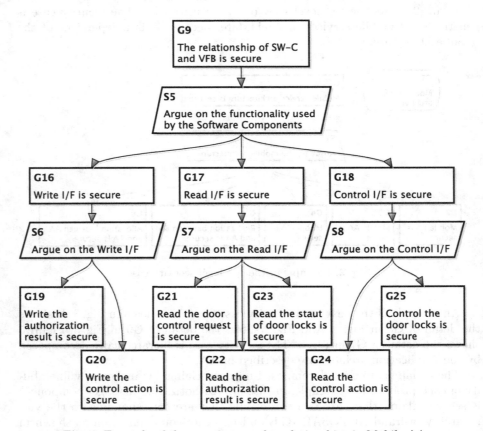

Fig. 4. Example of the security case for relationships in Mobile AA

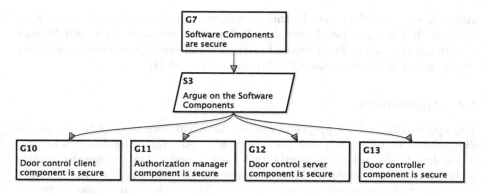

Fig. 5. Example of the security case for nodes in Mobile AA

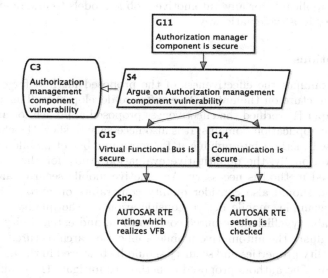

Fig. 6. Example of the evidence level security case

5   Discussion

In this section, we discuss on the effectiveness, applicability, and limitation of the proposed method.

5.1   Effectiveness

The case study was executed to evaluate the effectiveness of the proposed method [1] for the automotive software development based on AUTOSAR. The running example showed the derivation from the ArchiMate model to the security case was easy and exhaustive for the automotive software development as well as mobile service development. In this case study, the description of automotive AA was divided into two layers, i.e., Software Component layer and Virtual Functional Bus layer. The proposed method could create the security cases for the extended AA description with the same approach [1].

5.2 Applicability

The applicability of the proposed method to ArchiMate is clear by the above discussions. The BA, AA, and TA described in ArchiMate models can be easily analyzed by checking vulnerability for every node. Any automotive mobile architecture models in ArchiMate contain nodes and relationships among nodes. Therefore, the decomposition hierarchy defined by Table 1 can be applied to any automotive mobile service models of ArchiMate. Therefore, the proposed approach can be applicable for any automotive mobile models to assure automotive mobile security in a systematic way.

5.3 Limitations

This paper examines the effectiveness of the proposed method for one mobile example architecture on the automotive software development. This paper and the former paper [1] verified the effectiveness proposed approach for automotive and cell phone application domains. It is also necessary to show the effectiveness of the proposed method by applying it for more number of mobile application domains. Additionally, the quantitative evaluation study for the productivity of the proposed method is necessary. Automotive mobile security architecture design method should also consider quality constraints on automotive mobile devices. For example, mobile design consideration on the quality constraints, such as, portability, efficient resource consumption, and extensibility should be decided to evaluate the automotive mobile application architecture. These non-functional quality properties and security should be balanced in the mobile architectural design. The authors proposed a method to mitigate the conflict among non-functional softgoals including security and safety by using the weighted softgoal decomposition tree [33,34]. The integration of the mobile security assurance and quantitative softgoal weight evaluation approaches are necessary.

6 Conclusion

In this paper, a security case development method for automotive mobile services is evaluated to derive the argument decomposition structure based on the automotive ArchiMate model. The paper also provides the O-DA solution example for assuring security of business, application, and technology architecture of the automotive application domain. The example case study was evaluated for the automotive remote door lock service through a smartphone. Discussions based on the case study showed the effectiveness and appropriateness of the proposed method on automotive software development.

Future work includes the formalization of security case derivation process from ArchiMate models, more number of quantitative case studies of the proposed method, and the integration method with the weighted softgoal approach to balance quality attributes and security for designing mobile architectures.

Acknowledgment. This work was supported by KAKENHI (24220001). This work has been conducted as a part of "Research Initiative on Advanced Software Engineering in 2015" supported by Software Reliability Enhancement Center (SEC), Information Technology Promotion Agency Japan (IPA).

References

1. Yamamoto, S., Kobayashi, N.: Mobile security assurance through archimate. IT CoNvergence PRActice (INPRA) **4**(3), 1–8 (2016)
2. Josely, A.: ArchiMate®2.0, A Pocket Guide. The Open Group, Van Haren8 Publishing (2013)
3. Josely, A.: Togaf®version 9.1 a pocket guide (2011)
4. Real-Time, Systems, E.: Dependability through Assuredness™(O-DA) Framework. Open Group Standard (2013)
5. Jackson, D.: Software for dependable systems- sufficient evidence? National Research Council (2008)
6. DEOS: Deos project (2013). http://www.crest-os.jst.go.jp
7. DEOS: JST White Paper DEOS-FY2011-WP-03J. Japan Science and Technology Agency (2011). www.dependable-os.net/ja/topics/file/White_Paper_V3.0J.pdf
8. Tokoro, M. (eds.): Open Systems Dependability, Dependability Engineering for Ever-Changing Systems. CRC Press (2012). www.dependable-os.net/ja/topics/file/White_Paper_V3.0J.pdf
9. Kelly, T.: A Six-Step Method for the Development of Goal Structures. York Software Engineering (1997)
10. Kelly, T., McDermid, J.: Safety Case Construction and Reuse using Patterns. University of York (1997)
11. Kelly, T.: Arguing Safety, a Systematic Approach to Managing Safety Cases. Ph.D. thesis, Department of Computer Science, University of York (1998)
12. McDermid, J.: Software safety: where's the evidence? In: SCS 2001: Proceedings of the Sixth Australian Workshop on Safety Critical Systems and Software, pp. 1–6. Australian Computer Society Inc., Darlinghurst, Australia (2001)
13. Kelly, T., Weaver, R.: The goal structuring notation - a safety argument notation. In: Proceedings of the Dependable Systems and Networks 2004 Workshop on Assurance Cases (2004)
14. Bloomfield, R., Bishop, P.: Safety and assurance cases: past, present and possible future. In: Safety Critical Systems Symposium, Bristol, UK (2010)
15. Yamamoto, S., Matsuno, Y.: An evaluation of argument patterns to reduce pitfalls of applying Assurance Case. In: Assure 2013 (2013)
16. Howard, M., Leblanc, D.: Writing Secure Code. Microsoft Press, Redmond (2003)
17. Preschern, C., Kajtazovic, N., Kreiner, C.: Security analysis of safety patterns. In: PLoP 2013 (2013)
18. Yamamoto, S., Kaneko, T., Tanaka, H.: A proposal on security case based on common criteria. In: Mustofa, K., Neuhold, E.J., Tjoa, A.M., Weippl, E., You, I. (eds.) ICT-EurAsia 2013. LNCS, vol. 7804, pp. 331–336. Springer, Heidelberg (2013). https://doi.org/10.1007/978-3-642-36818-9_36

19. Patu, V., Yamamoto, S.: A model to capture security threat patterns by complying with standards and lesson learned. In: ISSRE2013, pp. 22–26, November 2013
20. Patu, V., Yamamoto, S.: Identifying and implementing security patterns for a dependable Security Case. In: CSE 2013, Australia, pp. 79–80, December 2013
21. Patu, V., Yamamoto, S.: How to develop Security Case by combining real life security experiences (evidence) with D-case. In: KES 2013, Kitakyushu, pp. 52–55, September 2013
22. Kaneko, T., Yamamoto, S., Tanaka, H.: CC-Case as an integrated method of security analysis and assurance over life-cycle process. Int. J. Cyber-Secur. Digital Forensics (IJCSDF) **3**(1), 49–62 (2014)
23. Kaneko, T., Yamamoto, S., Tanaka, H.: CC-Case for the system development over life-cycle process. In: ComSec 2014 (2014)
24. Kaneko, T., Yamamoto, S., Tanaka, H.: CC-Case as an efficient method of assurance case for the security risk management. In: ProMAC 2014 (2014)
25. Skovoroda, A., Gamayunov, D.: Securing mobile devices: malware mitigation methods. J. Wirel. Mobile Netw. **6**(2), 78–97 (2015)
26. Rashidi, B., Fung, C.: A survey of android security threats and defenses. J. Wirel. Mobile Netw. **6**(3), 3–35 (2015)
27. Kim, N.Y., Shim, J., Cho, S., Park, M., Han, S.: Android application protection against static reverse engineering based on multidexing. J. Internet Serv. Inform. Secur. (JISIS) **6**(4), 54–64 (2016)
28. Yamamoto, S.: An approach to assure dependability through ArchiMate. In: Koornneef, F., van Gulijk, C. (eds.) SAFECOMP 2015. LNCS, vol. 9338, pp. 50–61. Springer, Cham (2015). https://doi.org/10.1007/978-3-319-24249-1_5
29. Yamamoto, S.: Assuring security through attribute GSN. In: ICITCS 2015, pp. 1–5 (2015)
30. Heinecke, H., Schnelle, K.P., Fennel, H., Bortolazzi, J.: AUTomotive Open System ARchitecture-an industry-wide initiative to manage the complexity of emerging automotive E/E-architectures. In: Convergence (2004)
31. Cuenot, P., Frey, P., Johansson, R., Lönn, H.: Developing automotive products using the EAST-ADL2, an AUTOSAR compliant architecture description language. In: Embedded Real-Time Software Conference (2008)
32. Giese, H., Hildebrandt, S., Neumann, S.: Model synchronization at work: keeping SysML and AUTOSAR models consistent. In: Engels, G., Lewerentz, C., Schäfer, W., Schürr, A., Westfechtel, B. (eds.) Nagl Festschrift. LNCS, vol. 5765, pp. 555–579. Springer, Heidelberg (2010). https://doi.org/10.1007/978-3-642-17322-6_24
33. Yamamoto, S.: An approach for evaluating softgoals using weight. In: Khalil, I., Neuhold, E., Tjoa, A.M., Da Xu, L., You, I. (eds.) CONFENIS/ICT-EurAsia - 2015. LNCS, vol. 9357, pp. 203–212. Springer, Cham (2015). https://doi.org/10.1007/978-3-319-24315-3_20
34. Kobayashi, N., Morisaki, S., Atsumi, N., Yamamoto, S.: Quantitative Non Functional Requirements evaluation using softgoal weight. J. Internet Serv. Inform. Secur. (JISIS) **6**, 37–46 (2016)

A Generalized Data Inconsistency Detection Model for Wireless Sensor Networks

Tzu-Liang Kung[1,2(✉)] and Hsing-Chung Chen[1,2(✉)]

[1] Department of Computer Science and Information Engineering,
Asia University, Wufeng, Taichung City 413, Taiwan
{tlkung,cdma2000}@asia.edu.tw,
tlkueng@gmail.com, shin8409@ms6.hinet.net
[2] Department of Medical Research, China Medical University Hospital,
China Medical University, Taichung City 404, Taiwan

Abstract. A wireless sensor network is one popular candidate for the fundamental backbone of IoT (Internet of Things). Among the key technologies involved in wireless sensor networks, fault detection techniques are indispensable for maintaining the availability of sensor applications. To employ a distributed fault detection scheme, we address a generalized data inconsistency detection model and apply it to recognize data inconsistencies within a wireless sensor network. Then, we formally prove that data inconsistencies can be correctly recognized under the requisite conditions, and we evaluate the robustness of the generalized data inconsistency detection under the probability fault model. Our numerical result indicates that the degree of robustness eventually approaches to 1 if the node reliability is greater than 0.5. Moreover, we show that the tolerable defect rate of the generalized data inconsistency detection is strictly less than $\frac{1}{2}$, so its defect-free rate must be greater than $\frac{1}{2}$. All these results definitely imply that the generalized data inconsistency detection is sufficiently robust.

Keywords: Distributed computing · Fault detection
Data inconsistency · Sensor network

1 Introduction

A sensor network is one popular candidate for the fundamental backbone of IoT (Internet of Things) and ubiquitous computing [1,30,33]. Among the various kinds of communication networks, sensor networks have been widely applied in many areas such as the military, environment surveillance, agriculture, the healthcare industry, food industry, etc. Sensors in the network are usually created by incorporating sensing materials with integrated circuits. A sensor network is established by enhancing each sensor with wireless communication capability and networking the sensors together [14,22,31]. Furthermore, each sensor is not only a mobile host but also a router; in other words, the sensors are capable of forwarding the received data packages according to some routing protocol.

© Springer Nature Singapore Pte Ltd. 2018
I. You et al. (Eds.): MobiSec 2016, CCIS 797, pp. 21–31, 2018.
https://doi.org/10.1007/978-981-10-7850-7_3

However, a sensor network has no support of any fixed infrastructure so that there is no centralized administration mechanism in sensor networks.

Because sensor networks are essentially infrastructureless, it is more feasible to manage and update the topology of some substructure rather than the whole network. A potential substructure, for example, may be a ring, a path, a tree, a mesh, and so on. If all sensors in a substructure can be guaranteed to be fault-free, any procedure can still execute normally within the substructure even though there are many faulty sensors in the remainder of the network. In practice, the virtual backbone [23,32,35,36] has been proposed as an effective routing infrastructure of wireless networks so that routing messages are only exchanged between backbone nodes, instead of being broadcasted to all over the network. Such an approach is able to alleviate the broadcast storm problem in mobile ad hoc network [29]. Based on the similar spirit, Devipriya et al. [11] proposed a hashing-based backoff mechanism for IEEE 802.11 wireless networks, and Weng et al. [37] developed a proximity-based energy-efficient routing algorithm for wireless sensor networks.

The availability of a sensor network depends heavily upon the sensor reliability so that fault detection techniques are indispensable for maintaining the availability of sensor applications. Chen et al. [8] presented a distributed fault detection (DFD) scheme to identify hard faults, such as power failures, crash faults, etc., in a sensor network, and later Jiang [15] improved upon this scheme. Theoretical viewpoints of fault detection and diagnosis can be referred to in [13,17,19,21,24,25,39,41]. Furthermore, a variety of fault diagnosis methods were developed. For example, Chessa and Maestrini [9] introduced a correct and almost complete diagnosis method for square grids. Later, Caruso et al. [2–4] presented two correct and almost complete diagnosis algorithms, which are called EDARS and NDA, respectively. A lower bound to the worst-case diagnosis completeness for regular networks was discovered in [5]. In addition, Mánik and Gramatová [27,28] proposed the Boolean formalization for the syndrome-decoding process of the fault detection model. In this paper, we develop a more robust fault detection scheme and apply it to recognize potential inconsistencies among sensed data, which belongs to a frequent category of soft faults in sensor networks. The main contributions of this paper are highlighted as follows:

1. We formally prove that data inconsistencies can be correctly recognized under the requisite conditions.
2. Based on the probability fault model [6], the robustness evaluation of the generalized data inconsistency detection is addressed.
3. We present numerical results to validate the robustness of the generalized data inconsistency.
4. The tolerable defect rate of the generalized data inconsistency detection is strictly less than $\frac{1}{2}$, so the defect-free rate of the generalized data inconsistency detection must be greater than $\frac{1}{2}$.

The rest of this paper is organized as follows. Section 2 provides a preliminary background for distributed fault detection scheme. Section 3 introduces a generalized data inconsistency detection model, and Sect. 4 evaluates the robustness of the generalized data inconsistency detection. Finally, we draw a conclusion in Sect. 5.

2   Distributed Fault Detection Scheme

The underlying topology of a network system is modeled as a graph, and we follow the standard terminology given in [7].

In this paper, we assume that all sensors have the same sensing and transmission range; that is, every sensor senses and communicate with others within a unit distance, and the active areas of two sensors overlap if the two sensors can communicate with each other. Under this assumption, the underlying topology of a sensor network is modeled as a unit disk graph (UDG for short). A *unit disk* is a disk with radius one. A *unit disk graph* is associated with a set of unit disks in the Euclidean space. Each node represents the center of a unit disk. An edge joins two vertices u and v if and only if $|uv| \leq 1$, where $|uv|$ denotes the Euclidean distance between u and v. Such a formulation means that there is an edge between two vertices u and v if and only if u's disk covers v, and vice versa.

Chen et al. [8] proposed a distributed fault detection scheme to determine the status of a sensor: For two adjacent sensor nodes s_i and s_j, a test result at the moment t, $C_{i,j}^t$, is produced according to the comparison between data sensed by s_i and s_j. The data, such as temperature, humidity, etc., at the moment t should be very close to each other because they are near, and the difference $diff_{i,j}^t$ between these data should not exceed a certain threshold χ_1. Meanwhile, at the previous moment $t-1$, the difference between the data of s_i and s_j is $diff_{i,j}^{t-1}$, and the difference between $diff_{i,j}^{t-1}$ and $diff_{i,j}^t$ is $\Delta diff_{i,j}^t$, which should not exceed a certain threshold χ_2. If any one of these two conditions is violated, then s_i or s_j is very likely to be a faulty sensor, and the test result is assigned as $C_{i,j}^t = 1$; otherwise, $C_{i,j}^t = 0$.

- Phase I: For any sensor node s_i in a graph G, its comparison result with each node in $Nbd_G(s_i)$, the set of all neighbors of s_i in G, at the moment t is determined as follows: If $\sum_{j:s_j \in Nbd_G(s_i)} C_{i,j}^t > \frac{|Nbd_G(s_i)|}{2}$, then the initial status of node s_i is possibly faulty; otherwise, it may be possibly normal. Therefore, initial status of every node in the sensor network is available.
- Phase II: The status of s_i is adjusted according to the following criterion: for those nodes of $Nbd_G(s_i)$ whose initial status is possibly normal, subtract the number of nodes whose comparison result with s_i being 0 from the number of nodes whose comparison result with s_i being 1. Denote this value by ρ. If ρ is not less than $\frac{|Nbd_G(s_i)|}{2}$, then the status of s_i is normal; otherwise, the status of s_i is faulty.

Jiang [15] proposed an improved scheme via changing the criterion of Phase II. The new rule is as follows: For those nodes in $Nbd_G(s_i)$ whose initial status is possibly normal, if the number of nodes whose comparison result with s_i being 0 is not less than the number of nodes whose comparison result with s_i being 1, then the status of s_i is normal; otherwise, the status of s_i is faulty. It is noticed that there are many different types of sensors used for sensing various types of data in practice. For instance, a location sensor returns both the longitudinal and latitudinal information of the location, and a heart-rate sensor returns the present frequency of heart beats. It is meaningless to compare data sensed from a location sensor and a heart-rate one. In summary, the proposed fault detection scheme [8, 15] is applicable to detect inconsistency between homogeneous data.

3   Generalized Data Inconsistency Detection Model

In this section, a generalized data inconsistency detection model is presented: For any sensor node, its actual status may be either normal or faulty. Intuitively speaking, at least one of sensors s_i and s_j is faulty if $C_{i,j}^t = 1$. However, when $C_{i,j}^t = 0$, it may not definitely imply that both s_i and s_j are normal. Consider a special case that a faulty sensor is also likely to produce correct data occasionally. Then, $C_{i,j}^t$ may be 0 even though s_i or s_j is faulty. Table 1 summarizes the invalidation rules of the generalized data inconsistency detection model.

Table 1. Rules of the generalized data inconsistency detection model.

The status of sensor s_i	The status of sensor s_j	Comparison result $C_{i,j}^t$
Normal	Normal	0
Normal	Faulty	0 or 1
Faulty	Normal	0 or 1
Faulty	Faulty	0 or 1

The underlying detection scheme of Chen et al. [8] and Jiang [15] is based on a star structure, as shown in Fig. 1. Here we denote by $Star_G(s_i)$ a star structure rooted at the sensor node s_i in a graph G.

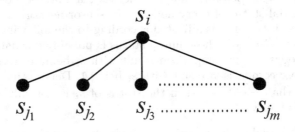

Fig. 1. The star structure $Star_G(s_i)$, in which m is the number of the neighbors of sensor node s_i.

Based on the generalized data inconsistency detection model, we prove the following theorem.

Theorem 1. *In Phase I of the distributed fault detection scheme, the sensor s_i is faulty if the following two conditions hold:*

1. $\sum_{j:s_j \in Nbd_G(s_i)} C_{i,j}^t > \frac{|Nbd_G(s_i)|}{2}$, *and*

2. the total number of faulty sensor nodes in $Star_G(s_i)$ does not exceed $\frac{|Nbd_G(s_i)|}{2}$,

where $Nbd_G(s_i)$ denotes the set of all neighbors of s_i in G.

Proof. Let $n_1 = \sum_{j:s_j \in Nbd_G(s_i)} C_{i,j}^t$ and $n_0 = |Nbd_G(s_i)| - n_1$. Since $n_1 > \frac{|Nbd_G(s_i)|}{2}$, we have $n_1 > n_0$. Suppose by contradiction that the sensor node s_i is normal. Accordingly, the total number of faulty sensor nodes in $Star_G(s_i)$ amounts to at least $n_1 > \frac{|Nbd_G(s_i)|}{2}$, contradicting the assumption that the total number of faulty sensor nodes in $Star_G(s_i)$ does not exceed $\frac{|Nbd_G(s_i)|}{2}$. Hence, the status of s_i has to be faulty, and the proof is completed.

4   Robustness Evaluation

In general, as the size of a network grows, the likelihood of fault occurrences in the network increases. Reliability is extensively applied to quantify the impact of systematic failures. The reliability of a network is defined as the probability that the network is fully functional in a given time session [16]. A number of reliability models have been proposed to assess the network reliability and/or availability [6,10,12,20,34,40]. For example, an explicit formula for the subcube reliability of the hypercube-based network was formulated by Das and Kim [10] under the random fault model, which assumes that there are exactly f faults distributed randomly in the hypercube. Later, Chang and Bhuyan [6] proposed a more efficient computational model, namely the probability fault model, for assessing the subcube reliability of the hypercube. Under the probability fault model, Wu and Latifi [38] analyzed the substar reliability in star networks, and Lin et al. [26] calculated the subgraph reliability of the arrangement graph. Recently, Kung and Hung [18] established the accurate lower and upper bounds on the subsystem reliability of the bubblesort network based on the probability fault model. In the rest of this section, we are going to evaluate the robustness of the generalized data inconsistency detection under the probability fault model.

The probability fault model [6] assumes that every node of a network system has a homogeneous node reliability, and node failures appear independently. Accordingly, we derive the robustness function $R(m,p)$ of the generalized data inconsistency detection based on $Star_G(s_i)$, where m is the number of sensor s_i's neighboring nodes, and p is the homogeneous node reliability. By Theorem 1, the sensor s_i produces inconsistent data if $\sum_{j:s_j \in Nbd_G(s_i)} C_{i,j}^t > \frac{|Nbd_G(s_i)|}{2}$, provided that the total number of faulty sensors in $Star_G(s_i)$ does not exceed $\frac{|Nbd_G(s_i)|}{2}$.

Let $F(Star_G(s_i))$ be the set of faulty sensors in $Star_G(s_i)$ Then, $R(m,p)$ is expressed as follows:

$$R(m,p) \cong P\left(|F(Star_G(s_i))| \leq \frac{|Nbd_G(s_i)|}{2}\right)$$

$$= P\left(|F(Star_G(s_i))| \leq \left\lfloor \frac{m}{2} \right\rfloor\right)$$

$$= \sum_{x=0}^{\lfloor \frac{m}{2} \rfloor} P(|F(Star_G(s_i))| = x)$$

$$= \sum_{x=0}^{\lfloor \frac{m}{2} \rfloor} \binom{m+1}{x} p^{m-x+1}(1-p)^x. \tag{1}$$

Obviously, $R(m, 0.5) = 0.5$ for $m \geq 1$. Figure 2 plots the curves of $R(m,p)$ for $p = 0.5, 0.49, 0.48$. It is clear to see that the value of the robustness function decays quickly as m increases, especially when the node reliability p is much less than 0.5.

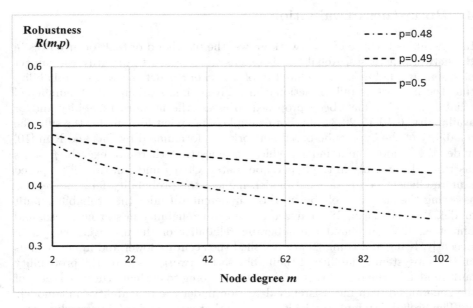

Fig. 2. Robustness function $R(m,p)$ of the generalized data inconsistency detection under the probability fault model for $p \leq 0.5$.

Figures 3 and 4 plot the curves of $R(m,p)$ for $p > 0.5$. In contrast with lower values of p (i.e., $p < 0.5$), the degree of robustness increases quickly as m goes larger and larger, especially when the node reliability p is much greater than 0.5. In addition, the higher value of p is, the faster $R(m,p)$ approaches to 1.

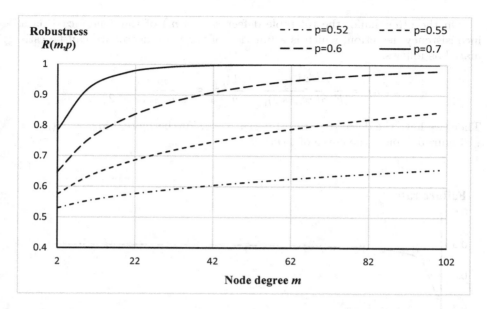

Fig. 3. Robustness function $R(m, p)$ of the generalized data inconsistency detection under the probability fault model for $p = 0.52, 0.55, 0.6, 0.7$.

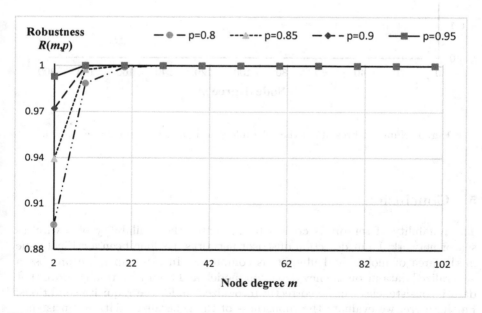

Fig. 4. Robustness function $R(m, p)$ of the generalized data inconsistency detection under the probability fault model for $p = 0.8, 0.85, 0.9, 0.95$.

On the other hand, the tolerable defect rate $\varphi(m)$ of the generalized data inconsistency detection, which is a function of the node degree m, can be estimated as follows:

$$\varphi(m) = \frac{\frac{|Nbd_G(s_i)|}{2}}{|F(Star_G(s_i))|} = \frac{\lfloor \frac{m}{2} \rfloor}{m+1} \approx \frac{m}{2(m+1)} < \frac{1}{2}. \tag{2}$$

Then, we have the defect-free rate $1 - \varphi(m) > \frac{1}{2}$. Furthermore, $\lim_{m \to \infty} \varphi(m) = \frac{1}{2}$. Figure 5 depicts the curve of $\varphi(m)$.

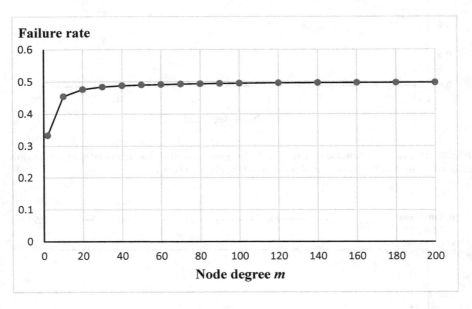

Fig. 5. Numerical results of the tolerable defect rate $\varphi(m)$ for $2 \leq m \leq 200$.

5   Conclusion

The reliability of sensors is critical to guarantee the availability of a wireless sensor network. Fault detection of sensor networks has long been a critical issue in the area of mobile and ubiquitous computing. In this paper, we propose a generalized data inconsistency detection model, and then we formally prove that data inconsistencies can be correctly recognized under the requisite conditions. Furthermore, we evaluate the robustness of the generalized data inconsistency detection under the probability fault model, and the presented numerical results validate that the robustness function $R(m, p)$ approaches to 1 as m increases if $p > 0.5$. An straightforward comparison between the curves of $R(m, p)$ also shows that the higher value of p is, the faster $R(m, p)$ approaches to 1. In addition, the estimated defect rate of the generalized data inconsistency detection is strictly less than $\frac{1}{2}$, so the defect-free rate of the generalized data inconsistency detection must be greater than $\frac{1}{2}$. All these results definitely imply that the generalized data inconsistency detection is sufficiently robust under the probability fault model.

Acknowledgments. The authors would like to express the most immense gratitude to the anonymous referees for their insightful and constructive comments. This work is supported in part by the Ministry of Science and Technology, Taiwan, Republic of China, under Grants MOST 104-2221-E-468-002 and MOST 104-2221-E-468-003.

References

1. Aram, S., Khosa, I., Pasero, E.: Conserving energy through neural prediction of sensed data. J. Wirel. Mobile Netw. Ubiquitous Comput. Dependable Appl. **6**(1), 74–97 (2015)
2. Caruso, A., Albini, L., Maestrini, P.: A new diagnosis algorithm for regular inter-connected structures. In: de Lemos, R., Weber, T.S., Camargo, J.B. (eds.) LADC 2003. LNCS, vol. 2847, pp. 264–281. Springer, Heidelberg (2003). https://doi.org/10.1007/978-3-540-45214-0_20
3. Caruso, A., Chessa, S., Maestrini, P.: Evaluation of a diagnosis algorithm for regular structures. IEEE Trans. Comput. **51**(7), 850–865 (2002)
4. Caruso, A., Chessa, S., Maestrini, P.: Fault-diagnosis of grid structures. Theoret. Comput. Sci. **290**(2), 1149–1174 (2003)
5. Caruso, A., Chessa, S., Maestrini, P.: Worst-case diagnosis completeness in regular graphs under the $\mathcal{PMC}$ model. IEEE Trans. Comput. **56**(7), 917–924 (2007)
6. Chang, Y., Bhuyan, L.N.: A combinatorial analysis of subcube reliability in hypercube. IEEE Trans. Comput. **44**(7), 952–956 (1995)
7. Chartrand, G., Ollermann, O.R.: Applied and Algorithmic Graph Theory. McGraw-Hill, New York (1993)
8. Chen, J.R., Kher, S., Somani, A.: Distributed fault detection of wireless sensor networks. In: Proceedings of the 2006 Workshop on Dependability Issues in Wireless Ad Hoc Networks and Sensor Networks (DIWANS 2006), Los Angeles, USA, pp. 65–72. ACM (2006)
9. Chessa, S., Maestrini, P.: Correct and almost complete diagnosis of processor grids. IEEE Trans. Comput. **50**(10), 1095–1102 (2001)
10. Das, C.R., Kim, J.: A unified task-based dependability model for hypercube computers. IEEE Trans. Parallel Distrib. Syst. **3**(3), 312–324 (1992)
11. Devipriya, M., Nithya, B., Mala, C.: Hashing based distributed backoff (HBDB) mechanism for IEEE 802.11 wireless networks. J. Internet Serv. Inform. Secur. **5**(3), 1–18 (2015)
12. Fitzgerald, K., Latifi, S.: Reliability modeling and assessment of the star-graph networks. IEEE Trans. Reliab. **51**(1), 49–57 (2002)
13. Hsu, G.H., Tan, J.J.M.: A local diagnosability measure for multiprocessor systems. IEEE Trans. Parallel Distrib. Syst. **18**(5), 598–607 (2007)
14. Intanagonwiwat, C., Govindan, R., Estrin, D.: Directed diffusion: a scalable and robust communication paradigm for sensor networks. In: Proceedings of the 6th Annual ACM/IEEE International Conference on Mobile Computing and Networking (MOBICOM 2000), Boston, USA, pp. 56–67. ACM/IEEE (2000)

15. Jiang, P.: A new method for node fault detection in wireless sensor networks. Sensors **9**(2), 1282–1294 (2009)
16. Kales, P.: Reliability: For Technology, Engineering, and Management. Prentice-Hall, New Jersey (1998)
17. Kung, T.L., Chen, H.C.: Toward the fault identification method for diagnosing strongly t-diagnosable systems under the $\mathcal{PMC}$ model. Int. J. Commun. Netw. Distributed Syst. **15**(4), 386–399 (2015)
18. Kung, T.L., Hung, C.N.: Estimating the subsystem reliability of bubblesort networks. Theoret. Comput. Sci. **670**, 45–55 (2017)
19. Kung, T.L., Teng, Y.H., Lin, C.K., Chen, H.C.: A localized fault identification algorithm for mobility management in the strongly t-diagnosable wireless ad hoc network under the comparison model. EURASIP J. Wirel. Commun. Networking **2016**(218), 1–11 (2016)
20. Kuo, S.Y., Huang, C.Y., Lyu, M.R.: Framework for modeling software reliability using various testing-efforts and fault-detection rates. IEEE Trans. Reliab. **50**(3), 310–320 (2001)
21. Lai, P.L.: A systematic algorithm for identifying faults on hypercube-like networks under the comparison model. IEEE Trans. Reliab. **61**(2), 452–459 (2012)
22. Leu, F.Y., Chen, H.L., Cheng, C.C.: Improving multi-path congestion control for event-driven wireless sensor networks by using TDMA. J. Internet Serv. Inform. Secur. **5**(4), 1–19 (2015)
23. Li, Y., Thai, M.T., Wang, F., Yi, C.W., Wan, P., Du, D.Z.: On greedy construction of connected dominating sets in wireless networks. J. Wirel. Commun. Mobile Comput. **5**(8), 927–932 (2005)
24. Lin, C.K., Kung, T.L., Tan, J.J.M.: Conditional-fault diagnosability of multiprocessor systems with an efficient local diagnosis algorithm under the $\mathcal{PMC}$ model. IEEE Trans. Parallel Distrib. Syst. **22**(10), 1669–1680 (2011)
25. Lin, C.K., Kung, T.L., Tan, J.J.M.: An algorithmic approach to conditional-fault local diagnosis of regular multiprocessor interconnected systems under the $\mathcal{PMC}$ model. IEEE Trans. Comput. **62**(3), 439–451 (2013)
26. Lin, L., Xu, L., Zhou, S., Wang, D.: The reliability of subgraph in the arrangement graph. IEEE Trans. Reliab. **64**(2), 807–818 (2015)
27. Mánik, M., Gramatová, E.: Boolean formalisation of the $\mathcal{PMC}$ model for faulty units diagnosis in regular multi-processor systems. In: Proceedings of the 11th International Symposium on Design and Diagnostics of Electronic Circuits and Systems (DDECS), pp. 1–2. IEEE (2008)
28. Mánik, M., Gramatová, E.: Diagnosis of faulty units in regular graphs under the $\mathcal{PMC}$ model. In: Proceedings of the 12th International Symposium on Design and Diagnostics of Electronic Circuits and Systems (DDECS), pp. 202–205. IEEE (2009)
29. Ni, S.Y., Tseng, Y.C., Chen, Y.S., Sheu, J.P.: The broadcast storm problem in a mobile ad hoc network. In: Proceedings of the 5th Annual ACM/IEEE International Conference on Mobile Computing and Networking (MOBICOM 1999), Seattle, USA, pp. 151–162. ACM/IEEE (1999)
30. Robles, T., Alcarria, R., Martin, D., Navarro, M., Calero, R., Iglesias, S., López, M.: An iot based reference architecture for smart water management processes. J. Wirel. Mobile Netw. Ubiquitous Comput. Dependable Appl. **6**(1), 4–23 (2015)
31. Sharma, V., Kumar, R., Rathore, N.: Topological broadcasting using parameter sensitivity-based logical proximity graphs in coordinated ground-flying ad hoc networks. J. Wirel. Mobile Netw. Ubiquitous Comput. Dependable Appl. **6**(3), 54–72 (2015)

32. Sinha, P., Sivakumar, R., Bharghavan, V.: Enhancing ad hoc routing with dynamic virtual infrastrutures. In: Proceedings of 20th Annual Joint Conference of the IEEE Computer and Communication Societies (INFOCOM 2001), Anchorage, AK, pp. 1763–1772. IEEE (2001)
33. Skarmeta, A.F., Moreno, M.V., Iera, A.: Smart things, big data technology and ubiquitous computing solutions for the future internet of things. J. Wirel. Mobile Netw. Ubiquitous Comput. Dependable Appl. **6**(1), 1–3 (2015)
34. Soh, S., Rai, S., Trahan, J.L.: Improved lower bounds on the reliability of hypercube architectures. IEEE Trans. Parallel Distrib. Syst. **5**(4), 364–378 (1994)
35. Thai, M., Wang, F., Liu, D., Zhu, S., Du, D.Z.: Connected dominating sets in wireless networks with different transmission ranges. IEEE Trans. Mob. Comput. **6**(7), 721–730 (2007)
36. Wan, P.J., Alzoubi, K.M., Frieder, O.: Distributed construction of connected dominating set in wireless ad hoc networks. In: Proceedings of 21st Annual Joint Conference of the IEEE Computer and Communication Societies (INFOCOM 2002), New York, USA, pp. 1597–1604. IEEE (2002)
37. Weng, C.E., Sharma, V., Chen, H.C., Mao, C.H.: PEER: proximity-based energy-efficient routing algorithm for wireless sensor networks. J. Internet Serv. Inform. Secur. **6**(1), 47–56 (2016)
38. Wu, X., Latifi, S.: Substar reliability analysis in star networks. Inf. Sci. **178**, 2337–2348 (2008)
39. Xu, M., Thulasiraman, K., Xu, X.D.: Conditional diagnosability of matching composition networks under the $\mathcal{PMC}$ model. IEEE Trans. Circ. Syst. II Express Briefs **56**(11), 875–879 (2009)
40. Zarezadeh, S., Asadi, M.: Network reliability modeling under stochastic process of component failures. IEEE Trans. Reliab. **62**(4), 917–929 (2013)
41. Zhu, Q., Guo, G., Wang, D.: Relating diagnosability, strong diagnosability and conditional diagnosability of strong networks. IEEE Trans. Comput. **63**(7), 1847–1851 (2014)

Building a Frame-Based Cyber Security Learning Game

Yuh-Jye Wang[1], Shian-Shyong Tseng[2(✉)], Tsung-Yu Yang[2], and Jui-Feng Weng[2]

[1] Department of Computer Science and Information Engineering,
Asia University,
Taichung, Republic of China
ecp@ms19.url.com.tw
[2] Department of Applied Informatics and Multimedia, Asia University,
Taichung, Republic of China
sstseng@asia.edu.tw, zongyu212@gmail.com, wengroy@gmail.com

Abstract. With the rapid growth of the Internet-based smart mobile phone applications, a variety of sophisticated threats or attacks have been developed on the Internet recently. Therefore, how to enhance the cyber-security literacy education to prevent or mitigate Internet crimes becomes a very important and challenging issue. In this paper, the frame structure of the knowledge base for the card game called iMonsters has been designed to help students to easily understand the attack or defense strategies and concepts in cyber-security domain, and the ontology crystallization method will be applied to refine the existing ontology. We then propose a rule generation algorithm to generate new rules based upon learning from examples approach, and the generated new rules can be used as the scaffoldings to help the users to learn the knowledge obtained from the real cases. 53 children have participated in the iMonster card game playing in 2015. Based upon the experimental results, we can find that the card game playing can assist students to learn the cyber-security knowledge.

Keywords: Cyber-security learning · Ontology crystallization
iMonster card game

1 Introduction

With the rapid development of information technology and network technology, the Internet-based services and applications of human daily life have been growing dramatically. According to Symantec's Norton 2015 Global Internet Security Threat Report, the direct and indirect economic losses caused have been increasing rapidly. Therefore, how to enhance the cyber-security literacy education to prevent or mitigate Internet crimes becomes a very important and challenging issue [5, 6]. Due to the popularity of smart mobile devices and Apps, sophisticated phishing attacks combined with APTs (Advanced Persistent Threats) to defraud victims of critical data and information are also increasing rapidly. In such cyber-attack context, the traditional way to develop the learning content usually requires a lot of efforts to acquire the domain knowledge from experts. In our previous research, we proposed an ontology crystallization method to gradually crystallize phishing ontology by analyzing newly obtained phishing cases and

© Springer Nature Singapore Pte Ltd. 2018
I. You et al. (Eds.): MobiSec 2016, CCIS 797, pp. 32–41, 2018.
https://doi.org/10.1007/978-981-10-7850-7_4

refining the existing knowledge base accordingly. Therefore, the resulting knowledge can be easily understood and explained. In this paper, the ontology crystallization method will be applied for the card game called iMonsters to help students to easily understand the attack or defense strategies and concepts.

In our previous studies [1–4], the APT has been modeled by the APT knowledge frames and APT scenario frames for describing nowadays APT attack, so that the created knowledge can be used to help users to distinguish APT attacks in real life. In this paper, we firstly apply the frame-based knowledge representation to model the three different roles of the iMonsters card game: attack card, defense card and resource card. During the game playing, the players take turns to use resources to summon monsters role card, or use role cards monster to attack or defense. We further propose a new rule generation algorithm based upon the learning from examples approach to generate the rules from the real cases in cyber-security domain. These rules will be used as the scaffoldings for helping students learn cyber-security. An experiment has been done to evaluate the effectiveness of the card game playing in Children's Network Security Learning Summer Camp in 2015. In our experiment, the students were engaged in the game-based learning activity. There are 37 children achieved the high learning performance. It shows game playing is a good way to help students to learn the Internet Literacy.

2 Related Work

Education is one of effective ways to protect users from attacks on Internet. Due to the low motivation of studying documental cyber security materials, some education games have been proposed for improving the learning motivation of users.

In [13, 14], the Game-based learning (GBL) which has gained considerable attention usually uses an interesting narrative and competitive exercises to motivate students learning according to specific designed learning objectives. Anti-Phishing Phil developed by Carnegie Mellon University allows users to play game to identify whether the link is legitimate or not by choosing to "eat" or "reject" the worm [11]. Paypal and VeriSign have also provided user quizzes to enhance learning motivation [15, 16]. CyberCIEGE [7–9] is a security awareness tool which offers a realistic virtual world in which players have to operate and defend a computer network. In our previous study, the cyber-security learning content pages which are composed of phishing attack knowledge and phishing scenario knowledge can be generated automatically by knowledge inference [16].

However, without realistic simulation, the games contain only general principles or limited cyber security knowledge, so students still hardly apply cyber security knowledge in real environment after the game-based learning. In the context of rapid changes in cyber-attacks, cyber-attack is more complex than traditional phishing attack and defense. Our goal is to make students understand the usage of the offensive and defensive strategies and tactics to enhance the effectiveness of the cyber-security learning.

Regular card game generally has a fixed number, just an extension of the change in the method of the game. The TCG (Trading Card Game) system having a fundamental set of rules describes the players' objectives, the categories of cards used in the game, and the basic rules by which the cards interact. The iMonsters is a TCG, in which each role card has additional text explaining its specific functionalities and the cards are named accordingly. Learner Master an understanding of the network of these possible interactions as they develop strategy.

3   iMonsters Card Game Knowledge Construction

For the Cyber-Security Ontology shown in Fig. 1 [4], the ontology crystallization method [18, 19] will be used to construct the whole cyber-security ontology with only little expert assistances.

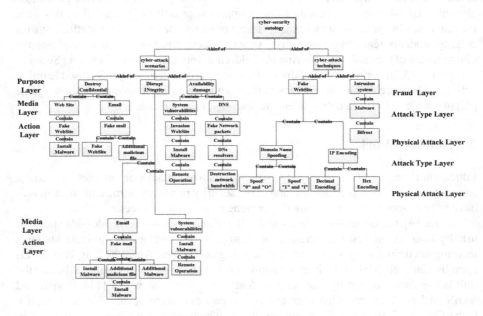

Fig. 1. Cyber-security ontology.

According to our observation, most of the recent cyber-attacks are the descendants of previous particular one. And the evolution could be the changing of the attacking media or attacking scenario. Therefore, tracing the history of the attacking technology is a good approach to model the attack knowledge. So, our idea is to trace the cyber-security history according to the evolution of attacking technologies. The cyber-security ontology can be refined by adding a new attribute called cyber-security event occurred date.

Therefore, the Cyber-Security Skeleton (CSS) consists of cyber-security event occurred date (OOD), the cyber-attack scenarios (CAS), and cyber-attack techniques (CAT). There are three layers in cyber-attack scenarios, including the Purpose Layer, Media Layer, and Action Layer. There are three layers in cyber-attack techniques, including the Fraud tips Layer, Attack type Layer, Physical attack Layer, as shown in Fig. 1.

3.1   The Design of the Roles in iMonsters Card Game

Based upon the Network attack and defense strategies ontology [13, 14], we further design the roles in the iMonsters card game [4]. As shown in Fig. 2, there are three different kinds of roles of the game, including attack card, defense card and resources card; attack cards includes passive attack, hacking and security vulnerability attack; defense cards includes prevention card and detection card.

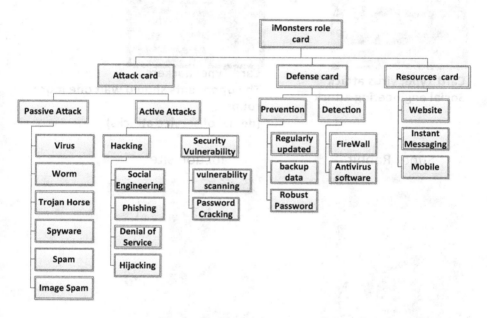

Fig. 2.   The structure of role cards

3.2   Frame of Role Card Knowledge Structure

During the game playing, the players take turns to use resources to summon monsters role card or use role cards monster to attack/defense by considering: the concepts of network attacks, the favorite strategies, the characters of role card, and the current status. Figure 3 shows four different types of role cards: phishing, hacker attacks, defending and network resources, each of which has the properties of type, name, the strength, etc.

Phishing Piggy

Card Type: virus attack
Social engineering attack

Script Kiddie

Card Type: hackers
The opponents should wait one more round
(denial of service attacks)

Super Rabbit

Card Type: virus attack
Social engineering attack

auction site

Cards Type: Website

Fig. 3. Properties of the role cards

Take the Phishing piggy card as an example, Fig. 4 introduces the slot name and the slot values of the phishing frame.

According to the frame shown in Fig. 4, the card role name "Phishing Piggy" is an instance of the traditional Phishing Frame, inherited from the frame called Phishing Frame. Figure 5 shows the relationship between the role card Phishing Piggy and the frame.

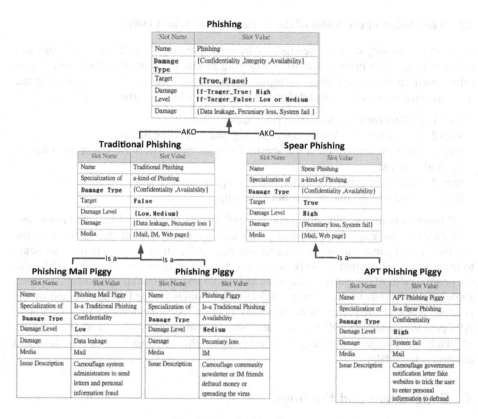

Phishing

Slot Name	Slot Value
Name	Phishing
Damage Type	{Confidentiality ,Integrity ,Availability}
Target	{True, Flase}
Damage Level	If-Trager_True: High If-Targer_False: Low or Medium
Damage	{Data leakage, Pecuniary loss, System fail }

——AKO——   ——AKO——

Traditional Phishing

Slot Name	Slot Value
Name	Traditional Phishing
Specialization of	a-kind-of Phishing
Damage Type	{Confidentiality ,Availability}
Target	False
Damage Level	{Low, Medium}
Damage	{Data leakage, Pecuniary loss }
Media	{Mail, IM, Web page}

Spear Phishing

Slot Name	Slot Value
Name	Spear Phishing
Specialization of	a-kind-of Phishing
Damage Type	{Confidentiality ,Availability}
Target	True
Damage Level	High
Damage	{Pecuniary loss, System fail}
Media	{Mail, Web page}

——Is a——   ——Is a——   ——Is a——

Phishing Mail Piggy

Slot Name	Slot Value
Name	Phishing Mail Piggy
Specialization of	Is-a Traditional Phishing
Damage Type	Confidentiality
Damage Level	Low
Damage	Data leakage
Media	Mail
Issue Description	Camouflage system administrators to send letters and personal information fraud

Phishing Piggy

Slot Name	Slot Value
Name	Phishing Piggy
Specialization of	Is-a Traditional Phishing
Damage Type	Availability
Damage Level	Medium
Damage	Pecuniary loss
Media	IM
Issue Description	Camouflage community newsletter or IM friends defraud money or spreading the virus

APT Phishing Piggy

Slot Name	Slot Value
Name	APT Phishing Piggy
Specialization of	Is-a Spear Phishing
Damage Type	Confidentiality
Damage Level	High
Damage	System fail
Media	Mail
Issue Description	Camouflage government notification letter fake websites to trick the user to enter personal information to defraud

Fig. 4. The phishing frame

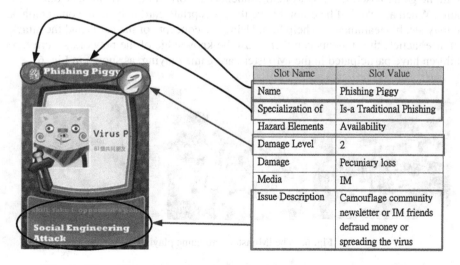

Slot Name	Slot Value
Name	Phishing Piggy
Specialization of	Is-a Traditional Phishing
Hazard Elements	Availability
Damage Level	2
Damage	Pecuniary loss
Media	IM
Issue Description	Camouflage community newsletter or IM friends defraud money or spreading the virus

Fig. 5. The relationship between the role card Phishing Piggy and the frame

3.3   The Design of the Rules of the Network Attack and Defense

In [3], cyber security case can be modeled by corresponding APT attack knowledge and scenario pages. We propose the following rule generation algorithm to generate new rules based upon learning from examples approach, and these new rules can help the users to learn the offensive and defensive knowledge obtained from the real cases.

Step 1: Collect the real cases of cyber-attacks.
Step 2: For each case, identify the attacking and defending actions.
Step 3: For each action, select the appropriate role card to perform the corresponding or similar action.
Step 4: Refine the cyber-security concept map, if necessary.
Step 5: Conduct the concept mapping learning assessment.

iMonsters is a strategic card game for multiplayer players and we can create new type cards to increase the complexity and the interestingness of the game. Use the iMonsters card game with role cards and new rules to illustrate ways of helping students to learn to play the game network security strategy and tactics concept. In addition to the general rules of the game contains the attack, advanced modular attacks used to teach students to understand the strategy and tactics of offensive and defensive use of the process. Has collected relevant news stories, contain loopholes through into the attack, APT penetration attacks, DDoS distributed attacks, worms, spyware and other categories of attacks, and the use of the algorithm proposed in this study to sort out the attack and defense-related table.

4   Experiment and Findings

With the game-based learning system, students can form a network alliance during the game. When attacked, if he did not have the appropriate card in hand to counterattack, he may ask his teammates to help him. Using the concepts of the cards and the attack/defense tactics, the students can then learn the knowledge of the network security. 53 children have participated in the iMonster card game playing, as shown in Fig. 6.

Fig. 6. The iMonster card game playing

Before the game playing, the children firstly learned the network security literacy from the lecture and the related multimedia films. As shown in Fig. 7 there are 37 children achieved the high learning performance.

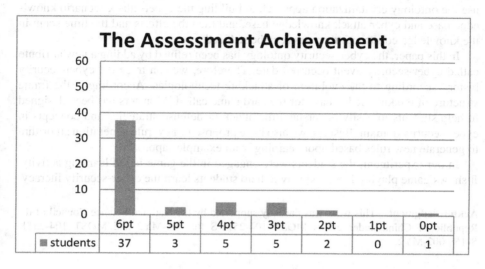

Fig. 7. The results of the assessment

As shown in Fig. 8, 13 students have "Phishing" misconception and 10 students have "combo-defense" misconception. It means that the card game playing can find the students' misconceptions and assist them to learn the network security knowledge.

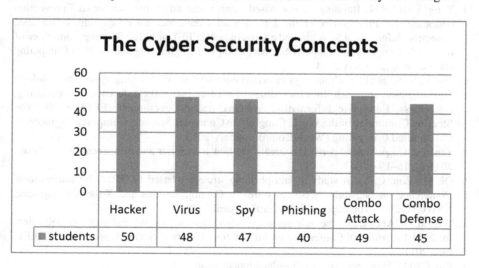

Fig. 8. The results of the concepts assessment

5 Conclusion

Due to the rapid changes of context in cyber-attack attacks, in our previous studies we use the ontology crystallization approach to building the cyber-attack scenario knowledge base and cyber-attack knowledge base, and then the efforts and the time spent in the knowledge construction process can be reduced.

In this paper, the cyber-security ontology has been refined by adding a new attribute called cyber-security event occurred date. Therefore, we can trace the cyber-security history according to the evolution of attacking technologies. Accordingly, the frame structure of the knowledge base for the card game called iMonsters has been designed to help students to easily understand the attack or defense strategies and concepts in cyber-security domain. Besides, we also have proposed a new rule generation algorithm to generate new rules based upon learning from examples approach.

In our experiment, the students were engaged in the game-based learning activity. It shows game playing is a good way to help students learn the cyber-security literacy.

Acknowledgment. This work was partially supported by the National Science Council of the Republic of China under grants MOST 104-2511-S-468-005-MY2 and MOST 104-2511-S-468-002-MY2.

References

1. Tseng, S.S., Ku, C.H., Lee, T.J., Geng, G.G., Wang, Y.J.: Building a frame-based anti-phishing model based on phishing ontology. In: Proceedings of the AIT 2013 (2013)
2. Lee, T-J., et al.: Game-based anti-phishing training. In: Proceedings of the TWELF (2010)
3. Tung, Y.-H., et al.: Building a frame-based content generation approach for APT prevention education. In: Proceedings of the International Conference on e-Learning, e-Business, Enterprise Information Systems, and e-Government (EEE), p. 1. The Steering Committee of the World Congress in Computer Science, Computer Engineering and Applied Computing (WorldComp), January 2014
4. Tseng, S.-S., et al.: Building a game-based internet security learning system by ontology crystallization approach. In: Proceedings of the International Conference on e-Learning, e-Business, Enterprise Information Systems, and e-Government (EEE), p. 98. The Steering Committee of the World Congress in Computer Science, Computer Engineering and Applied Computing (WorldComp), January 2015
5. Tankard, C.: Advanced persistent threats and how to monitor and deter them. Netw. Secur. **2011**(8), 16–19 (2011)
6. Qi, M., Zou, C.-Y.: A study of anti-phishing strategies based on TRIZ. In: International Conference on Networks Security, Wireless Communications and Trusted Computing, NSWCTC 2009, vol. 2, pp. 536–538. IEEE, April 2009
7. Wilson, C., Argles, D.: The fight against phishing: technology, the end user and legislation. In: 2011 International Conference on Information Society (i-Society), pp. 501–504. IEEE, June 2011
8. Bay (2011). http://pages.ebay.com/education/spooftutorial
9. Microsoft (2011). http://www.microsoft.com/athome/security/email/phishing.mspx

10. Dennis, D., William, R.: "Games are made for fun": lessons on the effects of concept maps in the classroom use of computer games. Comput. Educ. **56**(3), 604–615 (2011)
11. OnGuardOnline (2011). http://www.onguardonline.gov/games/phishing-scams.aspx
12. Gorling, S.: The myth of user education. In: Virus Bulletin Conference, vol. 11, p. 13, October 2006
13. Admiraal, W., et al.: The concept of flow in collaborative game-based learning. Comput. Hum. Behav. **27**(3), 1185–1194 (2011)
14. Papastergiou, M.: Digital game-based learning in high school computer science education: impact on educational effectiveness and student motivation. Comput. Educ. **52**(1), 1–12 (2009)
15. Sheng, S., Magnien, B., Kumaraguru, P., Acquisti, A., Cranor, L.F., Hong, J., Nunge, E.: Anti-phishing phil: the design and evaluation of a game that teaches people not to fall for phish. In: Proceedings of the 3rd Symposium on Usable Privacy and Security, pp. 88–99. ACM, July 2007
16. Paypal (2011). https://www.paypal.com/au/cgi-bin/webscr?cmd=xpt/Marketing/securitycenter/antiphishing/CanYouSpotPhishing-outside
17. VeriSign (2011). https://www.phish-no-phish.com/default.aspx
18. Weng, J.-F.: A self-organizing behavior modeling on programming e-Learning. Ph.D. dissertation, Department of Computer Science, National Chiao Tung University, Hsinchu, Taiwan, R.O.C., December 2010
19. Lin, H.N., Tseng, S.S., Weng, J.F., Lin, H.Y., Su, J.M.: An iterative, collaborative ontology construction scheme. In: Second International Conference on Innovative Computing, Information and Control, ICICIC 2007, p. 150. IEEE, September 2007

Personal Identification Using Time and Frequency Domain Features of ECG Lead-I

Gyu Ho Choi[1], Hae Min Moon[2], and Sung Bum Pan[3(✉)]

[1] Department of Control and Instrumentation Engineering, Chosun University,
Gwangju, Republic of Korea
choiguho@gmail.com
[2] Soongsil University, Seoul, Republic of Korea
bombilove@gmail.com
[3] Department of Electronics Engineering, Chosun University,
Gwangju, Republic of Korea
sbpan@chosun.ac.kr

Abstract. Recently, people are increasingly interested in biometrics using wearable device-based biosignals. Biosignals are better than fingerprints, iris, and faces because of less objection, and easy perpetuation and continuation with biosignals. This paper proposes a system for personal identification using ECG which is a biosignal. The proposed system uses ECG signals and extracts features by convergence in the time domain and the frequency domain. The ECG-based method of personal identification analyzes performance change depending on enrolment data, recognition data and the number of feature parameters by 1:N matching to analyze performance. The experiment revealed personal identification performance of 98% in ECG data of 10 persons obtained while they felt comfortable.

Keywords: Wearable device · Biometrics · Bio-signal · ECG
Personal identification

1 Introduction

It is a recent trend to study biometric authentication system technology which converges IT with BT by using wearable devices [5,9]. A wearable device is worn to let users use freely both of their hands, and free them from temporal and special limitations. That is, a wearable device can collect bio-information including body temperature, blood pressure and ECG without hindering user's daily living once the user wears it [4]. The collected personal bio-information is used for various services, for example, authentication technology, medical purpose, health care and the like [19].

The biometric authentication technology is excellent in terms of security and convenience [3,8]. The process of recognizing individual persons by using bio-information of fingerprints and iris involves user's objection and inconvenience

© Springer Nature Singapore Pte Ltd. 2018
I. You et al. (Eds.): MobiSec 2016, CCIS 797, pp. 42–53, 2018.
https://doi.org/10.1007/978-981-10-7850-7_5

when used. However, the strength of using bio signals is that they are robust to the external environment and users do not need to assume a given action to obtain data. It is hard to counterfeit ECG, a representative biosignal, because it has each person's unique features by the electrophysiologic factors, the position and size of hearts, and physical conditions [2, 7, 10, 25].

Biometric authentication studies are reported for using ECG with the technologies for the number of data channels, changes in measurement state, and types of heart diseases. The method of using multiple channels of ECG enhances recognition ratios by obtaining data according to the Standard 12 Leads Method, and recognizing individual persons by using the Pan-Tompkins algorithm [16, 17]. With ECG signals, it is possible to classify types of personal heart diseases, for example, ischaemic heart diseases, dilated cardiomyopathy, hypertrophic cardiomyopathy, and angina pectoris [23]. In addition, the technology is studied for classifying emotional changes depending on personal stress, exercises, sleeping, and excitement [6, 22]. Although various studies for using ECG are currently in progress, they focus on personal diseases and emotional classification rather than personal identification. Personal identification using ECG of multiple channels experiences lowered accuracy where the number of channels is reduced for the convenience purpose.

This paper proposes a system for personal identification using just ECG signals of a single channel for minimizing the number of electrodes and in consideration of user-friendliness. The proposed algorithm is composed of an enrolment process and a recognition process. In the enrolment process and the recognition process, personal ECG signals are used to convert them to a time domain and a frequency domain after preprocessing them to extract features. The dimension of extracted features is reduced through FLDA for finding unique values and unique vectors. For the classifier for personal identification, Euclidean distance is applied which implements Multi Class Similarity. For the method proposed for analyzing performance, ECG signals were obtained from 10 persons while they felt comfortable. The experiment revealed the best personal identification performance of 98% when every individual had 40 enrolment data and 10 recognition data.

2   Biometrics System Using ECG

Figure 1 shows the architecture of biometrics technology using ECGs. Step 1 is for obtaining, enrolling biosignal data and segmenting them into recognized data; step 2 is for processing data signals by removing noise, setting up and segmenting into a reference point and non-reference points; step 3 is for extracting features matching the biosignals, reducing the feature vector dimension to analyze the data in real time; and step 4 is for applying machine learning which is a final classifier to evaluate user authentication performance.

The first task carried out in biometrics is to build an ECG DB. MIT-BIH & PTB is usually used in PhysioNet which is an official database, or the ECG DB is built by measuring ECGs by means of the developed instrument, medical instruments, wearable devices and mobile devices [1, 12].

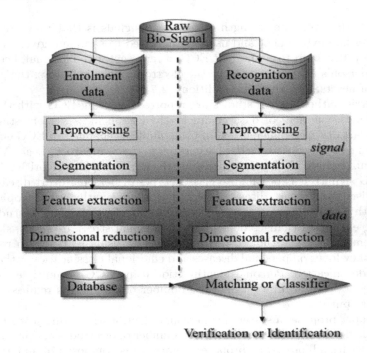

Fig. 1. Biometrics system blocks using ECG

The ECGs obtained from the common database and measured have noise because they are measured by instruments, and signal processing is thus essential. Noise in the electrocardiogram is present in the 60 Hz band of the power supply line generated by the measuring equipment, broadband white noise (power line noise), peripheral noise due to peripherals or movement of the measurer, and baseline fluctuation noise due to respiration of the measurer [18,24]. To remove the aforementioned noises, it is essential to conduct filtering and normalization. Filtering is conducted to remove noise with a frequency filter and through wavelet decomposition. Exemplary frequency filters include high-pass filter, low-pass filter, and band-pass filter-based Butterworth, Chebyshev and Notch filters. Wavelet decomposition is subdivided into the steps to remove noise components after transform by means of the function for wavelet transform, and the noise components are removed by excluding the noise component coefficient in the subdivided steps. Normalization is conducted through up-sampling, down-sampling and over-sampling based on re-sampling by using thresholds proposed in this paper. As a result, raw ECGs are used to output constant clean signals. Segmentation by using ECGs pre-processed for extracting time and features in biometrics establishes sections through the method for setting up a reference point and non-reference points. The reference point is enrolled and segmented to match the recognition time by setting up its initial point and end point by using P, QRS and T waves in the whole ECG. The non-reference points are enrolled without consideration of their end point and end point and segmented just in consideration of the recognition time in the whole ECG.

Data analysis by using the segmented ECG is composed of feature extraction and dimensional reduction by discriminant analysis. Features are selectively extracted by means of the proposed algorithm from the time, frequency and phase domains. Discriminant analysis is conducted to reduce dimensions by using extracted features. Exemplary discriminant analysis includes principal component analysis and linear discriminant analysis. The principle component analysis is to find an axis for reducing a dimension the most efficiently, and reducing the dimension with the axis to extract features [15]. The linear discriminant analysis is to collect internal distributed data while protecting dimensional data and reduce external distributed data by finding the axis going farther away. Deep learning for extracting features and reducing feature dimensions in parallel is now applied after using a neural network to apply it [20].

Machine learning is a classifier for evaluating user authentication and identification performance by using dimension-reduced data, and classified into supervised learning and unsupervised learning. Supervised learning is a method for using a correct answer set (class) established in advance and learning for prediction. Unsupervised learning does not have a correct answer set (class), and clusters sets with similar patterns. Unsupervised learning is composed of the parametric method and the non-parametric method. The SVM (support vector machine) is an exemplary type of supervised learning and a classification modeling method for determining which category a new data belongs to and presenting it as a boundary in a mapped space. Other exemplary methods include the decision tree learning method, KNN (K-Nearest Neighbors algorithm) and Random Forests. The GMM (Gaussian Mixture Model) is a parametric method for modeling data distribution to know the probability that an identified data is selected for a given Gaussian. The k-average algorithm is a non-parametric method and a clustering algorithm for using k average vectors.

3   Personal Identification Algorithm

Figure 2 shows the process of personal identification using ECG Lead-I. The proposed structure is divided into an enrolment process and a recognition process. The enrolment process is composed of a preprocessing process of receiving ECG Lead-I signals as input, removing noise and adjusting a baseline, a process of extracting features from the time domain, a process of storing features in a database for enrolling data, and an Fisher Linear Discriminant Analysis (FLDA) process of reducing the domain of features. The recognition process is composed of a preprocessing process of receiving ECG Lead-I signals as input, removing noise and adjusting a baseline, a process of extracting features from the time domain, an FLDA process of reducing the domain of features and a classification process of final personal identification.

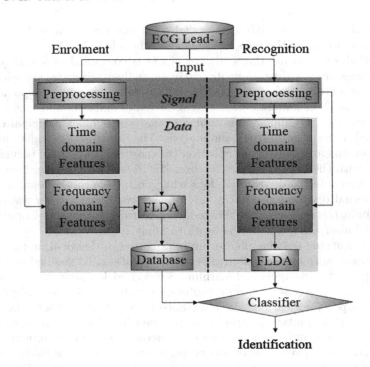

Fig. 2. The block diagram of personal identification based on ECG-lead-I

3.1 Preprocessing

In this study, it is a method to remove noise by preprocessing process using raw ECG Lead-I signal acquired as shown in Fig. 3(a). Two noises are removed from the ECG in the frequency band between 0.05 Hz and 100 Hz. For the power line noise that may generate distortion in a specific section, the high-pass butterworth filter as shown in Fig. 3(b) is applied to specify the frequency not smaller than 60 Hz as a cutoff frequency to remove it. The baseline wander noise due to respiration at low frequency is removed by applying the low-pass butterworth filter to specify the frequency not greater than 0.4 Hz as a cut-off frequency. The small noise present in the frequency-filtered ECG Lead-I is removed by an averaging filter as shown in Fig. 3(c). The R wave peak using the ECG Lead-I with the noise removed for the 5 s segment was detected as shown in Fig. 3(d).

3.2 Time Domain Features

The features in the time domain are extracted with preprocessed local segments and AC. The local segments are extracted with data which exist for 5 s, starting with the peak of R waves. AutoCorrelation(AC) is an approach of finding the existence of possible correlation of error terms always successive in the time domain [11]. The error term of the corresponding time at a specific time includes

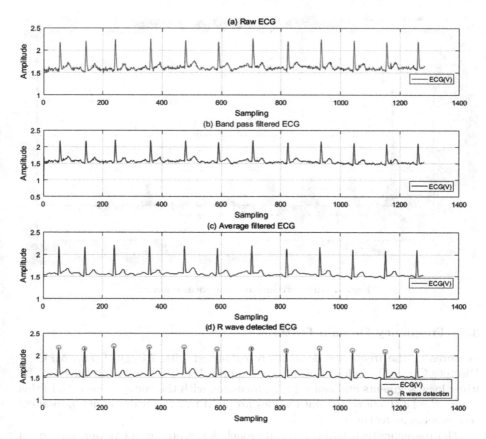

Fig. 3. Preprocessing using ECG: (a) raw ECG Lead-I, (b) band pass filtered ECG Lead-I, (c) average filtered ECG Lead-I, (d) R wave detected ECG Lead-I

the effect transferred due to impact from the previous state as well as the impact at the corresponding time. Therefore, it is known how much the voltage value at the time t_1 is correlated with the voltage value at the time t_2. Autocorrelation exists between the value at the time t_1 and the value at the time t_2. Figure 4 shows AC using local segments. The correlation function representing autocorrelation is calculated with the harmonic mean by multiplying the value at t_1 by the value at t_2. Two limit lines made by the calculated value are composed of an upper limit line and a lower limit line. The upper limit line is a positive limit line, and the lower limit line is a negative limit line. The limit lines are used to know whether the ECG voltage values existing in the time axis are random or not, or estimate future values with the current values. If the autocorrelation value above or below a limit line means not random, they are periodical data. This paper decides that values above and below the limit line are periodical components and extract features.

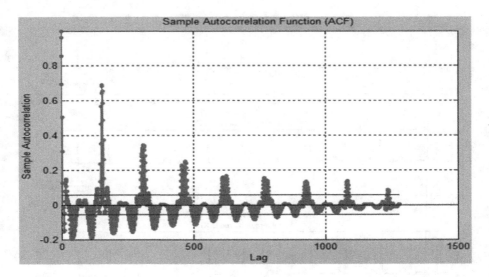

Fig. 4. Autocorrelation using local segments

3.3   Frequency Domain Features

Features in the frequency domain are extracted with AC/DCT and MFCCs. Discrete Cosine Transform(DCT) is an approach of FFT with the time axis by using local segments and again FFT processing with the voltage axis [14]. In this study, the DCT-converted data values are used to extract data with periodical components as features.

Mel-frequency cepstrum is an approach for representing power spectra of short section signals in the time domain, and is obtained through cosine transformation of log power spectra in the frequency domain of non-linear Mel-scale [13]. The frequency band is divided equally in a general cepstrum, but divided equally at the Mel-scale in MFCC. The Mel Filterbank composed of Mel-scale is obtained in respective banks by using the frequency band to divide it into a plurality of filter banks. Mel is calculated

$$M(f) = 1125ln(1 + \frac{f}{700}) \tag{1}$$

by using log as illustrated in Eq. (1). $M(f)$ calculated with Eq. (1) finds cepstrum in the secondary frequency domain through the DCT process.

The bandwidth of respective filters is determined by the critical bandwidth. Therefore, Mel energy is converted to the number of degrees of uncorrelated M-order for the Mel-scale energy through DCT. Figure 5 illustrates a graph of coefficients for which the local segments passing the M-scale filter bank changes into MFC. In this paper, MFCCs which are coefficients by gathering MFCs are extracted as features.

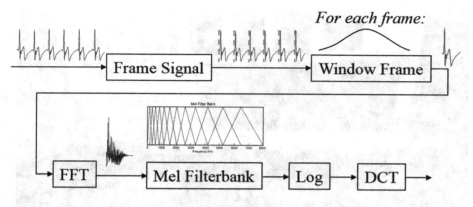

Fig. 5. MFCCs algorithm based on ECG by Mel-scale filter bank

3.4 FLDA and Euclidean Distance

FLDA is an approach of normalizing the difference between average values with a variance in a class to represent and maximize it as an objective function. Fishers linear discriminant function finds linear transformation matrices W for maximizing the objective function. The transformation matrices W are a matrix of projecting specimens of the same classes adjacently but samples of different classes as far as possible. In this study, extracted features in the time domain and the features in the frequency domain are used to find W matrices to reduce dimensions thereof through FLDA.

For the process after dimension reduction, it is essential to group individuals similar each other in the same category or cluster to classify or cluster the individual features. Euclidean Distance similarity is used to measure the level of similarity between individuals with a numerical measure. Euclidean Distance is an algorithm to find a distance between two points in the P dimension with higher similarity as the two individuals resemble more. It is essential to satisfy Eq. (2) to consider corresponding observation values are similar if the two points are close in terms of distance.

$$d(x, y) = \sqrt{\sum_{i=1}^{P} (x_i - y_i)^2} \tag{2}$$

x and y are points at a dimension. In this study, the personal identification ratio is calculated with a Euclidean distance similarity for the feature points of which the dimension between enrolment data and recognition data is reduced.

4   Experiment Result

As shown in Fig. 6, ECG Lead-I was obtained from software tool BrainBay [21] by using BioAMP which is a research and development device. Table 1 shows

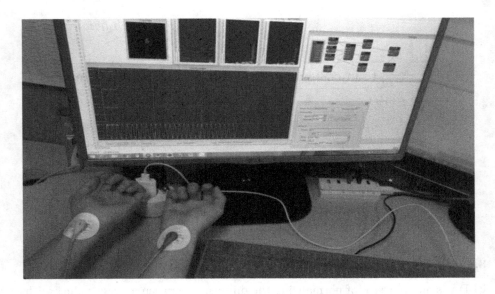

Fig. 6. Acquired ECG Lead-I using BioAMP

Table 1. ECG data information

Information	Data
Participants (persons)	10
Sampling rate (Hz)	256
Data (number)	50
Acquisition time (sec/data)	10
Data usage time (sec/data)	5
Situation	Normal

data of participants in the experiment of 10 persons of 9 males and 1 female, between 24 and 34 years old. The ECG Lead-I signal was sampled at 256 Hz for 10 s, and 50 data were obtained with a time difference of a few days. Actually, the data were obtained for more than 10 s, but it was 5 s for the used data, and the data were measured while participants sat and felt comfortable.

This paper analyzed performance depending on the number of enrolment data, the number of recognition data and the number of features of individuals for personal identification which is a 1:N matching approach. Table 2 illustrates personal identification performance as the number of enrolment data increases. The number of enrolment data was fixed to the minimum number required, and the number of feature parameters was fixed to 182 which is the number of best performance. As the number of enrolment data increases, the personal identification accuracy performance increased from 88.72% to 98%.

Table 2. Accuracy of personal identification with different number change (Enrolment data)

Number of enrolment data	Number of recognition data	Number of feature data	Accuracy
10	40	182	88.72%
15	35	182	90.11%
20	30	182	92.48%
25	25	182	95.13%
30	20	182	96.77%
35	15	182	97.60%
40	10	182	98.00%

The experiment result is that the personal identification was 98% which is the best performance for 40 enrolment data, 10 recognition data and 182 feature parameters. Higher performance is expected as the number of feature parameters increases.

5   Conclusions

This paper proposes a system for personal identification using personal ECG Lead-I signals. The proposed system uses ECG which is a biosignal to analyze performance of personal identification for security authentication systems based on wearable devices. ECG is divided into 12 biosignals in accordance with the Standard 12 Leads Method, among which the Lead-I signal can be obtained from both wrists. Therefore, this paper used the ECG Lead-I signal to analyze the performance of the proposed system. BioAMP which obtained the ECG Lead-I signal for a short time measured signals of 10 participants for experiment while they sat and thus felt comfortable with the equipment for research and development. The experiment reveals the best performance of 98% for personal identification with 40 enrolment data, 10 recognition data and 182 feature parameters per person. The proposed system used the ECG Lead-I signal for a short time and identified the potential personal identification. Better personal identification performance was implemented as enrolment data increased, and lower performance was shown as the recognition data increased. There was not shown a great difference for the change depending on the number of feature parameters. Future plan is to increase the number of experiment data and the number of participants for experiment of this study to study the ECG Lead-I signal-based biometric authentication system and the personal identification system interworking with wearable devices.

References

1. Amiruddin, A.B., Khalifa, O.O., Rabih, F.A.F.: Performance evaluation of human identification based on ECG signal. In: 2015 International Conference on Computing, Control, Networking, Electronics and Embedded Systems Engineering (ICC-NEEE), pp. 479–484. IEEE, September 2015
2. Skarmeta, A.F., Victoria Moreno, M., Iera, A.: Guest editorial: smart things, big data technology and ubiquitous computing solutions for the future internet of things. J. Wirel. Mob. Netw. Ubiquit. Comput. Depend. Appl. 6(1), 1–3 (2015)
3. Adkins, L.D.: Biometrics: weighing convenience and national security against your privacy. Mich. Telecommun. Tech. Law Rev. 13, 541–555 (2007). Spring
4. Sanz-Izquierdo, B., Huang, F., Batchelor, J.C., Sobhy, M.: Compact antenna for WLAN on body applications. In: 36th European Microwave Conference, England, pp. 815–818. IEEE, September 2006
5. Chen, C., Anada, H., Kawamoto, J., Sakurai, K.: A hybrid encryption scheme with key-cloning protection: user/terminal double authentication via attributes and fingerprints. J. Internet Serv. Inf. Secur. (JISIS) 6(2), 37–52 (2016)
6. Hardani, D.N.K., Wahyunggoro, O., Nugroho, H.A., Faisal, N.: Analysis of emotional condition based on electrocardiogram signals. In: 2014 International Conference on Electrical Engineering and Computer Science (ICEECS), pp. 152–157. IEEE, November 2014
7. Di Crescenzo, G., Graveman, R., Ge, R., Arce, G.: Approximate message authentication and biometric entity authentication. In: Patrick, A.S., Yung, M. (eds.) FC 2005. LNCS, vol. 3570, pp. 240–254. Springer, Heidelberg (2005). https://doi.org/10.1007/11507840_22
8. Yang, H., Oleshchuk, V., Prinz, A.: Verifying group authentication protocols by Scyther. J. Wirel. Mob. Netw. Ubiquit. Comput. Depend. Appl. 7(2), 3–19 (2016)
9. Janakiraman, R., Zhang, M.: Technological convergence of IT and BT: evidence from patent analysis. ETRI J. 34(3), 226–231 (2012)
10. Sidek, K., Sufi, F., Khalil, I., Al-Shammary, D.: An efficient method of biometric matching using interpolated ECG data. In: 2010 IEEE EMBS Conference on Biomedical Engineering and Sciences (IECBES), pp. 330–335. IEEE, December 2010
11. Legendre, P.: Spatial autocorrelation: trouble or new paradigm? Ecology 74(6), 1659–1673 (1993)
12. Dar, M.N., Akram, M.U., Shaukat, A., Khan, M.A.: ECG based biometric identification for population with normal and cardiac anomalies using hybrid HRV and DWT features. In: 2015 5th International Conference on IT Convergence and Security (ICITCS), pp. 1–5. IEEE, August 2015
13. Murty, K., Yegnanarayana, B.: Combining evidence from residual phase and MFCC features for speaker recognition. IEEE Signal Process. Lett. 13(1), 52–55 (2006)
14. Ahmed, N., Natarajan, T., Rao, K.R.: Discrete cosine transfom. IEEE Trans. Comput. 23(1), 90–93 (1974)
15. Boumbarov, O., Velchev, Y., Sokolov, S.: Personal biometric identification based on ECG features. J. Inf. Technol. Control 4(3), 11–18 (2008)
16. Pan, J., Tomkins, W.J.: Personal identification based on vectorcardiogram derived from limb leads electrocardiogram. J. Appl. Math. 2012(ID 904905), November 2012
17. Pan, J., Tompkins, W.J.: A real-time QRS detection algorithm. IEEE Trans. Biomed. Eng. BME-32(3), 230–236 (1985)

18. Fattah, S.A., Shahnaz, C., Jameel, A.S.M.M., Goswami, R.: ECG signal based human identification method using features in temporal and wavelet domains. In: TENCON 2012–2012 IEEE Region 10 Conference, pp. 1–4. IEEE, November 2012
19. Aram, S., Shirvani, R.A., Pasero, E.G., Chouikha, M.F.: Implantable medical devices; networking security survey. J. Internet Serv. Inf. Secur. (JISIS) **6**(3), 40–60 (2016)
20. Pathoumvanh, S., Airphaiboon, S., Prapochanung, B., Leauhatong, T.: ECG analysis for person identification. In: 2013 6th Biomedical Engineering International Conference (BMEiCON), pp. 1–4. IEEE, October 2013
21. Collins, T., Woolley, S.I., Rawson, N.C., Haroon, L.: Final-year projects using open source openEEG. Comput. Appl. Eng. Educ. **24**(1), 156–164 (2015)
22. Kato, T., Kawanaka, H., Bhuiyan, M.S., Oguri, K.: Classification of positive and negative emotion evoked by traffic jam based on electrocardiogram (ECG) and pulse wave. In: 2011 14th International IEEE Conference on Intelligent Transportation Systems (ITSC), pp. 1217–1222. IEEE, October 2011
23. Nazmy, T.M., El-Messiry, H., Al-Bokhity, B.: Adaptive neuro-fuzzy inference system for classification of ECG signals. In: 2010 The 7th International Conference on Informatics and Systems (INFOS), pp. 1–6. IEEE, March 2010
24. Shen, T.W., Tompkins, W.J., Hu, Y.H. (eds.): One-Lead ECG for Identity Verification, vol. 1. IEEE, October 2002
25. Wang, Y., Agrafioti, F., Hatzinakos, D., Plataniotis, K.N.: Analysis of human electrocardiogram for biometric recognition. EURASIP J. Adv. Sig. Process. **2008**, 1–11 (2007). Springer

A Secure Color-Code Key Exchange Protocol for Mobile Chat Application

Hsing-Chung Chen[1,2(✉)], Hong Chang[3], Tzu-Liang Kung[1(✉)],
Yung-Fa Huang[4(✉)], Ze-Min Lin[1], Pei-Chi Yeh[1], and Qiu-Hua Ruan[1]

[1] Department of Computer Science and Information Engineering,
Asia University, Taichung, Taiwan
{cdma2000, tlkung}@asia.edu.tw
[2] Department of Medical Research, China Medical University Hospital,
China Medical University, Taichung, Taiwan
shin8409@ms6.hinet.net
[3] School of Information Engineering, Xiamen Nanyang College, Xiamen, China
104703620@qq.com
[4] Department of Information and Communication Engineering,
Chaoyang University of Technology, Taichung, Taiwan
yfahuang@cyut.edu.tw

Abstract. This paper proposes a secure color-code key exchange protocol for secure mobile chat applications (MC APPs). This proposed protocol in this paper is a novel approach which the exchanged color-code coding session keys are selected from the assigned color-code sets, which each color-code key is determined by according to a random number and generated by using simple exclusive-or operations for each session. Furthermore, some distinct color codes are chosen randomly and represented as passwords for the distinct session, which are exchanged via a Mobile Chat Server (MCS). In addition, the exchanged color-code session key is used for the encryption and decryption algorithm which could provide an easy approach to protect the communicated messages between the two clients' MC APP for each session. Finally, it could be applied efficiently to be a novel secure key exchange mechanism on a MC APP.

Keywords: Mobile Chat · Instant Message Service
Color-code key exchange protocol · Secure key exchange protocol

1 Introduction

Due to the rapid developments of the technologies for high speed wireless communications and their supporting software, some newly various mobile applications (APPs) providing convenient and efficient instant messaging service (IMS) have become higher popularly for 4G mobile communications networks. IMS allows people

This version is extended from the original paper titled as 'A Secure Color-Code Key Exchange Protocol' presented in the MobiSec2016 workshop, Taichung, Taiwan, July 13–16, 2016.

© Springer Nature Singapore Pte Ltd. 2018
I. You et al. (Eds.): MobiSec 2016, CCIS 797, pp. 54–64, 2018.
https://doi.org/10.1007/978-981-10-7850-7_6

to use Internet Chat Conversation (ICS) to relay information back and forth in real time. As a result, ICS almost replaces the traditional voice call. Because it's popularity in 4G mobile communication networks, the privacy issues and insecurity problems (Chen et al. 2016b, Kurokawa et al. 2016, Yang et al. 2016, Chakraborty et al. 2016) are more and more dangerous while using IMS on 4G mobile communication networks. It is an urgent task to provide some countermeasures for the user privacy protection and securely exchanged instant messages.

Therefore, we propose an appropriate security protocol for the IMS applications which could provide a securely message exchange method by using the secure color-code key exchange (SCCKE) protocol. In fact, it is the secure color-code key exchange protocol which is first proposed for secure mobile chat applications (MC APPs). In the other words, it is a novel approach in which the exchanged color-code session key selected from the assigned color-code sets. Each color-code session key is generated by according to a random number and some simple exclusive-or operations for each session. Additionally, the two clients' distinct color codes are chosen randomly and represented as passwords for the distinct secure session, which are exchanged via a Mobile Chat Server (MCS). Furthermore, the exchanged color-code session key is then used for the encryption and decryption algorithm which could provide an approach to protect the communicated messages between the two clients' MC APP, individually. Finally, it could be applied efficiently to be a novel secure key exchange mechanism on a MC APP.

The remainder of this paper is organized as follows: In Sect. 2, we introduce the preliminary works. In Sect. 3, we first present SCCKE protocol. Security analyses are discussed in Sect. 4. Finally, we draw our conclusions in Sect. 5.

2 Preliminary

Red, green and blue are three basic colors in color science, which could be mixed in different proportions can produce different colors. In this paper, each color has its own color code represented as an 8-bits binary digital value. For example, some popular color codes are shown Table 1 in which each color coding is represented as 8-bits binary digital value and its decimal value, individually. To mix the different proportions of red color and green color and blue color could produce some new colors out. It could be used to color code encryption and decryption functions in this paper.

At first, we assume that if a mobile user u_i wants to use the MC services, she/he needs to download and install the client application (APP for short) of the MC from an APP store, which the scenario was proposed in the secure End-to-End Mobile Chat (SE2E-MC) scheme (Chen 2014) and the secure group-based mobile chat (SGMC) protocol (Chen et al. 2016a). In this paper, we will follow the same scenarios mentioned above that the users (or called clients) will also initiate the client's registration phase in a MCS after downloading the corresponding secure MC APP, where each user has to apply a new account consisting of a distinct identification u_i. Finally, each user will be assigned a secure information set consisting of an initial random number set, a RNG procedure, a large-size serial random number and a hash information shared and kept secure by the MCS and her/himself.

Table 1. An example for some popular color codes table

Color(s)	Index No.	Color code	Red color		Green color		Blue color	
	Deci-mal	Hex	Binary	Deci-mal	Binary	Deci-mal	Binary	Deci-mal
	1	FF9900	11111111	255	10011001	153	00000000	0
	2	DD3441	11011101	221	00110100	52	01000001	65
	3	FF00FF	11111111	255	00000000	0	11111111	255
	4	99CC00	10011001	153	11001100	204	00000000	0
	5	6A8BD D	01101010	106	10001011	139	11011101	221
	6	66CC99	01100111	103	11001100	204	10011001	153
	7	333300	00110011	51	00110011	51	00000000	0
	8	B7BF9 C	10110111	183	10111111	191	10011100	156
	9	0066FF	00000000	0	01100110	102	11111111	255

3 Secure Color-Code Key Exchange Protocol

The SCCKE protocol is first introduced in this section. There are three phases consisting of *User Registration Phase*, *Color-Code Session Key Generation Phase* and *Secure Messages Encryption and Decryption Phase* which are proposed in this section.

3.1 User Registration Phase

Assume a user u_i wants to register an account from MCS to be a member for this color-code key exchanging system. The user u_i will perform the following steps. The user's registration phase is shown below.

1. The user u_i send his or her identity u_i to MCS for registration;
2. MCS generates a large-size serial random number R_i with hexadecimal digitals via a random number generator (RNG), where the size of the serial random number is a large hexadecimal digitals, *e.g.* $R_i =$ DD3441FF9900FF00FF. . . .;
3. MCS generates the large-size color code set CCS^{u_i} consisting of n color-codes $\left\{ CC^{u_i}_{x\in\{1,2,\ldots,l,\ldots,k,\ldots,n\}} \right\}$, where each color-code $CC^{u_i}_{x\in\{1,2,\ldots,l,\ldots,k,\ldots,n\}}$ is chosen randomly from the serial random number R_i for the user u_i. In the other words, $\text{CCS}^{u_i} = \left\{ CC^{u_i}_1, CC^{u_i}_2, \ldots, CC^{u_i}_l, \ldots, CC^{u_i}_k, \ldots, CC^{u_i}_n \right\} = \left\{ CC^{u_i}_{x\in\{1,2,\ldots,l,\ldots,k,\ldots,n\}} \right\}$, where

each color-code $CC^{u_i}_{x\in\{1,2,\ldots,l,\ldots,k,\ldots,n\}}$ with six hexadecimal digitals is represented as $CC^{u_i}_{x\in\{1,2,\ldots,l,\ldots,k,\ldots,n\}} = \{r^{u_i}_x||g^{u_i}_x||b^{u_i}_x\}$; $r^{u_i}_x$, $g^{u_i}_x$ and $b^{u_i}_x$ are represented as sub color-codes: red color, green color and blue color, separately. The size of each sub color-code is 256 bits; the symbol "$||$" denotes the concatenation operator to connect the messages. For instance, a serial random number $R_i =$ 'DD3441FF9900 FF00FF....' is generated by RNG, then a subset of the color code set could be denoted as $CCS^{u_i}=\{CC^{u_i}_1, CC^{u_i}_2,\ldots, CC^{u_i}_5\}=\{CC^{u_i}_{x\in\{1,2,\ldots,5\}}\}$, where $CC^{u_i}_{x=1} = \{r^{u_i}_1||g^{u_i}_1||b^{u_i}_1\} = \{DD||34||41\}_{HEX}$ is shown in Table 1, if the first color-code $x = 1$;

4. MCS generates an initial random number set $\{ir^{u_i,s}_{CA,\alpha\in\{1',2',\ldots,k'\}}\}$, where $ir^{u_i,s}_{CA,\alpha} = \{ir^{u_i}_{\alpha_1}||ir^{u_i}_{\alpha_2}||ir^{u_i}_{\alpha_3}\}$, $\alpha \in (1',2',\ldots,k')$ and k' is a prime number, e.g. $ir^{u_i,s}_{CA,1'} = \{59||EF||38\}$.
5. MCS chooses a hash function $f_i(\bullet)$ for the user u_i.
6. MCS sends securely a secure information set consisting of the initial random number set $\{ir^{u_i,s}_{CA,\alpha\in\{1',2',\ldots,k'\}}\}$, a RNG procedure, a large-size serial random number R_i and a hash information $\{f_i(\bullet)||k'\}$ to the user u_i;

3.2 The Exchanged Color-Code Session Key Generation Phase

Assume a user u_i wants to secure exchange messages to a user u_j. First, the user u_i will perform the following steps. The color-code session key generation phase is described below.

1. The user u_i generates a random number $rn^{u_i}_s = \{r^{u_i}_1||r^{u_i}_2||r^{u_i}_3\}$ via RNG procedure for a session s, where each $r^{u_i}_1, r^{u_i}_2$ or $r^{u_i}_3$ is the number with two hexadecimal digitals, e.g. $rn^{u_i}_{s=1} = \{8B||39||2F\}$.
2. The user u_i calculates the index number by using the hash equation $f_i(rn^{u_i}_s) = f_i(r^{u_i}_1||r^{u_i}_2||r^{u_i}_3) \bmod k'$, where $f_i(\bullet)$ is the hash function created and assigned by MCS in user's registration phase. For instance, $f(rn^{u_i}_s) = f(8B||39||2F) \bmod k'$. The user u_i then gets the index number set as $\{f_i(rn^{u_i}_s),f_i(rn^{u_i}_s) + 1,\ldots,f_i(rn^{u_i}_s) + (\beta' - 1)\}$. Thus, we assume that there are total β' members for this index set.
3. The user u_i selects a client's color-code subset $\{CC^{u_i}_{f_i(rn^{u_i}_s)}, CC^{u_i}_{f_i(rn^{u_i}_s)+1},\ldots,$ $CC^{u_i}_{f_i(rn^{u_i}_s)+(\beta'-1)}\}$ according to the index number set $\{f_i(rn^{u_i}_s),f_i(rn^{u_i}_s) + 1,\ldots,$ $f_i(rn^{u_i}_s) + (\beta' - 1)\}$ from the color code set $CCS^{u_i}=\{CC^{u_i}_1, CC^{u_i}_2,\ldots, CC^{u_i}_n\}=\{CC^{u_i}_{x\in\{1,2,\ldots,n\}}\}$ made and chosen by the large-size serial random number R_i for the session s.
4. The user u_i selects the initial random number $ir^{u_i,s}_{CA,l} = \{ir^{u_i}_1||ir^{u_i}_2||ir^{u_i}_3\}$ from the initial random number set $\{ir^{u_i,s}_{CA,\alpha\in\{1',2',\ldots,k'\}}\}$, where each random number

$ir_1^{u_i}, ir_2^{u_i}$, or $ir_3^{u_i} \in \{1, 2, \ldots, \beta'\}$ is selected by according to the sequence of the index number $\{1', 2', \ldots, k'\}$ for the session s.

5. User u_i computes the session key $k_s^{u_i} = \left(ir_{CA,l}^{u_i,s} \oplus rn_s^{u_i}\right)(\mathrm{mod}\,256)$. Thus, the session key is calculated as

$$
\begin{aligned}
k_s^{u_i} &= \left(ir_{CA,l}^{u_i,s} \oplus rn_s^{u_i}\right)(\mathrm{mod}\,256) \\
&= \left\{ir_1^{u_i}\|ir_2^{u_i}\|ir_3^{u_i}\right\} \oplus \left\{rn_1^{u_i}\|rn_2^{u_i}\|rn_3^{u_i}\right\}(\mathrm{mod}\,256) \\
&= \left\{(ir_1^{u_i} \oplus rn_1^{u_i})(\mathrm{mod}\,256)\|(ir_2^{u_i} \oplus rn_2^{u_i})(\mathrm{mod}\,256)\|(ir_3^{u_i} \oplus rn_3^{u_i})(\mathrm{mod}\,256)\right\} \\
&= \left\{k_1^{u_i}\|k_2^{u_i}\|k_3^{u_i}\right\}(\mathrm{mod}\,256)
\end{aligned}
$$

by using the exclusive-or operation for the initial random number $ir_{CA,l}^{u_i,s} = \left\{ir_1^{u_i}\|ir_2^{u_i}\|ir_3^{u_i}\right\}$ and the random number $rn_s^{u_i} = \left\{rn_1^{u_i}\|rn_2^{u_i}\|rn_3^{u_i}\right\}$ for the session s.

6. The user u_i selects an exchanged color-code subset $\left\{CC_{f_i(k_s^{u_i})}^{u_i}, CC_{f_i(k_s^{u_i})+1}^{u_i}, \ldots, \right.$
$\left. CC_{f_i(k_s^{u_i})+(\beta'-1)}^{u_i}\right\}$ from the color code set $CCS^{u_i} = \left\{CC_1^{u_i}, CC_2^{u_i}, \ldots, CC_n^{u_i}\right\} = \left\{CC_{x\in\{1,2,\ldots,n\}}^{u_i}\right\}$ for the session s according to the index number set $\{f_i(k_s^{u_i}), f_i(k_s^{u_i})+1, \ldots, f_i(k_s^{u_i})+(\beta'-1)\}$, where the first index number is calculated by using the hash equation $f_i(k_s^{u_i}) = f_i((ir_l^{u_i} \oplus rn_1^{u_i})\| (ir_l^{u_i} \oplus rn_2^{u_i})\|(ir_l^{u_i} \oplus rn_3^{u_i}))\,\mathrm{mod}\,k'$, where $f_i(\bullet)$ is the hash function created by MCS in user's registration phase.

7. User u_i then calculates the exchanged color-code key set $\left\{cck_{l\in\{1',2',\ldots,\beta'\},s}^{u_i}\right\}$ for session s by the exclusive-OR operation below, individually.

$$
\begin{aligned}
&\left\{cck_{l\in\{1',2',\ldots,\beta'\},s}^{u_i}\right\}(\mathrm{mod}\,256) \\
&= \left\{CC_{f_i(m_s^{u_i})}^{u_i}, CC_{f_i(m_s^{u_i})+1}^{u_i}, \ldots, CC_{f_i(m_s^{u_i})+(\beta'-1)}^{u_i}\right\} \oplus \left\{CC_{f_i(k_s^{u_i})}^{u_i}, CC_{f_i(k_s^{u_i})+1}^{u_i}, \ldots, CC_{f_i(k_s^{u_i})+(\beta'-1)}^{u_i}\right\} \\
&= \left\{\left(CC_{f_i(m_s^{u_i})}^{u_i} \oplus CC_{f_i(k_s^{u_i})}^{u_i}\right), \left(CC_{f_i(m_s^{u_i})+1}^{u_i} \oplus CC_{f_i(k_s^{u_i})+1}^{u_i}\right), \ldots, \left(CC_{f_i(m_s^{u_i})+(\beta'-1)}^{u_i} \oplus CC_{f_i(k_s^{u_i})+(\beta'-1)}^{u_i}\right)\right\}
\end{aligned}
$$

8. Next, the user u_i send the messages $\left\{u_i\|u_j\|\left\{cck_{l\in\{1',2',\ldots,\beta'\},s}^{u_i}\right\}\|k_s^{u_i}\|s\right\}$ to MCS, where the user with identity u_j who is the invitee requested by the user u_i.

9. After receiving the messages $\left\{u_i\|u_j\|\left\{cck_{l\in\{1',2',\ldots,\beta'\},s}^{u_i}\right\}\|k_s^{u_i}\|s\right\}$ sent by the user u_i, MCS then verifies the legitimacy for the user u_i and u_j. If both them are legitimate members, then MCS will send the request to the user u_j. If u_j does not a member, MCS will invite her or him to register an account and to be a member via *User Registration phase*.

10. The user u_j send the messages $\left\{u_j\|u_i\|\left\{cck_{l\in\{1',2',\ldots,\beta'\},s}^{u_j}\right\}\|k_s^{u_j}\|s\right\}$ back to MCS, if user u_j is one of the members.

11. After receiving the messages $\left\{u_j||u_i||\left\{cck_{l\in\{1',2',\ldots,\beta'\},s}^{u_j}\right\}||k_s^{u_j}||s\right\}$ from the user u_j, MCS will then perform the *Algorithm 1: Shadow color-code key generation algorithm*.

Algorithm 1: Shadow color-code key generation algorithm

STEP 1: MCS finds the initial random number subsets $ir_{CA,l}^{u_i,s} = \left\{ir_1^{u_i}||ir_2^{u_i}||ir_3^{u_i}\right\}$ and $ir_{CA,l}^{u_j,s} = \left\{ir_1^{u_j}||ir_2^{u_j}||ir_3^{u_j}\right\}$ from the initial random number sets $\left\{ir_{CA,\alpha\in\{1',2',\ldots,k'\}}^{u_i,s}\right\}$ and $\left\{ir_{CA,\alpha\in\{1',2',\ldots,k'\}}^{u_j,s}\right\}$, where each random number $ir_1^{u_i}, ir_2^{u_i}$, or $ir_3^{u_i} \in \{1,2,\ldots,\beta'\}$ and $ir_1^{u_j}, ir_2^{u_j}$, or $ir_3^{u_j} \in \{1,2,\ldots,\beta'\}$ is selected by according to the corresponding sequence of the index number $\{1',2',\ldots,k'\}$ for the session s, respectively.

STEP 2: MCS computes the clients' random numbers by using the session keys $k_s^{u_i} = \left(ir_{CA,l}^{u_i,s} \oplus rn_s^{u_i}\right)$, $k_s^{u_j} = \left(ir_{CA,l}^{u_j,s} \oplus rn_s^{u_j}\right)$ and initial random numbers $ir_{CA,l}^{u_i,s} = \left\{ir_1^{u_i}||ir_2^{u_i}||ir_3^{u_i}\right\}$ and $ir_{CA,l}^{u_j,s} = \left\{ir_1^{u_j}||ir_2^{u_j}||ir_3^{u_j}\right\}$ for the session s, respectively. Thus, the random numbers are calculated below.

$$
\begin{aligned}
rn_s^{u_i} &= \left(ir_{CA,l}^{u_i,s} \oplus k_s^{u_i}\right)(\bmod\,256) \\
&= \left\{ir_1^{u_i}||ir_2^{u_i}||ir_3^{u_i}\right\} \oplus \left\{k_1^{u_i}||k_2^{u_i}||k_3^{u_i}\right\}(\bmod\,256) \\
&= \left\{(ir_1^{u_i} \oplus k_1^{u_i})(\bmod\,256)||(ir_2^{u_i} \oplus k_2^{u_i})(\bmod\,256)||(ir_3^{u_i} \oplus k_3^{u_i})(\bmod\,256)\right\} \\
&= \left\{rn_1^{u_i}||rn_2^{u_i}||rn_3^{u_i}\right\}(\bmod\,256);
\end{aligned}
$$

and

$$
\begin{aligned}
rn_s^{u_j} &= \left(ir_{CA,l}^{u_j,s} \oplus k_s^{u_j}\right)(\bmod\,256) \\
&= \left\{ir_1^{u_j}||ir_2^{u_j}||ir_3^{u_j}\right\} \oplus \left\{k_1^{u_j}||k_2^{u_j}||k_3^{u_j}\right\}(\bmod\,256) \\
&= \left\{(ir_1^{u_j} \oplus k_1^{u_j})(\bmod\,256)||(ir_2^{u_j} \oplus k_2^{u_j})(\bmod\,256)||(ir_3^{u_j} \oplus k_3^{u_j})(\bmod\,256)\right\} \\
&= \left\{rn_1^{u_j}||rn_2^{u_j}||rn_3^{u_j}\right\}(\bmod\,256).
\end{aligned}
$$

STEP 3: MCS finds the two clients' color-code subsets $\left\{CC_{f_i(rn_s^{u_i})}^{u_i},\right.$ $CC_{f_i(rn_s^{u_i})+1}^{u_i},\ldots,CC_{f_i(rn_s^{u_i})+(\beta'-1)}^{u_i}\right\}$ and $\left\{CC_{f_j(rn_s^{u_j})}^{u_j}, CC_{f_j(rn_s^{u_j})+1}^{u_j},\ldots,\right.$ $\left.CC_{f_j(rn_s^{u_j})+(\beta'-1)}^{u_j}\right\}$ from the color code set CCS^{u_i} and CCS^{u_j} according to the index number sets $\{f_i(rn_s^{u_i}), f_i(rn_s^{u_i})+1,\ldots,f_i(rn_s^{u_i})+(\beta'-1)\}$ and $\{f_j(rn_s^{u_j}), f_j(rn_s^{u_j})+1,\ldots,f_j(rn_s^{u_j})+(\beta'-1)\}$, where $f_i(rn_s^{u_i}) = f_i(r_1^{u_i}||r_2^{u_i}||r_3^{u_i})\bmod k'$ and $f_j(rn_s^{u_j}) = f_j(r_1^{u_j}||r_2^{u_j}||r_3^{u_j})\bmod k'$ for the session s, respectively.

STEP 4: MCS finds the exchanged color-code subsets $\left\{ CC^{u_i}_{f_i(k^{u_i}_s)}, CC^{u_i}_{f_i(k^{u_i}_s)+1}, \right.$

$\left. \ldots, CC^{u_i}_{f_i(k^{u_i}_s)+(\beta'-1)} \right\}$ and $\left\{ CC^{u_j}_{f_j(k^{u_j}_s)}, CC^{u_j}_{f_j(k^{u_j}_s)+1}, \ldots, CC^{u_j}_{f_j(k^{u_j}_s)+(\beta'-1)} \right\}$
from the color code sets CCS^{u_i} and CCS^{u_j} for the session s according to
the index number sets $\{f_i(k^{u_i}_s), f_i(k^{u_i}_s)+1, \ldots, f_i(k^{u_i}_s)+(\beta'-1)\}$ and
$\{f_j(k^{u_j}_s), f_j(k^{u_j}_s)+1, \ldots, f_j(k^{u_j}_s)+(\beta'-1)\}$, where the first index number is also calculated by using the hash equation $f_i(k^{u_i}_s) =$
$f_i\left((ir^{u_i}_1 \oplus rn^{u_i}_1) || (ir^{u_i}_1 \oplus rn^{u_i}_2) || (ir^{u_i}_1 \oplus rn^{u_i}_3) \right) \bmod k'$ and $f_j(k^{u_j}_s) =$
$f_j\left((ir^{u_j}_1 \oplus rn^{u_j}_1) || (ir^{u_j}_1 \oplus rn^{u_j}_2) || (ir^{u_j}_1 \oplus rn^{u_j}_3) \right) \bmod k'$ for the session s,
respectively.

STEP 5: MCS then calculates the color-code session key set $\left\{ cck^{u_i}_{l \in \{1', 2', \ldots, \beta'\}, s} \right\}$
and $\left\{ cck^{u_j}_{l \in \{1', 2', \ldots, \beta'\}, s} \right\}$ by the exclusive-OR operations below,
individually.

$$\left\{ cck^{u_i}_{l \in \{1', 2', \ldots, \beta'\}, s} \right\} (\bmod\ 256)$$
$$= \left\{ CC^{u_i}_{f_i(m^{u_i}_s)}, CC^{u_i}_{f_i(m^{u_i}_s)+1}, \ldots, CC^{u_i}_{f_i(m^{u_i}_s)+(\beta'-1)} \right\} \oplus \left\{ CC^{u_i}_{f_i(k^{u_i}_s)}, CC^{u_i}_{f_i(k^{u_i}_s)+1}, \ldots, CC^{u_i}_{f_i(k^{u_i}_s)+(\beta'-1)} \right\}$$
$$= \left\{ \left(CC^{u_i}_{f_i(m^{u_i}_s)} \oplus CC^{u_i}_{f_i(k^{u_i}_s)} \right), \left(CC^{u_i}_{f_i(m^{u_i}_s)+1} \oplus CC^{u_i}_{f_i(k^{u_i}_s)+1} \right), \ldots, \left(CC^{u_i}_{f_i(m^{u_i}_s)+(\beta'-1)} \oplus CC^{u_i}_{f_i(k^{u_i}_s)+(\beta'-1)} \right) \right\}$$

and

$$\left\{ cck^{u_j}_{l \in \{1', 2', \ldots, \beta'\}, s} \right\} (\bmod\ 256)$$
$$= \left\{ CC^{u_j}_{f_j(m^{u_j}_s)}, CC^{u_j}_{f_j(m^{u_j}_s)+1}, \ldots, CC^{u_j}_{f_j(m^{u_j}_s)+(\beta'-1)} \right\} \oplus \left\{ CC^{u_j}_{f_j(k^{u_j}_s)}, CC^{u_j}_{f_j(k^{u_j}_s)+1}, \ldots, CC^{u_j}_{f_j(k^{u_j}_s)+(\beta'-1)} \right\}$$
$$= \left\{ \left(CC^{u_j}_{f_j(m^{u_j}_s)} \oplus CC^{u_j}_{f_j(k^{u_j}_s)} \right), \left(CC^{u_j}_{f_j(m^{u_j}_s)+1} \oplus CC^{u_j}_{f_j(k^{u_j}_s)+1} \right), \ldots, \left(CC^{u_j}_{f_j(m^{u_j}_s)+(\beta'-1)} \oplus CC^{u_j}_{f_j(k^{u_j}_s)+(\beta'-1)} \right) \right\}.$$

STEP 6: MCS generates a color-code session key set $\left\{ cck^{CA}_{l \in \{1', 2', \ldots, \beta'\}, s} \right\}$ for the
session s, where $\left\{ cck^{CA}_{l \in \{1', 2', \ldots, \beta'\}, s} \right\} = \left\{ CC^{CA}_{1', s}, CC^{CA}_{2', s}, \ldots, CC^{CA}_{\beta', s} \right\}$ for the
session s.

STEP 7: MCS computes the two shadow color-code key sets $\left\{ cck^{u_i \oplus CA}_{l \in \{1', 2', \ldots, \beta'\}, s} \right\} =$
$\left\{ cck^{u_i}_{l \in \{1', 2', \ldots, \beta'\}, s} \right\} \oplus \left\{ cck^{CA}_{l \in \{1', 2', \ldots, \beta'\}, s} \right\}$ and $\left\{ cck^{u_j \oplus CA}_{l \in \{1', 2', \ldots, \beta'\}, s} \right\} =$
$\left\{ cck^{u_j}_{l \in \{1', 2', \ldots, \beta'\}, s} \right\} \oplus \left\{ cck^{CA}_{l \in \{1', 2', \ldots, \beta'\}, s} \right\}$ for the session s, respectively. □

12. Finally, MCS then send the shadow color-code key set $\left\{ cck^{u_i \oplus CA}_{l \in \{1', 2', \ldots, \beta'\}, s} \right\}$ to user
u_i, and send the shadow color-code key set $\left\{ cck^{u_j \oplus CA}_{l \in \{1', 2', \ldots, \beta'\}, s} \right\}$ to the user u_j for the
session s, respectively.

13. After receiving the shadow color-code key set $\left\{ cck^{u_j \oplus CA}_{l \in \{1', 2', \ldots, \beta'\}, s} \right\}$, the user u_i
generates the final exchanged color-code session key set $\left\{ cck^{u_i \oplus u_j \oplus CA}_{l \in \{1', 2', \ldots, \beta'\}, s} \right\}$ for the

session s, where each exchanged color-code session key is calculated by the Eq. (1).

$$
\begin{aligned}
\left\{cck_{l\in\{1',2',\ldots,\beta'\},s}^{u_i\oplus u_j\oplus CA}\right\} &= \left\{cck_{l\in\{1',2',\ldots,\beta'\},s}^{u_i}\right\} \oplus \left\{cck_{l\in\{1',2',\ldots,\beta'\},s}^{u_j\oplus CA}\right\} \\
&= \left\{cck_{l\in\{1',2',\ldots,\beta'\},s}^{u_i}\right\} \oplus \left\langle \left\{cck_{l\in\{1',2',\ldots,\beta'\},s}^{u_j}\right\} \oplus \left\{cck_{l\in\{1',2',\ldots,\beta'\},s}^{CA}\right\}\right\rangle \\
&= \left\{cck_{l\in\{1',2',\ldots,\beta'\},s}^{u_i}\right\} \oplus \left\{cck_{l\in\{1',2',\ldots,\beta'\},s}^{u_j}\right\} \oplus \left\{cck_{l\in\{1',2',\ldots,\beta'\},s}^{CA}\right\}
\end{aligned}
\tag{1}
$$

14. After receiving the shadow color-code key set $\left\{k_{s\in\{1',2',\ldots,k'\}}^{u_i\oplus CA}\right\}$, the user u_j generates the final exchanged color-code session key set $\left\{cck_{l\in\{1',2',\ldots,\beta'\},s}^{u_j\oplus u_i\oplus CA}\right\}$, where each exchanged color-code session key is calculated by the Eq. (2).

$$
\begin{aligned}
\left\{cck_{l\in\{1',2',\ldots,\beta'\},s}^{u_j\oplus u_i\oplus CA}\right\} &= \left\{cck_{l\in\{1',2',\ldots,\beta'\},s}^{u_j}\right\} \oplus \left\{cck_{l\in\{1',2',\ldots,\beta'\},s}^{u_i\oplus CA}\right\} \\
&= \left\{cck_{l\in\{1',2',\ldots,\beta'\},s}^{u_j}\right\} \oplus \left\langle \left\{cck_{l\in\{1',2',\ldots,\beta'\},s}^{u_i}\right\} \oplus \left\{cck_{l\in\{1',2',\ldots,\beta'\},s}^{CA}\right\}\right\rangle \\
&= \left\{cck_{l\in\{1',2',\ldots,\beta'\},s}^{u_i}\right\} \oplus \left\{cck_{l\in\{1',2',\ldots,\beta'\},s}^{u_j}\right\} \oplus \left\{cck_{l\in\{1',2',\ldots,\beta'\},s}^{CA}\right\} \\
&= \left\{cck_{l\in\{1',2',\ldots,\beta'\},s}^{u_i\oplus u_j\oplus CA}\right\}
\end{aligned}
\tag{2}
$$

3.3 Secure Messages Encryption and Decryption Phase

Assume both the user u_i and the user u_j want to communicate securely to each other, where the color-code session keys belonging to them, where they have been exchanged after *Color-Code Session Key Generation Phase*. If the user u_i wants to send securely the plaintext messages $M = \{m_1, m_2, \ldots, m_{\beta'}\}$ to the user u_j, he or she will calculate the messages via any traditional symmetric cryptosystem by using one by one session key which is selected from the final exchanged color-code session key sets $\left\{cck_{l\in\{1',2',\ldots,\beta'\},s}^{u_i\oplus u_j\oplus CA}\right\}$ and $\left\{cck_{l\in\{1',2',\ldots,\beta'\},s}^{u_j\oplus u_i\oplus CA}\right\}$, individually, where each exchanged color-code session key in $\left\{cck_{l\in\{1',2',\ldots,\beta'\},s}^{u_i\oplus u_j\oplus CA}\right\}$ equals the corresponding exchanged color-code session key in $\left\{cck_{l\in\{1',2',\ldots,\beta'\},s}^{u_j\oplus u_i\oplus CA}\right\}$ according to Eq. (2). Finally, each sensitive information $m_i \in M = \{m_1, m_2, \ldots, m_{\beta'}\}$ will be encrypted by the following the encryption algorithm $c_i = E_{cck_l^{u_iu_jCA}}(m_i) \in C = \{c_1, c_2, \ldots, c_{\beta'}\}$. Then, the corresponding ciphertext information $c_i \in C$ will be decrypted by the following decryption algorithm $m_i = E_{cck_l^{u_ju_iCA}}(c_i) = E_{cck_l^{u_iu_jCA}}(c_i) \in M$.

4 Security Analysis

In this section, the proposed scheme in this paper is discussed and analyzed, which could prevent the session key guessing attack and replay attack. The details of the discussions and analyses are described.

4.1 Prevent the Session Key Guessing Attack

In the subsection, the proposed scheme is analyzed in order to prevent the password guessing attack. Generally, an attacker may use the detectable/undetectable online guessing attacks to get the password of users. Sensitive information such as $E_{cck_l^{u_iu_jCA}}(m_i)$ and $E_{cck_l^{u_ju_iCA}}(c_i)$ are protected by using the final exchanged color-code session key sets $\left\{cck_{l\in\{1',2',\ldots,\beta'\},s}^{u_i\oplus u_j\oplus CA}\right\}$ together with $\left\{cck_{l\in\{1',2',\ldots,\beta'\},s}^{u_j\oplus u_i\oplus CA}\right\}$, the random numbers $rn_s^{u_i} = \left\{r_1^{u_i}||r_2^{u_i}||r_3^{u_i}\right\}$, $rn_s^{u_j} = \left\{r_1^{u_j}||r_2^{u_j}||r_3^{u_j}\right\}$ and a color-code session key set $\left\{cck_{l\in\{1',2',\ldots,\beta'\},s}^{CA}\right\}$ for a session s. Therefore, the attacker doesn't know the random numbers $rn_s^{u_i} = \left\{r_1^{u_i}||r_2^{u_i}||r_3^{u_i}\right\}$, $rn_s^{u_j} = \left\{r_1^{u_j}||r_2^{u_j}||r_3^{u_j}\right\}$ and the MCS's color-code session key set $\left\{cck_{l\in\{1',2',\ldots,k'\}}^{CA}\right\}$ for the session s via variously guessing attacks. However, each client has her/his large-size serial random number R_i or R_j which is only shared by the MCS server. If the authentication procedure fails, the request will be rejected. Thus, the proposed schemes could be protected effectively the offline password guessing attack.

4.2 Prevent to Replay Attack

For preventing the replay attack, the user u_i and u_j select his or her client's color-code subset $\left\{CC_{f_i(rn_s^{u_i})}^{u_i}, CC_{f_i(rn_s^{u_i})+1}^{u_i}, \ldots, CC_{f_i(rn_s^{u_i})+(\beta'-1)}^{u_i}\right\}$ and $\left\{CC_{f_j(rn_s^{u_j})}^{u_j}, CC_{f_j(rn_s^{u_j})+1}^{u_j}, \ldots, CC_{f_j(rn_s^{u_j})+(\beta'-1)}^{u_j}\right\}$ from the color code set CCS^{u_i} and CCS^{u_j}, individually, according to the index number set $\left\{f_i(rn_s^{u_i}), f_i(rn_s^{u_i})+1, \ldots, f_i(rn_s^{u_i})+(\beta'-1)\right\}$ and $\left\{f_j(rn_s^{u_j}), f_j(rn_s^{u_j})+1, \ldots, f_j(rn_s^{u_j})+(\beta'-1)\right\}$ which the protection and security are relied on the two random numbers $rn_s^{u_i} = \left\{r_1^{u_i}||r_2^{u_i}||r_3^{u_i}\right\}$ and $rn_s^{u_j} = \left\{r_1^{u_j}||r_2^{u_j}||r_3^{u_j}\right\}$ via RNG procedure for each session s. In addition, the user u_i and u_j generates the session keys $k_s^{u_i} = \left(ir_{CA,l}^{u_i,s} \oplus rn_s^{u_i}\right)(\mathrm{mod}\,256)$ as well as $k_s^{u_j} = \left(ir_{CA,l}^{u_j,s} \oplus rn_s^{u_j}\right)(\mathrm{mod}\,256)$ are also depending on the security of two random numbers $rn_s^{u_i} = \left\{r_1^{u_i}||r_2^{u_i}||r_3^{u_i}\right\}$, $rn_s^{u_j} = \left\{r_1^{u_j}||r_2^{u_j}||r_3^{u_j}\right\}$ and the initial random number set $\left\{ir_{CA,\alpha\in\{1',2',\ldots,k'\}}^{u_i,s}\right\}$.

Moreover, MCS generates a color-code session key set $\left\{cck_{l\in\{1',2',\ldots,\beta'\},s}^{CA}\right\}$ and computes the two shadow color-code key sets $\left\{cck_{l\in\{1',2',\ldots,\beta'\},s}^{u_i\oplus CA}\right\} = \left\{cck_{l\in\{1',2',\ldots,\beta'\},s}^{u_i}\right\} \oplus \left\{cck_{l\in\{1',2',\ldots,\beta'\},s}^{CA}\right\}$ and $\left\{cck_{l\in\{1',2',\ldots,\beta'\},s}^{u_j\oplus CA}\right\} = \left\{cck_{l\in\{1',2',\ldots,\beta'\},s}^{u_j}\right\} \oplus \left\{cck_{l\in\{1',2',\ldots,\beta'\},s}^{CA}\right\}$

for the session s, respectively. However, the two shadow color-code key sets are protected by the two random numbers $rn_s^{u_i} = \{r_1^{u_i}||r_2^{u_i}||r_3^{u_i}\}$, $rn_s^{u_j} = \{r_1^{u_j}||r_2^{u_j}||r_3^{u_j}\}$ and the initial random number set $\{ir_{CA,\alpha\in\{1',2',...,k'\}}^{u_i,s}\}$ which only are kept securely and shared between the MCS server and the corresponding users u_i or u_j, respectively. When attackers want to break the corresponding the users' exchanged session color-code keys and the two shadow color-code keys, they need to get the three random numbers via RNG procedure. However, attackers are hard to get them. Owing to the fact that each message is encrypted by the corresponding exchanged color-code session key for each session s, where all of the session key are kept secure only by the MCS server. Therefore, the attackers could not generate the encrypted message via replay the previous the encrypted messages in the same session s or next session $s + 1$. Therefore, the proposed scheme could resist the replay attack.

5   Conclusions

A secure color-code key exchange protocol for mobile chat application (MC APP) in this paper. It could be used to design a visual approach which the exchanged color-code coding session key are selected from the assigned color-code sets in user registration phase. In the other words, each client selects some color codes represented as an initial session color code key in order to exchange and generate the shadow color code session key as well as exchanged color code session key. Subsequently, the exchanged color-code session key is used to encrypt and decrypt the messages by each client of MC APP. Hence, this paper focuses on how to generate the shadows and the exchanged color code session key via choosing randomly and then calculating its hash value as the index number in order to pick the corresponding color-codes for each session s, respectively. Finally, it is a novel key exchange mechanism which could be applied to any secure MC APP.

Acknowledgment. The authors would like to express the most immense gratitude to the anonymous referees for their insightful and constructive comments. This work was supported in part by Asia University and China Medical University Hospital, China Medical University, Taiwan under Grant ASIA-105-CMUH-04. This work was also supported in part by the Ministry of Science and Technology, Taiwan, Republic of China, under Grant MOST 104-2221-E-468-002.

References

Chen, H.C.: A Rotation session key based transposition cryptosystem scheme applied to mobile text chatting. In: Proceedings of Frontiers of Information Technology, pp. 497–503 (2014)

Chen, H.C., Mao, C.H., Lin, Y.T., Kung, T.L., Weng, C.E.: A secure group-based mobile chat protocol. J. Ambient Intell. Humanized Comput. 7(5), 693–703 (2016a). https://doi.org/10.1007/s12652-016-0368-1

Chen, C., et al.: A hybrid encryption scheme with key-cloning protection: user/terminal double authentication via attributes and fingerprints. J. Internet Serv. Inf. Secur. (JISIS) **6**(2), 23–36 (2016b)

Kurokawa, T., et al.: On the security of CBC mode in SSL3.0 and TLS1.0. J. Internet Serv. Inf. Secur. (JISIS) **6**(1), 2–19 (2016)

Yang, H., et al.: Verifying group authentication protocols by Scyther. J. Wirel. Mob. Netw. Ubiquit. Comput. Dependable Appl. (JoWUA) **7**(2), 3–19 (2016)

Chakraborty, S., et al.: A pairing-free, one round identity based authenticated key exchange protocol secure against memory-scrapers. J. Wirel. Mob. Netw. Ubiquit. Comput. Dependable Appl. (JoWUA) **7**(1), 1–22 (2016)

Design and Implementation of SPEEX Speech Technology on ARM Processor

Chia-Chi Chang[✉] and Yen-Hao Shih

Chaoyang University of Technology, Taichung, Taiwan
ccchang@cyut.edu.tw

Abstract. The goal of this paper is to implement SPEEX speech compression technology on ARM processor. SPEEX is a speech compression technology based on the Code Excited Linear Prediction (CELP) algorithm. It has a low bit rate, high resolution, and supports a variety of signal sampling rates, so the voice can effectively compression and also preserve speech integrity. For hardware part, we abandon high cost, high power digital signal processors (DSPs), but we select the ARM processor of STM32 series produced by STMicroelectronics. SPEEX voice compression technology will be transplanted to the STM32 processor, and SPEEX encoded data transmitted through the transmitter to the receiver; and finally through the decoding side the encoded data is restored to playback. The experiment is divided into two parts. First through the SPEEX encoded sine wave signal, we input data to the ARM decoder, and use the oscilloscope to compare the difference after encoding and decoding signals. The other is through the PESQ for voice quality verification, and is compared with the traditional ADPCM voice quality.

Keywords: SPEEX · CELP · STM32 · Bluetooth · PESQ

1 Introduction

With the rapid development of semiconductor technology, it makes the performance of microprocessors in the implementation substantially increase; in the ARM architecture, microprocessors are indeed more obvious in the performance of computing performance, and in power loss, which can achieve the current requirements of high performance, low power consumption standards. ARM microprocessors of STM32 series produced by STMicroelectronics belong to the single-chip of ARM Cortex-M series, which can reach the maximum operating frequency of 72 MHz, and the memory capacity of 512 Kb; coupled with peripheral hardware support, it can be used to replace the digital signal Processor to achieve SPEEX voice compression technology. SPEEX [1] is a speech compression technology based on CELP [2]. Its main feature is low bit rate, and can compress 128 kbps to 8 kbps, 16: 1 compression ratio, and support narrowband (8 kHz), wideband (16 kHz), and Ultra-wideband (32 kHz) frequencies. By use of the above features, t we can use Bluetooth wireless transmission for voice playback. Bluetooth is a wireless technology standard, and Bluetooth protocol [3] is developed by the Bluetooth SIG; it has a fast transfer rate, high stability, and high security. Originally,

© Springer Nature Singapore Pte Ltd. 2018
I. You et al. (Eds.): MobiSec 2016, CCIS 797, pp. 65–79, 2018.
https://doi.org/10.1007/978-981-10-7850-7_7

Bluetooth provides voice transmission support functions, but the transmission power consumption, and now Bluetooth 4.0 architecture implements the low power consumption as shown in Fig. 1 to reduce the large portion of problems of Bluetooth transmission power consumption, and also down support early Bluetooth architecture, Making Bluetooth 4.0 wireless transmission have more advantages in the future. Voice transmission through wireless transmission of voice packets may result in poor voices, and finally the PESQ voice detection technology is used to verify the quality of voice quality. Compared with the traditional ADPCM [4] voice quality, it is found through verification results that voice quality is well achieved.

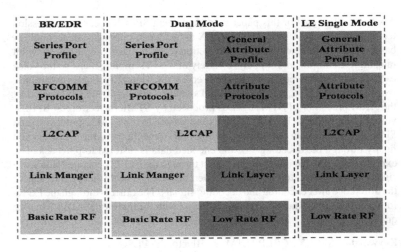

Fig. 1. Bluetooth 4.0 architecture

2   System Architecture

System architecture is divided into hardware and software parts; the hardware part mainly introduces the hardware core of STM32 microprocessor, and wireless transmission module CC254x of two cores and audio amplifier circuits; the software part mainly introduces the speech coding and the research using the SPEEX voice compression technology.

2.1   Hardware Architecture

For hardware architecture, we first introduce the system core ARM processor of STM32 series, which is used to study the implementation of SPEEX decoding processor. Since speech signal processing is to be performed, the implementation of capacity, peripheral functions and memory are in line with the conditions, and this is what we choose this processor as the core of this study. CC254x communication chip is selected in the wireless transmission, mainly for the chip provides a variety of peripheral functions, coupled with a built-in control core, and can accelerate the hardware performance.

2.1.1   STM32 Processor

Hardware core selects ARM processor of STM32 series produced by STMicroelectronics semiconductor company, and this series of processors belong to ARM-Cortex M3 architecture [5, 6]. With working clock up to 72 MHz, and the memory storage capacity of 128 Kb, this Chip provides a lot of peripheral functions, such as: ADC, Timer, DMA, UART, etc. The above-mentioned functions allow us to save lot of time and cost.

2.1.2   CC254x

The transmission hardware is based on a communications chip [7] manufactured by Texas Instruments, which supports the Bluetooth 4.0 standard protocol with a 2.4 GHz transmit band; The CC254x is internal with a group of high-performance low-power 8051 module, which internally provides UART, Timer, I2C and other peripheral functions, so that the circuit design can have a higher scalability, and support 250 kbps, 500 kbps, 1 Mbps, 2 Mbps data transfer rate, which is more flexible for audio transmission.

We will transplant the Bluetooth module to the STM32 development board, as shown in Fig. 2. The circuit board planning software is used to draw CC254x circuit board, and this circuit board can be combined with the STM32 development board, so as to be free from the environment limit. In the Bluetooth receive distance range it is able to process voice broadcast.

Fig. 2. Combining CC254x and STM32 development board

2.1.3   Audio Amplifier Circuit

Audio amplifier circuit is mainly used by the company OLIMEX LTD design [8], and Figs. 3 and 4 are the audio input and audio output circuits, respectively. The audio input circuit uses the Microchip MCP601 operational amplifier [9], and its main feature is that it is manufactured by complementary metal oxide semiconductor (CMOS) so as to have the operation speed and low power loss. Audio output circuits use STMicroelectronics TS4871 audio power amplifier [10], and its main feature is to restore and enlarge the signal after decoding process. Because it is through the pulse width modulation (PWM) for signal conversion, it must pass through the low-pass filter which sets the cutoff frequency signal at 4000 Hz. Most people's speech frequency will not exceed 4000 Hz, so as to effectively restore the signal integrity.

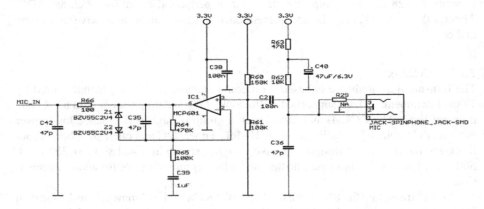

Fig. 3. Audio input circuit

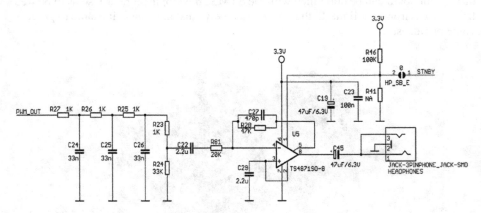

Fig. 4. Audio output circuit

2.2 Software Architecture

At first, software architecture begins to introduce the voice coding type and advantages and disadvantages, and then will explore in detail the use of SPEEX voice compression technology.

SPEEX is the voice compression technology developed by the Xiph.Org Foundation. The Xiph.Org Foundation is a non-profit organization dedicated to the development of multimedia compression technologies, which are frees for developers to use Xiph.Org developed multimedia formats including FLAC, Vorbis, Opus…, etc. The SPEEX voice compression technology used in this paper can effectively compress the data, and also restore the integrity of the voice signal without distortion.

2.2.1 Speech Coding

Voice coding is divided into three categories: waveform encoding, sound source coding, and mixed coding, and the main waveform encoding is used to record the pulse of the sound waveform. The sound is sampled, quantized, and encoded, and the sound uses a fixed bit length to represent the waveform amplitude; the advantage is high fidelity sound, but the disadvantage is the high bit rate, which requires a lot of memory space to access. Waveform coding represents pulse-code modulation (PCM).

Sound source coding, also known as parameter encoding, mainly uses mathematical models to simulate human speech architecture, and the voice feature values of voice signals are recorded through the sound box. Since the audio characteristic parameters are recorded, the bit rate is lower than that of the waveform encoding, but the resultant sound is inferior to the waveform code. Sound source coding technology is a linear predictive coding (LPC).

Hybrid coding combines the advantages of waveform coding and sound source coding, and uses a post-analysis synthesis coding architecture. The hybrid coding architecture mainly uses a specific excitation source, and then synthesizes it through long-range and short-range correlation synthesis filters so that after encoding voice achieves low bit rate, and sound fidelity is high. The hybrid coding technique is codebook-excited linear predictive coding.

2.2.2 SPEEX

SPEEX is mainly based on CELP-based voice compression technology, so the coding architecture is also a type of mixed coding. The CELP speech model is based on the analysis-by-synthesis framework. The analysis mainly uses the linear prediction method to predict the speech signal. Then, the difference between the predictive signal and the input speech signal is calculated. The results obtained through the code book search get the corresponding code, and the corresponding code will be synthesized through the synthesis filter, and decoded and restored to the original voice signal.

CELP has two main characteristics; the first feature is the use of linear prediction, and linear prediction is based on the Source-Filter model to simulate the body's vocal structure; the human voice is produced by air of the lungs through the glottis, so vocal cord vibration produces sound waves that resonate through the mouth, throat, and nasal cavity to amplify the volume, and finally produce our voice through the tongue and lips. The variability of the voice in a short time is small, indicating the high correlation between the signals, so this feature is used for signal prediction to collect the first few sampling signals, and get the next signal through the linear weighting method.

The second feature uses the codebook search to generate the excitation signal, which is divided into an Adaptive Codebook and a Fixed Codebook. Adaptive codebook is mainly for the sound with a periodic part on behalf of the sound generated through the throat vibration, and fixed codebook is for noise (gas, consonant) part according to the sound characteristics through the codebook search; finally, adaptive codebook coding is combined with fixed codebook code to generate the excitation signal (Fig. 5).

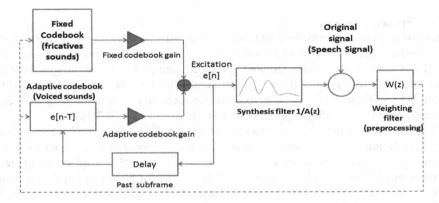

Fig. 5. SPEEX encoding block diagram [1]

Excitation signals are restored through the synthesis filter to the voice signal. The synthesis filter is all-pole filter, whose features can effectively restore the voice signal and reduce the computational complexity; the biggest difference between encoding and decoding is that the input signal will first through the $W(z)$ weight filter, which is mainly used to eliminate the input signal noise (Fig. 6).

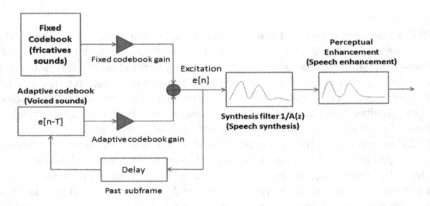

Fig. 6. SPEEX decoding block diagram [1]

3   Experimental Method

The SPEEX codec is implemented on the ARM processor. We split the study into two experimental sections. The first part will be SPEMP codecs transplanted to the STM32 processor, and the second part is that the wireless transmission part will be added to the research structure, so that the research system can achieve wireless communication. This section will explore the two experimental methods.

3.1   Voice Compression Technology Transplantation

In this study, SPEEX voice compression technology is ported to the STM32 processor, and first it needs the signal processing which must be through analog to digital conversion. Converted digital signals are processed by the processor to perform encoding and decoding operations, and then through the digital analog conversion are converted into analog signals for the speaker to play out.

In this experiment, SPEEX voice compression technology must be transplanted before the analog signal processing by digital conversion, and analog digital conversion processing goes through three steps: sampling, quantization, coding (See Fig. 7), Sampling is the analog signal converted into a discrete signal, and the sampling frequency must be in accordance with the sampling theorem defined to be twice the sampling frequency. Quantization is the instantaneous value of the discrete amplitude of the sampled signal, using the nearest potential value to represent. The signal obtained after sampling quantization is the quantized pulse signal.

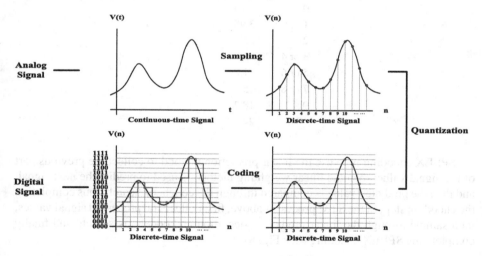

Fig. 7. Analog-to-digital conversion

Coding makes the quantized signal potential value represented by the bit number. STM32 processor provides analog to digital converter (ADC) function, so that the microphone collects the voice signal (analog signal) through the ADC conversion, and the converted digital signals are input to SPEEX for voice compression processing.

3.2   SPEEX Encoding

Before SPEEX encoding, you need to set the relevant parameters. The parameters are quality and complexity. The above parameters are used to determine the complexity of SPEEX voice compression technology calculation. Therefore, it must be determined based on hardware operation efficiency and data Transmission rate. Quality setting is to control the bit rate. As shown in Table 1, the quality parameter is set to 1; the bit rate is 2.15 kbps; the larger the quality parameter is set, the larger the bit rate is, the more memory is occupied. We will set the quality parameters in four bit rate of 8 kbps, not taking up too much memory space, but also restoring the voice signal without distortion. Complexity setting is to determine the encoding operation and codebook search speed; the higher the complexity setting, the more codec operation time will increase; therefore, according to the hardware capacity to set, we will set the complexity parameter.

Table 1.   Quality setting to control the bit rate

Quality	Bit-rate (kbps)
0	2.15
1	3.95
2	5.95
3 or 4	8.00
5 or 6	11.0
7 or 8	15.0
9	18.2
10	24.6

SPEEX encoding is to use the linear prediction method to collect the previous part of the signal value; then the linear weighting method is used to predict the next signal, and then the predicted value is compared through the codebook search, thus completing the encoding step. In the STM processor above, first collect 160 processed signal values, then sample through the linear prediction operation and codebook search, and finally complete the SPEEX encoding (See Fig. 8).

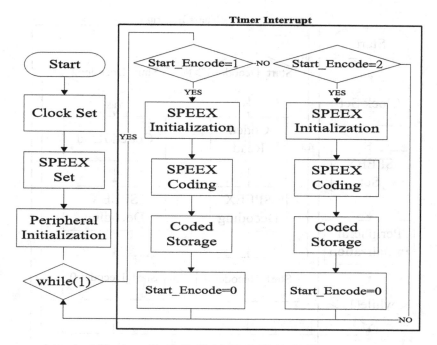

Fig. 8. SPEEX encoding end program flow chart

3.3 Voice Playback

SPEEX encoding must be decoded to restore the voice signal (See Fig. 9), and SPEEX decoding is through the codebook search signal and the linear weighted excitation signal; and finally the excitation signal is through the synthesis filter for speech synthesis, synthesis and decoding to restore the voice signal.

In order to allow the voice after SPEEX decoding played, the firmware must process digital to analog processing. However, most of processors have not built-in digital to analog converter (DAC), so it must purchase an additional chip to process the DAC. Since DACs are expensive to handle, we use Pulse Width Modulation (PWM) instead of DACs. Pulse width modulation is a technique used to convert analog signals into pulse waves by changing the duty cycle to control the duty cycle so that analog signals are required. In order to achieve good voice playback quality, we have to add a low-pass filter circuit design, so as to complete the voice playback.

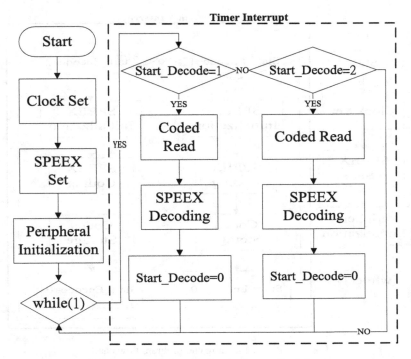

Fig. 9. SPEEX decoding end program flow chart

3.4 Wireless Transmission Processing

After migrating SPEEX speech compression technology to the STM32, we want to extend the use range of this speech system, so we add wireless transmission technology to this study. Nowadays, Wireless technology has a very wide variety, and we often hear wireless technology has Wi-Fi, Bluetooth, Zigbee, and so on. Although the Wi-Fi transmission distance is relatively far, but the power consumption is higher than the other two technologies. The transmission distance between Bluetooth and Zigbee has little difference, but Zigbee in the number of nodes and power consumption is much better than Bluetooth. This advantage is limited to the more traditional Bluetooth above, but after the announcement of the Bluetooth 4.0 specification, Bluetooth 4.0 is comparable to Zigbee.

The new specification of Bluetooth 4.0 adds low-power features, according to the official power consumption test, a button battery can work for several years. In addition to its low power consumption, it is also backward compatible with the previous version of Bluetooth; coupled with future support for Bluetooth devices with other support, Zigbee has a strong advantage in terms of cost and scalability.

In order for Bluetooth 4.0 to achieve low power consumption, the packet format has been adjusted, and Bluetooth packet format is shown in Fig. 10 below. Preamble packet length is 1 Byte, used to make the receiver do the time synchronization and transmission power measurement. Access Address is the length of the packet, which is a fixed value

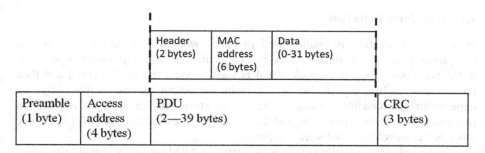

Fig. 10. Bluetooth 4.0 transport packet format

for the broadcast channel. The value of the data transmission channel is randomly generated or set by the developer. PDU is mainly used to transmit data, which contains the header (Header), MAC address, and data. The last CRC is used to check if the packet has a data error.

Preamble: The Preamble used for synchronization and timing estimation at the receiver.

Access address: The Access Address is also fixed for broadcasted packets.

PDU: The packet payload consists of a header and payload. The header describes the packet type and the PDU Type defines the purpose of the device.

CRC: error-detecting code used to validate the packet for unwanted alterations.

Voice data encoded after SPEEX has only 20 Bytes in size, so you can write data to the transfer field of PDU data of Bluetooth 4.0; the user inputs through the microphone voice signal, and then uses the ADC encoding to process signals. Then the converted signal is encoded by SPEEX, and SPEEX encoded data will be transmitted through the UART to the CC2541 transmitter. This is handled through a queue in the middle so as to ensure packet integrity.

Through the Bluetooth transmission to the receiver, the receiver will receive some of the encoded data transmitted to the decoding side through using UART transmission, and the decoder side will decode encoded data through SPEEX decoding; after decoding, the decoded data are converted into voice signals through the PWM, and finally playback through the speaker.

4   Experimental Results

The results of this study verify the quality of voice playback and Bluetooth data integrity testing. The quality of voice playback is verified by two test methods: the first inspection method uses oscilloscope waveforms, and the second method uses the PESQ software for voice quality testing.

4.1 Waveform Detection

Waveform verification is mainly used to check whether the output waveform is completely restored, and through the signal generator sine wave signals are input to the ARM processor. Then the output signal is used to view the oscilloscope, and then comparative analysis are carried out for input and output signals. In this study, the experiment is divided into two stages. The first stage tests whether ARM processor signal processing waveform is complete, and the second stage tests after testing SPEEX codec whether the waveform results are complete.

The first phase of the experiment is to verify the ARM processor signal processing. The sine wave signals through the analog to digital conversion (ADC) are converted into digital signals, and then digital signals through pulse code modulation (PWM) are directly converted into analog signals to verify whether both waveforms are the same.

The signal generator is input with 500 Hz sine wave signal, and through the ARM processor signal processing, the oscilloscope detects the output results; the two waveform comparison results are the same as shown in Fig. 11.

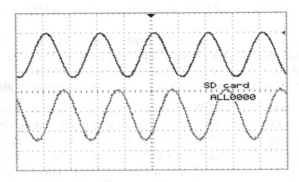

Fig. 11. Waveform detection results for phase 1 (yellow for output waveform, and blue for input waveform) (Color figure online)

In the second stage, SPEEX is added to the ARM processor. The analog signal is converted into the digital signal through ARM signal processing, and the digital signal is processed by SPEEX codec. Finally, the result of the operation is processed by the signal processing from digital signals converted into analog signals.

Signal generator inputs sine wave signals, and the frequency is 500 Hz. The signal after codec uses the oscilloscope to verify the decoder output signals and input signals for comparison, and verification results show that the input signals and output signals only have small errors, but the errors are still under recognition range (Fig. 12).

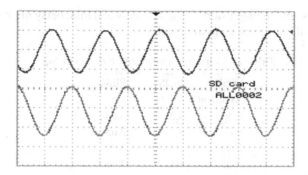

Fig. 12. Waveform detection results for phase 2 (yellow for output waveform, and blue for input waveform) (Color figure online)

4.2 PESQ Voice Quality Detection

PESQ developed by the Dutch KNP and British Telecom is used to develop voice measurement mode. In 2001, the ITU was defined as the standard speech quality measurement method ITU-T P.862 [11], and PESQ was a set of automated and objective evaluation of voice quality standards, whose purpose obtained time-consuming subjective testing methods. PESQ operation method is shown in Fig. 13. Basically, the difference between the original voice signal and the degraded signal between the devices under test (DUT) is compared, and the MOS score is calculated from the comparison result.

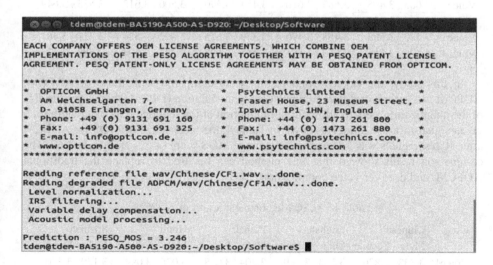

Fig. 13. PESQ measurement window [12]

PESQ measurement result is the difference between the ideal speech model and the real output voice signal, and is quantified by MOS score, as Table 2. The factors affecting the PESQ scores are: coding distortion packet delay and loss, delay jitter, and the background noise of the measuring environment.

Table 2. Comparison between MOS and PESQ

Quality	MOS	PESQ
Excellent	4.5	4.5
Good	4.3	3.88
Fair	4.0	3.65
Poor	3.6	3.40
Bad	3.1	3.31

According to the ITU-T P.862 standard, the PESQ test uses the following types of sources: five major international languages (English, Chinese, Spanish, French, Hindi), each with four different voice paragraphs, half male and female voice, and a total of forty test signals.

In the beginning of the experiment, 40 test signals and SPEEX codec files were tested with PESQ. The average score of PESQ MOS was 3.62 points after the measurement as shown in Table 3. Through the MOS corresponding PESQ table, it can detect that the voice quality results are not bad.

Table 3. PESQ Measurement results of SPEEX [12]

Lang.	Chinese		English		French		Hindi		Spanish	
Sex	Male	Female	Male	Female	Male	Female	Male	Female	Male	Female
Voice1	3.603	3.495	3.683	3.616	3.454	3.590	3.500	3.613	3.573	3.649
Voice2	3.715	3.437	3.499	3.628	3.456	3.594	3.530	3.418	3.552	3.660
Voice3	3.520	3.588	3.468	3.490	3.379	3.615	3.492	3.524	3.721	3.481
Voice4	3.470	3.516	3.679	3.581	3.455	3.633	3.235	3.494	3.588	3.473

In this study, the experimental results were compared with those of ADPCM. ADPCM is a variant of differential pulse-code modulation (DPCM) that varies the size of the quantization step, to allow further reduction of the required data bandwidth for a given signal-to-noise ratio. As shown in Table 4, the mean score of MOS for ADPCM after 40 test signals was 3.166, and the average MOS score of this study was 3.62. The comparison result showed that this method can be used to replace the traditional ADPCM, and used for voice compression.

Table 4. PESQ Measurement results of ADPCM

Lang.	Chinese		English		French		Hindi		Spanish	
Sex	Male	Female	Male	Female	Male	Female	Male	Female	Male	Female
Voice1	3.333	2.870	3.353	3.149	3.304	3.068	3.036	3.094	3.130	3.340
Voice2	3.501	3.114	2.908	3.283	3.309	3.196	3.032	2.908	3.066	3.226
Voice3	3.518	3.018	3.326	2.877	3.024	3.135	3.027	3.086	3.509	3.012
Voice4	3.494	3.055	3.384	3.230	3.064	3.155	2.911	3.159	3.546	2.911

5 Conclusion

In this study, SPEEX was successfully ported to the ARM processor, and voice data transmission was through the Bluetooth mode; and finally through the oscilloscope PESQ detection software was used to verify the quality of voice playback. The system first used the microphone to collect the voice signal, and the voice signal was input to the encoding side encoding; and then by the sender to transmit data to the receiver, the receiver received the voice data to the decoding side. At the decoder side SPEEX decoding was carried out at 125us time interval. Finally, the decoded speech was played back. Experimental PESQ voice quality verification results MOS score of 3.6 points. The experimental result of the PESQ voice quality verification shows that MOS average score is about 3.6 points or so. Compared with the traditional ADPCM voice quality, the result shows that the voice quality is superior to ADPCM.

SPEEX in voice compression and voice quality is superior to traditional ADPCM. In the future research and development, we hope that this study can be combined with environmental sensing to enhance the environmental sensing network application, and the research system can be used in the future life.

References

1. Valin, J.M.: The Speex Codec Manual Version 1.2 Beta 3, 8 December 2007
2. Schroeder, M.R., Atal, B.S.: Code-excited linear prediction (CELP): high-quality speech at very low bit rates. In: ICASSP 1985, pp. 937–940 (1985)
3. Bluetooth SIG Regulatory Committee, Bluetooth Low Energy Regulatory Aspects, 26 April 2011
4. ITU-CCITT G.726: 40,32,24,16 kbit/s Adaptive Differential Pulse Code Modulation (ADPCM). In: International Telecommunication Union, Geneva, Switzerland (1990)
5. STMicroelectronics RM0008 Reference manual, STM32F101xx, STM32F102xx, STM32F103xx, STM32F105xx and STM32F107xx advanced ARM ®-based 32-bit MCUs, Rev. 15, June 2014
6. STMicroelectronics Product Specifications, Medium-density performance line ARM-based 32-bit MCU interfaces, Rev. 16, August 2013
7. Texas Instruments, CC254x System-on –Chip for 2.4-GHz Bluetooth® low energy Applications, April 2014
8. OLIMEX.https://www.olimex.com/Products/ARM/ST/STM32-103STK/resources/STM32-103STK-REV-B-sch.gif
9. Microchip, "MCP601/1R/2/3/4:2.7 V to 6.0 V Single Supply CMOS Op Amps," Chandler, Arizona, United States (2007)
10. STMicroelectronics, "TS4871:Output Rail to Rail 1 W Audio Power Amplifier With Standby Mode," Geneva, Switzerland (2015)
11. ITU-T P862 Corrigendum, Perceptual Evaluation of Speech Quality(PESQ): An objective method for end-to-end speech quality assessment of narrow-band telephone networks and speech codecs, October 2007
12. Chang, C.C., Shih, Y.H., Wang, P.M.: Design and implement SPEEX decoder on ARM processor. In: International Congress on Image and Signal Processing BioMedical Engineering and Informatics (2016)

A Discrete Wavelet Transformation Based Fast and Secure Transmission of Images for Group Communication

M. Sridevi[1](✉), C. Mala[1], and S. Lakshmi Prabha[2]

[1] Department of Computer Science and Engineering,
National Institute of Technology, Trichy 620015, Tamil Nadu, India
{msridevi,mala}@nitt.edu
[2] Department of Computer Application,
National Institute of Technology, Trichy 620015, Tamil Nadu, India
jaislp111@gmail.com

Abstract. Security breaches such as confidentiality, authenticity and integrity are considered for transmission of vital information in the network. This paper proposes a fast and secure transmission of primary images in the network. The proposed schemes use Discrete Wavelet Transformation (DWT) with a traditional symmetric encryption algorithm. From the results, it is inferred that the proposed algorithms are fast and secured for transmission of significant images in a group.

Keywords: Discrete Wavelet Transformation · Image
Group communication and security

1 Introduction

Technology has grown in the recent past to tamper digital images transmitted across networks. When these images are for sensitive applications like medical, telemedicine, defense, journalism, scientific publication, biometrics, digital forensic, etc., it is required to provide secured transmission for the images. With the help of latest technology, the information can be easily trapped, modified and circulated over the network. Hence, it is essential to integrate security mechanisms. The transmitted data has to be protected from both external and internal intrusion attacks. Different techniques are used to protect confidentiality of a digital image from unauthorized access [1–6,10,14]. Further, the operations such as deleting, adding, hiding a region in an image can make it unauthentic. Many image authentication techniques [3,8,14] were proposed to detect and prevent forgery in the information content. These techniques are widely applied in law, defense, journalism, scientific publication, etc.

Transmission of digital images can be done in a secure manner by using any one of the four methods namely cryptography [1,2,4,7], steganography [14], digital signature [8] and watermarking [3] as shown in Fig. 1. The information are

© Springer Nature Singapore Pte Ltd. 2018
I. You et al. (Eds.): MobiSec 2016, CCIS 797, pp. 80–94, 2018.
https://doi.org/10.1007/978-981-10-7850-7_8

changed into an unreadable format in cryptography during its transfer whereas in case of steganography, the meaningful information is hidden within other information. Digital signature is used to authenticate the information sent by the user. Watermarking method uses a symbol or signature embedded within the digital data to provide copyright and ownership for the data.

Fig. 1. Image security mechanisms and methods

Even though many techniques are available for transmitting the image in an authentic and confidential way in a network, they take more time and consume large amount of bandwidth for transmission due to the huge size of the image [8]. Moreover, with the help of modern technologies, the transmitted information across the network can be trapped easily, manipulated and then distributed. While transferring secret information, it has to be protected from the intruders. Hence, it is essential to incorporate security during transmission of important digital images. Image encryption is applied in many applications such as internet communication, multimedia systems, medical imaging, telemedicine, journalism, scientific publication, military, digital forensic, law etc.

2 Related Work

The information transferred via the network should be free from malicious attacks. Different methods were developed by many researchers [1–5,7–14,19] to incorporate security features. The methods may use encryption or hiding techniques such as cryptography [1,2,4,7], watermarking [3], digital signature [8], compression [9] or steganography [14]. The encryption schemes can be either applied to spatial [9,10] or frequency domain [11–13,19].

Any secret information has to be protected while transmission. There are various fool proof methods to safe guard such information. [20] discusses about the traditional steganography method of incorporating the secret information by Camouflaging it inside an image. It also discusses about the additional security measures incorporated while transmitting and receiving information using steganography with multi user.

The portion of the quadtree compressed data are encrypted using partial encryption [9]. The most significant information are encrypted which leads to possibility of brute force attack. In [10], the image is scrambled using a random vector and substitution method is adapted to change the pixel values. This method is suitable only for gray scale images and is also susceptible to attacks. The chaotic map is used for changing the pixel position in [5,6] which uses permutation and diffusion mechanism. It has the ability to detect image tampering and ensures authenticity. Image encryption using new spatiotemporal chaotic system is proposed in [17] by defining the local non linear map with chaotic algorithm through the mechanism of permutation and diffusion. It resists various attacks to the image during transfer.

The security of medical images in digital form is another major content that has to be protected while transferring over a network. In such cases, [18] proposes a chaos based medical image encryption that provides an increase in efficiency compared to the classic permutation substitution type of image ciphers. The proposed method introduces a substitution mechanism in the permutation level. A new approach was proposed in [24] and named as Certificate-Based Encryption with Keyword Search (CBEKS). The approach is used in medical application to conceal the medical documents. The proposed scheme is highly secured for all kind of attacks.

The encryption in frequency domain [11–13,19] gives high level of security due to its complex computations. In [11], encryption is performed based on Discrete Cosine Transformation (DCT) coefficients. The bits are encrypted using DES or IDEA algorithms. It is applicable only to JPEG images. It is very difficult to predict the original information. Hence it is highly secured.

Asymmetric image encryption is used in [12] based on matrix transformation. Each block of original image is scrambled and key is generated based on the transformation. The scrambled image is encrypted using private key. The encrypted information is decrypted using public key at receiver side.

Multilevel partial image encryption is proposed in [13]. It uses Discrete Fourier Transformation (DFT). The computed image coefficients are permuted and the resultant is used for encryption. The encrypted image is obtained after applying wavelet reconstruction and compression. If higher frequency coefficients are known, then outliners of the original image can be viewed. Therefore, it is not secure.

In case of insecure network or a wireless network, it is very difficult to ensure authenticity of an image. In [8], a content based image authentication scheme is proposed to address these issues. The proposed scheme is robust and improves security against forgery attacks using digital signature and key dependent parametric wavelet filters respectively.

In [23], the authors adopted a technique to solve key cloning problem based on terminal fingerprints. The solution uses a hybrid encryption scheme which uses both attribute and RSA based encryption scheme. It depicts high level of security but takes more computational time to perform the encryption and decryption operations.

In [25], the authors proposed a privacy preserving mechanism for a video surveillance to detect the unauthorized persons. Two implementations (for authentication and usage control) were done in a real time scenario to test the proposed frame work. The insider attacks were explained in [15,16,26]. The insider threats are studied in [26] using signalling game theoretic model.

Image tampering is very sensitive and the modified data becomes invalid. The sensitive image data stored need to be highly confidential and available to valid users at all times. Attackers may tamper the data for fun to professional smugglers or intentionally modify or hide important information. Hence, security must be high to prevent damage of the data. In case of defense and medical imaging, if the security of the image is lost, it will lead to damage of the information present in the image. When a photograph or video of a missile launch is communicated over network, an intruder may modify sensitive or important portion of the image such as name of the missile, country name which in turn will lead to misinterpretation in the image at the receiver side. In medical applications, the cause will be even more dangerous if the sensitive information is tampered. In case of organ transplant, a donor organ tissue may be modified to be shown as non donor or the organ donor matches can be drugged and robbed. This might lead to death of the patient. Hence, security is needed for transmission of vital information in the network. To solve these issues, this paper proposes an algorithm for transmitting the sensitive image in a secured manner.

The remainder of the paper is organized as follows: Sect. 3 discusses about the proposed algorithm. Experimental results and analysis are discussed in Sect. 4. Section 5 concludes the paper.

3   Proposed Method

Due to recent development in multimedia and networking technologies, huge number of applications involve transfer of information in a distributed network environment, which makes the data (image, video, multimedia, etc.) more vulnerable to the attack. This paper proposes an algorithm which transfers the information (digital image or video) and protects it from attack. To ensure confidentiality and faster transmission of the image, it is transformed to frequency domain using Discrete Wavelet Transform (DWT). The image is decomposed to j levels and the coefficients are determined. The size of the image is reduced to 2^j levels. The resultant coefficients (horizontal, vertical, diagonal and approximated) are encrypted using maximum values for each column of their corresponding coefficients. Row vectors are formed as a result of encryption. The size of the encrypted image is less and hence they require less memory and bandwidth for transmission. The encrypted coefficients are sent to n different receivers. At the receiver side, reverse process of encryption and transformation takes place to get back the original image.

3.1   FAST Algorithm

To maintain secrecy during transmission, encryption scheme is used for the image data. This section proposes an algorithm called FAST (Fast And Secure Transmission) algorithm and it is given in Algorithms 1 and 2 for both single sender and multiple receivers to protect the image from attack. The proposed FAST algorithm consists of three modules as shown in Fig. 2. They are

- Sender module
- Secure transmission module (Transformation and Encryption)
- Receiver module

In the sender module, first an input image of size M x N is converted from spatial to frequency domain using Discrete Wavelet Transform (DWT). The major

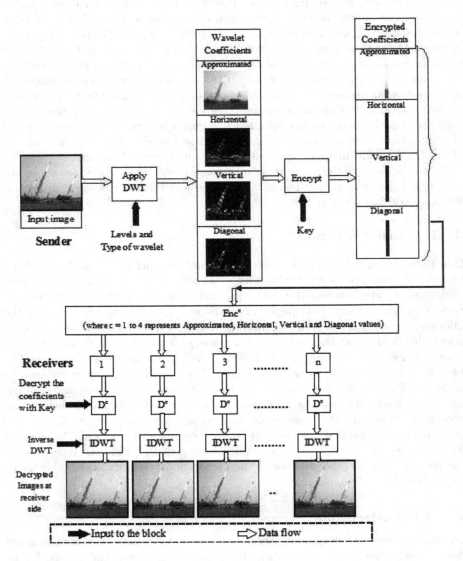

Fig. 2. Flow diagram of proposed FAST algorithm using symmetric key

advantages of using wavelet transformation are its (1) compact representation, (2) tolerance to color intensity shift, (3) ability to capture shape and texture information of the image and (4) computation in linear time. The four coefficients W_ϕ^c such as horizontal, vertical, diagonal and approximation are computed from the image using multi level decomposition [21]. The outliners of the image can be obtained if higher frequency coefficients are known. Hence, the frequency domain coefficients are sent in a secured way by encrypting and then transmitting them which provides better confidentiality to the coefficients.

The symmetric encryption algorithm [22] is used for encryption and decryption of the frequency domain coefficients. At the sender side, private key is generated which is used for encrypting the four coefficient values by determining maximum of W_ϕ^c for each coefficient using the Eqs. 1 – 3.

$$\text{Enc}^c = W_\phi^c/k \tag{1}$$

where Enc^c is Encrypted coefficient, i denotes coefficient values in horizontal, vertical, diagonal and approximated image, W_ϕ^c is the result of DWT and k is the key as given in Eq. 2.

$$k = max(\mathrm{W}_\phi^c) \tag{2}$$

$$\text{Enc}^c = \text{avg}\,(W_\phi^c)/\text{avg}(\max(W_\phi^c)) \tag{3}$$

Finally, the encrypted coefficients (Enc^c) are sent to n receivers (insiders). The insiders are the people in a group who have legal permission to access the data. Whenever an image is sent from one person in the network to others in the group, it has to be received by other persons within the group without any modification. But there is a possibility for an insider to trap the confidential information sent within the group. The trapped information can be edited and manipulated to make them insecure and also create damage to the organization. The damage will be hazardous and irrecoverable for transmission of information related to medical and defense applications.

At the receiver side, the proposed FAST algorithm performs decryption and inverse transformation for the received data for n receivers. The encrypted coefficients are decrypted (D^c) with private key to obtain details of four coefficients namely horizontal, vertical, diagonal and approximated. Then Inverse DWT (IDWT) is applied to the decrypted coefficients (D^c) for j levels to reconstruct the original image. The perfect reconstruction of the image can be verified by comparing the reconstructed image at receiver side with the original image at the sender side using the Eq. 4. If the result yields zero, then it indicates perfect reconstruction of the image.

$$max(max(abs(f - g))) \tag{4}$$

where f is the original image and g is the reconstructed image after IDWT.

Algorithm 1. FAST algorithm at single sender
Input to the algorithm: An image of size (M x N)
Output of the algorithm: Encrypted coefficients $(1 \times M/2^j)$
The steps involved in sender side are given as follows:

1. Apply DWT for j levels to the input image of size M x N.
2. Determine (W_ϕ^c) coefficients of DWT which is of size M/j x N/j
3. Find maximum of (W_ϕ^c) which results in row vector containing maximum value from each column.
4. Encrypt the coefficients (Enc^c) with the values obtained in step 3. The resultant will be of size $1 \times M/2^j$
5. Send (Enc^c) to n users.

Algorithm 2. FAST algorithm at multiple receivers
Input to the algorithm: Encrypted coefficients from sender.
Output of the algorithm: Reconstructed image (M x N) at each receiver.
The following two steps are repeated by all n receivers:

1. Decrypt the encrypted information to get D^c using secret key.
2. Apply IDWT for the decrypted information to get back the image (M x N).

Let the image be of the size M x N and the size of coefficient be $M/2^j \times N/2^j$ with decomposition level j by using Algorithm 1. After encryption, the size of encrypted image is $1 \times M/2^j$. The size of the image is drastically reduced from M x N to $1 \times M/2^j$. Therefore, the encrypted image information requires less memory and bandwidth for transmission to n receivers. By this reduction in size, the encrypted information can be sent faster.

In the proposed algorithm, the image is first transformed into frequency domain to ensure confidentiality. Frequency domain coefficients are computed using complex calculations [21]. Hence, it provides better security to the image when compared to spatial domain [11–13]. The image is decomposed into many levels to reduce the image size. The image size is inversely proportional to levels used for decomposition as inferred from Eq. (5). The size of encrypted information (coefficients) is a vector which is less than the size of the image. From Eq. (6), it is inferred that the memory and bandwidth required for transmission is also less. Hence, the proposed method transfers the image information faster and in a secured manner.

$$Size\ of\ image \propto \tfrac{1}{j} \tag{5}$$

$$Size\ of\ Enc^c \propto Transmission\ speed \tag{6}$$

4   Results and Discussion

This section discusses about the experimental results and analyses the proposed FAST algorithm in the subsequent sections from 4.1 to 4.2.

4.1 Experimental Results

The proposed algorithms are tested with two different image data sets namely, defense and medical data sets. The results of defense and medical images are shown in Sects. 4.1.1 and 4.1.2 respectively.

Fig. 3. Image to be sent

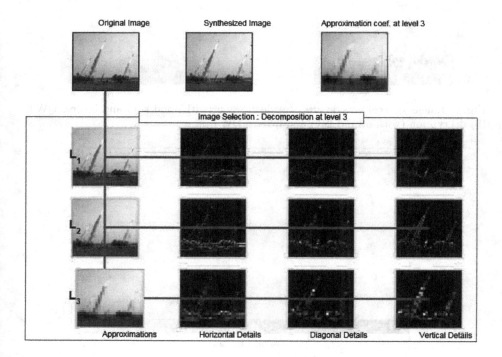

Fig. 4. DWT for three different levels

4.1.1 Defense Dataset

A missile launching image is taken as an input image as shown in Fig. 3, which is transmitted through the network. An intruder might hack the transmitted information such as missile name, country name, etc. to modify and misinterpret the image. To protect important and sensitive information in images and

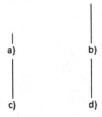

Fig. 5. Encrypted coefficients (a) Approximated, (b) Horizontal, (c) Vertical, (d) Diagonal

Fig. 6. Image at receiver side after (a) decryption (with valid key) and inverse DWT (b) decryption (with invalid key) and inverse DWT

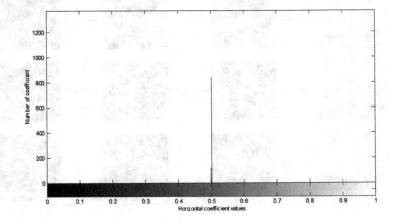

Fig. 7. Horizontal coefficient at level 1

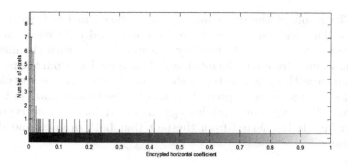

Fig. 8. Histogram plot for encrypted horizontal coefficients

to provide secured transmission, the image is encrypted using proposed FAST algorithm as explained in Sect. 3.1. DWT is used to convert the image into frequency domain coefficients. The detailed coefficients for three different decomposition levels are shown in Fig. 4. The coefficients namely approximation, horizontal, vertical and diagonal are encrypted to provide security. Figure 5 shows the encrypted image coefficients. From the results in Fig. 5, it is inferred that the size of encrypted information is very less. Hence, the memory and bandwidth required for the transmission of encrypted coefficients are also low which ultimately results in speedy transmission of image using the proposed FAST algorithm. The encrypted image is sent to a group. n receivers are there in a group. Each and every receiver will have their own private key to decrypt the

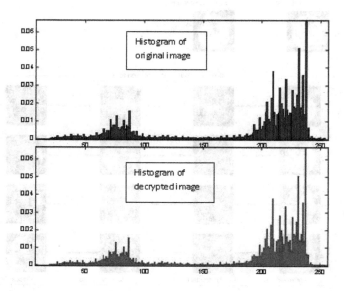

Fig. 9. Histogram plots of original and decrypted images with correct key

message. The result of the decrypted image is shown in Fig. 6 with valid and invalid keys. The original image can be reconstructed only when valid key is used for decryption process. As this key is available only with the insiders, the algorithm is secured from outside intruders. This is evident from the result of the decrypted image with an invalid key as shown in Fig. 6(b). Histogram plot of horizontal coefficient and its encrypted coefficient for level 1 are shown in Figs. 7 and 8 respectively. Figure 9 represents histograms of original and decrypted image with proper key. It is inferred from the plot that both original and decrypted values are same.

4.1.2   Medical Dataset

Medical image security is an important issue when digital images and their respective patient information are transmitted across public networks. With secure image transmission and communication, diagnosis can be done from long

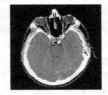

Fig. 10. Image to be sent

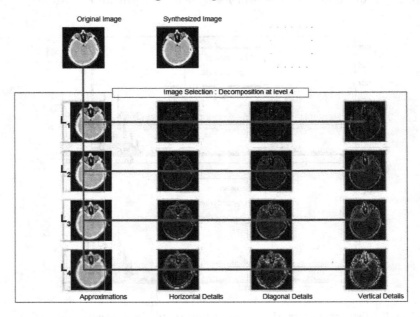

Fig. 11. Result of discrete wavelet transform for four levels

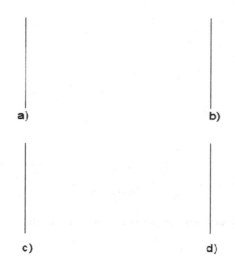

Fig. 12. Encrypted coefficients for the image shown in Fig. 10

Fig. 13. Results of medical image (a) Decrypted with valid key (b) Decrypted with invalid key

distances where superior medical facility is available. Ease of access is also provided to patients. They do not have to always burn a CD in order to take their information to another consultant. Cross communication across the globe for research and educational purposes can be enabled. Data privacy and confidentiality for every patient record is important. The availability of electronic data within the modern health information infrastructure presents significant benefits for medical providers and patients, including enhanced patient autonomy, improved clinical treatment, advances in health research and public health surveillance. The experiment was conducted for a medical image (brain) as shown in Fig. 10 to validate the proposed algorithms. The results are shown from Figs. 11, 12 and 13.

4.2 Analysis

The proposed FAST algorithm is analysed with respect to the bandwidth required for transmission of an image as shown in Fig. 14. From Fig. 14, it is inferred that the memory requirement decreases with the increase in the number of decomposition levels.

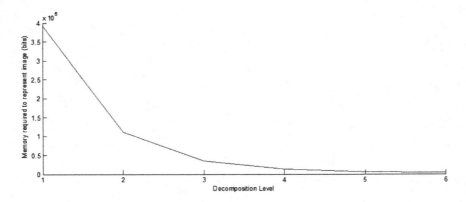

Fig. 14. Bandwidth required for an image at different levels

5   Conclusion

Novel algorithm was proposed in this paper to incorporate security in transmission of digital images. The proposed algorithm prevents external attack. The bandwidth and memory required for transmission are computed for the proposed schemes and are found to be very less due to the usage of DWT. Hence the proposed methods can be adopted for faster and secured transmission of images in video conferencing, medical, military, defense and scientific applications.

References

1. Liao, X., Lai, S., Zhou, Q.: A novel image encryption algorithm based on adaptive wave transmission. Sig. Process. **90**(9), 2714–2722 (2010). Elsevier
2. Kumar, H.S.S., Panduranga, H.T., Kumar, S.K.N.: A two stage combinational approach for image encryption. In: Meghanathan, N., Nagamalai, D., Chaki, N. (eds.) Advances in Computing and Information Technology. AISC, vol. 177, pp. 843–849. Springer, Heidelberg (2013). https://doi.org/10.1007/978-3-642-31552-7_86
3. Wong, P.W.: A public key watermark for image verification and authentication. In: International Conference on Image Processing, Chicago, vol. 1, pp. 455–459 (1998)
4. Pareek, N.K., Patider, V., Sud, K.K.: Diffusion substitution based gray image encryption scheme. Digit. Signal Proc. **23**(4), 894–901 (2013). Elsevier
5. Hakhshandeh, A., Eslami, Z.: An authenticated image encryption scheme based on chaotic maps and memory cellular automata. Opt. Lasers Eng. **51**(6), 665–673 (2013). Elsevier
6. Wang, Y., Wong, K.W., Liao, X., Chen, G.: A new chaos based fast encryption algorithm. Appl. Soft Comput. **11**(1), 514–522 (2011). Elsevier
7. Shah, J., Saxena, V.: Performance study on image encryption schemes. Int. J. Comput. Sci. **8**(1), 349–356 (2011)

8. Charles, S., Govardhan, A., Sultana, F.: A tamper proof noise resilient end to end image based authentication system over wireless transmission with AWGN channel using wavelet based templates and AES. Int. J. Comput. Sci. Netw. Secur. **13**(5), 41–49 (2013)

9. Cheng, H., Li, X.: Partial encryption of compressed images and videos. IEEE Trans. Sig. Process. **48**(8), 2439–2451 (2000)

10. Kulkarni, N.S., Gupta, I., Kulkarni, S.N.: A robust image encryption technique based on random vector. In: International Conference on Emerging Trend in Engineering and Technology (ICETET), 16–18 July 2008, pp. 15–19 (2008)

11. Van Droogenbroeck, M., Benedett, R.: Techniques for a selective encryption of uncompressed and compressed images. In: Proceedings of Advanced Concepts for Intelligent Vision Systems (ACIVS), Ghent, Belgium, 9–11 September 2002, pp. 90–97 (2002)

12. Shuihua, H., Shuangyan, Y.: An asymmetric image encryption based on matrix transformation. ECTI Trans. Comput. Inf. Technol. **1**(2), 126–133 (2005)

13. Odibat, O.M., Abdallah, M.H., Al-Zoubi, M.B.R.: New techniques in the implementation of partial image encryption. In: International Multi-conference on Computer Science and Information Technology, Amman (2006)

14. Khamrui, A., Mandal, J.K.: A wavelet transform based image authentication approach using genetic algorithm (AWTIAGA). In: Satapathy, S., Avadhani, P., Udgata, S., Lakshminarayana, S. (eds.) ICT and Critical Infrastructure: Proceedings of the 48th Annual Convention of Computer Society of India- Vol I. AISC, vol. 248, pp. 251–258. Springer, Cham (2014). https://doi.org/10.1007/978-3-319-03107-1_28

15. Salem, M.B., Hershkop, S., Stolfo, S.J.: A survey of insider attack detection research. In: Stolfo, S.J., Bellovin, S.M., Keromytis, A.D., Hershkop, S., Smith, S.W., Sinclair, S. (eds.) Insider Attack and Cyber Security. Advances in Information Security, vol. 39, pp. 69–90. Springer, Boston (2008). https://doi.org/10.1007/978-0-387-77322-3_5

16. Li, M.: Analysis of the insider attack issue in the movie, banking, and computer industries. Compsci 725 SC 05 team paper, pp. 1–13 (2005)

17. Songa, C.-Y., Qiao, Y.-L., Zhang, X.-Z.: An image encryption scheme based on new spatiotemporal chaos. Optik **124**, 3329–3334 (2013). Elsevier

18. Fu, C., Meng, W., Zhan, Y., Zhu, Z., Lau, F.C.M., Tse, C.K., Ma, H.: An efficient and secure medical image protection scheme based on chaotic maps. Comput. Biol. Med. **43**, 1000–1010 (2013). Elsevier

19. Tedmodi, S., Al-Najdawi, N.: Loseless image cryptograph algorithm based on Discrete Cosine Transform. Int. Arab J. Inf. Technol. **9**(5), 471–478 (2012)

20. Kumar, P.P.P., Amirtharajan, R., Thenmozhi, K., Rayappan, J.B.B.: Steg-OFDM blend for highly secure multi-user communication. In: Wireless VITAE, IEEE Conference Proceedings, pp. 1–5 (2011)

21. Gonzalez, R.C., Woods, R.E., Eddins, S.L.: Digital Image Processing, 3rd edn. Pearson, Upper Saddle River (2008)

22. Stallings, W.: Cryptography and Network Security, 4th edn. Pearson, Noida (2006)

23. Chen, C., Anada, H., Kawamoto, J., Sakurai, K.: A hybrid encryption scheme with key-cloning protection: user/terminal double authentication via attributes and fingerprints. J. Internet Serv. Inf. Secur. (JISIS) **6**(2), 23–36 (2016)

24. Gritti, C., Susilo, W., Plantard, T.: Certificate-based encryption with keyword search enabling secure authorization in electronic health record. J. Internet Serv. Inf. Secur. (JISIS) **6**(4), 1–34 (2016)

25. Carniani, E., Costantino, G., Marino, F., Martinelli, F., Mori, P.: Enhancing video surveillance with usage control and privacy-preserving solutions. J. Wirel. Mob. Netw. Ubiquitous Comput. Dependable Appl. **7**(4), 20–40 (2016)
26. Casey, W., Morales, J.A., Mishra, B.: Threats from inside: dynamic utility (mis)alignments in an agent based model. J. Wirel. Mob. Netw. Ubiquitous Comput. Dependable Appl. **7**(1), 97–117 (2016)

An Automated Graph Based Approach to Risk Assessment for Computer Networks with Mobile Components

Elena Doynikova[1,2] and Igor Kotenko[1,2(✉)]

[1] St. Petersburg Institute for Informatics and Automation of the Russian Academy of Sciences (SPIIRAS), St. Petersburg, Russia
[2] St. Petersburg National Research University of Information Technologies, Mechanics and Optics, St. Petersburg, Russia
{doynikova,ivkote}@comsec.spb.ru

Abstract. The paper suggests an automated approach to risk assessment for computer networks with mobile components. The approach is based on the modeling of attacks against computer network as attack graphs and application of open databases of attack patterns and vulnerabilities. Distinctive features of the attacks against networks with mobile components are analyzed. On the base of this analysis we develop the technique of attack graph generation taking into account vulnerabilities of software and hardware for mobile access points as well as weaknesses of mobile devices and mobile connection channels. The technique for calculation of risk assessment metrics is suggested. Operation of the technique for the attack graph generation and calculation of risks is shown on a sample network with mobile components.

Keywords: Mobile networks · Mobile security · Risk analysis · Risk assessment
Attack graphs · Security metrics

1 Introduction

Modern computer networks comprise various elements including mobile components. The distribution of mobile technologies leads to new risks for computer network security including risks from the attacks against wireless connections and wireless clients (that comprise mobile and fixed devices). Attacks of this type are becoming more attractive for the malefactors because of the confidential corporate data stored on wireless clients and new possibilities to penetrate enterprise computer networks.

The fact that the number of attacks against mobile devices in order to compromise the enterprise computer networks increases is confirmed, for example, by the report of Check Point Software Technologies Ltd. company [3]. Their list of top-10 attacks against computer networks contains Android malware HummingBad (a persistent mobile chain attack). There are also other serious malware for mobile devices: Xcode-Ghost, AndroRAT, BrainTest, etc. [3]. It is critical as soon as currently mobile devices can store confidential data and fulfill critical processes. Besides, mobile devices provide additional entry points to computer networks: if an attacker will be able to get privileges on a mobile device, he/she can further compromise all connected network. That is why

© Springer Nature Singapore Pte Ltd. 2018
I. You et al. (Eds.): MobiSec 2016, CCIS 797, pp. 95–106, 2018.
https://doi.org/10.1007/978-981-10-7850-7_9

it is necessary to consider wireless clients in security awareness. Whereas fixed devices (desktops and workstations) can be controlled, it is more difficult to control mobile devices (laptops, smartphones). Owners of the mobile devices usually do not pay sufficient attention to the security: a lot of devices are not equipped with antivirus; users store not encrypted data, and connect to public Wi-Fi.

In this paper we consider possible attacks against networks with mobile components in the process of security assessment. For security assessment of mobile components we extend our approach suggested earlier for security assessment of fixed computer networks which is based on the analytical modeling and open standards [13, 14]. We review some features of mobile networks and analyze an opportunity of consideration of these features in case of application of the following open standards for security assessment: CAPEC [4] - for the attack pattern representation, CVE [6] - for the vulnerability representation, and CVSS [15] - for the vulnerability assessment. The technique for modeling of attacks against mobile networks and assessment of appropriate risks is suggested. It takes into account vulnerabilities of software and hardware of mobile access points (APs), weaknesses of mobile devices and mobile connection channels. The operation of the technique is demonstrated on an example. Thereby, the main contribution of the paper consists in the development and analysis of the risk assessment technique that considers mobile components.

This paper is an extended version of the paper presented on MobiSec 2016 [8]. Contrary to [8] the particularities of approach for security assessment of mobile components, and algorithms for models generation and assessment are provided.

The paper is organized as follows. Section 2 reviews related researches. Section 3 describes the suggested risk assessment technique for mobile components. In Sect. 4 the approach implementation is shown on an example. Conclusion analyzes the paper results and provides insight into the future research.

2   Related Work

There is a number of research works on the detection, analysis and defense against mobile attacks. Theoharidou et al. [20] consider a risk assessment technique for smartphones. It includes identification of assets, definition of assets criticalities, identification of possible threats, and definition of probabilities of threats considering required permissions. Risk for assets is defined on the basis of attack probabilities and assets criticalities using a risk matrix. Frei [9] reviews a tabular procedure of qualitative risk assessment and controls selection for mobile devices. It is based on existing solutions. The author provides some unique considerations connected with business requirements for the mobile risk assessment. He outlines possible threats for mobile devices and then defines their impacts to business, their likelihood of occurrence and possible controls, and considers risks before and after control implementation for a case study. But the techniques in [20] and [9] are not automated and do not consider in details risks of mobile devices compromise for the whole network.

There are automated techniques of risk assessment for mobile applications. In [22] the tool on the base of Natural Language Processing is suggested. It serves to define the compliance of the application description and the required application permissions. Authors suppose that further on this basis the security risks of the application installation on mobile devices can be assessed. Jing et al. [19] describe a tool for the automated risk assessment of mobile applications on the base of machine-learned ranking. User should rank the permission groups according to their relevance to the applications of different type. The tool continuously assesses deviation of the required permissions from the expected baseline and defines risks of mobile applications according to the relevance of required permissions. Unfortunately, these works do not consider criticality of mobile devices security for the enterprise computer networks.

Security assessment of mobile networks is considered in [21]. Authors analyze typical components of mobile networks and possible threats. On the base of these data they assess the risk on a quantitative scale considering threat probability, network vulnerabilities and attack impact. Though [21] provides comprehensive analysis of mobile network components considering different protocols and architectures, it does not review automated risk analysis for corporative networks.

In this paper we suggest the technique for the automated risk assessment of the networks with mobile components on the base of analytical modeling and open standards. Main features of the approach are: (1) application of attack graphs to model possible steps of an attacker; (2) application of open standards to represent the input data, including CVE [6] - for vulnerabilities representation, CAPEC [4] - for attack patterns representation, CPE [18] - to represent software and hardware, CVSS [15] - to assess vulnerabilities; (3) application of open databases of vulnerabilities and attacks, including NVD [16] and CAPEC [4]; (4) application of quantitative metrics for security assessment. We suppose that this approach allows to outline weak places of computer networks introduced by unsecured mobile components, and further to increase common security level of networks.

3   Risk Assessment Technique

We suggested an approach to the automated security assessment of fixed computer networks earlier [13, 14]. The approach includes the stages: (1) data gathering (including links between network elements, software and hardware in the CPE format [18], vulnerabilities in the CVE format [6] and weaknesses in the CWE format [7], security events); (2) models generation; (3) calculation of the security metrics; (4) definition of the security level. We divide metrics on groups according to the models used for their calculation: metrics of the topological level are calculated on the base of the network model; metrics of the attack graph level – on the base of the attack model; metrics of the attacker level – on the base of the attacker model; metrics of the events level – on the base of the event model. For the security assessment the metrics of the topological level are mandatory and metrics of other levels are optional and can refine assessments.

In the previous research distinctive features of the wireless network components were not considered. In this paper we fill this gap. The modified processes of our approach and the appropriate data are: the input data gathering process and resulting input data (links between network elements, software and hardware, vulnerabilities and weaknesses); the models generation process and generated models (network model, attack graph); the security metrics calculation process and generated metrics (attack probability, attack impact, security risk).

To describe particularities of the input data gathering we provide an example of the wireless network architecture in Fig. 1(a). In Fig. 1(b) the attack graph for the example network is provided (it will be described later). The network consists of the Wi-Fi APs (Wi-Fi router and Wi-Fi bridge) and the Wi-Fi clients (mobile devices). Wireless connections are represented with dashed lines. We get input data on the network components from networks scanning tools and administrators.

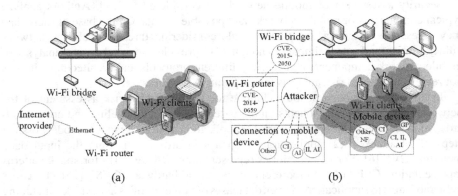

(a)   (b)

Fig. 1. Example of a wireless network (a) and the attack graph for the example network (b)

An important feature of our approach is the application of open standards and databases. We analyzed opportunity to use them for wireless clients and wireless APs.

Hardware and software of the wireless APs (wireless routers and other devices) can be represented in the CPE format, and its vulnerabilities in the CVE format can be found in the open databases.

For example: Dap-1350: D-Link Wireless Router/AP (in the CPE format: cpe: 2.3:o:d-link:dap-1350_firmware:1.10:*:*:*:*:*:*:*). The appropriate vulnerability instance from the NVD database [16]: CVE-2014-3872 (7.5 – HIGH) in the format: CVE_ID (BaseScore – BaseScore_Qual), where CVE_ID – id of the vulnerability; BaseScore – its quantitative CVSS score; BaseScore_Qual – its qualitative CVSS score. CVSS_Vector for this vulnerability incorporates CVSS indexes and their values [15]: AV:N/AC:L/Au:N/C:P/I:P/A:P, where AV defines access to the vulnerability (N – network, A – adjacent network, L – local), AC – access complexity for the vulnerability (L – low, M – medium, H – high), Au defines if additional authentication is required for the vulnerability exploitation (M – multiple, S – single, N – none), C, I, A – confidentiality, integrity and availability impact from the vulnerability exploitation accordingly (C – complete, P – partial, N – none).

Hardware and software of mobile devices can be also represented in the CPE format, and its vulnerabilities in the CVE format can be found in the open databases. But there is a challenge: new mobile devices can connect to the network and disconnect from it depending on the access policy. So mobile devices and connection channels stay uncovered. To represent attacks against these objects we chose the CAPEC dictionary [4]. CAPEC database contains various attack patterns including attack patterns for mobile devices and mobile channels. Besides, the CAPEC database provides details on the attack patterns that can be used for security assessments: attack severity, required attacker skills, attack prerequisites and attack impact. CAPEC View that incorporates attacks on mobile devices is named "Mobile Device Patterns" (view id 553) [2]. This set can be complemented with attack patterns from CAPEC category "Communications" (id 512) [1]. In Table 1 these attack patterns are provided with fields of the CAPEC scheme that we will use for security assessment. We added field "Target" to separate attacks against mobile devices from the attacks against wireless channels. It can take values "channel" and "device". We fill this field manually, analyzing the attack pattern description. Field "Typical severity" defines an attack impact level. Field "Attacker skills" defines an attack complexity. These fields can take values: L (low), M (medium), H (high). Field "Attack prerequisites" provides a keyword that defines attack prerequisites ("none" – there is no prerequisites for this attack, "yes" – prerequisites exist). Field "Attack consequences" defines what security property is damaged. To determine it we map its values in the CAPEC database on the impact for the security properties: execute unauthorized code or commands – CI (confidentiality impact), II (Integrity impact), AI (availability impact); DoS: resource consumption – AI; modify application data – II; read application data – CI; other – other; bypass protection mechanism – GP (get privileges). We use this information to generate model of attacks against wireless devices and channels.

The particularities of the *models generation stage* are provided below. Initial network model is generated on the base of network hosts, their hardware and software, their vulnerabilities, and links between them. Model of the network with mobile components additionally contains nodes for the wireless devices, link type, and applicable CAPEC patterns for the wireless devices and channels. On the base of the network model the attack model in the form of an attack graph is generated. Nodes of the graph represent attack actions (exploitation of the vulnerabilities or attack patterns), edges – transitions from the attack action to the next one [12]. Attack actions against wireless APs are automatically included into the model. To model attack actions against other components of the network with wireless components (wireless devices and wireless channels) we generate nodes of the specific type for the attack graph. These nodes contain fields that we outlined in the previous section: "Target", "Typical severity", "Attacker skills", "Attack prerequisites", "Attack consequences". For the attack graph generation we use fields "Target" and "Attack consequences" of the CAPEC scheme. We divide the nodes on two groups: "Connection to mobile device" and "Mobile device". Each group is defined on the base of filed "Target": attack patterns with value "channel" are added to the "Connection to mobile device" group, attack patterns with value "device" are added to the "Mobile device" group. Further attack actions are grouped according to their consequences on the base of "Attack consequences" field: CI; II; AI; NF (not filled); GP; other. Group 1: GP; group 2: CI, II, AI; group 3: CI, II; group 4: CI, AI; group 5: II, AI; group 6: CI; group 7: II; group 8: AI; group 9: other/NF. Attack patterns of these groups are outlined with different colors in Table 1: from the darkest color for the group 1 to the lightest color for the group 9. Field "Attack consequences" is used to link the

Table 1. Mobile attack patterns from the CAPEC dictionary

Name	Target	Typical severity	Attacker skills	Attack prereq-uisites	Attack conse-quences
CAPEC-187: Malicious Automated Software Update	device	H	-	none	-
CAPEC-498: Probe iOS Screenshots	device	-	-	yes	-
CAPEC-499: Intent Intercept	device	-	-	yes	AI, II, CI
CAPEC-501: Activity Hijack	device	-	-	-	-
CAPEC-502: Intent Spoof	device	-	-	yes	-
CAPEC-604: Wi-Fi Jamming	channel	L	L	yes	AI
CAPEC-605: Cellular Jamming	channel	L	L	yes	AI
CAPEC-606: Weakening of Cellular Encryption	device	H	M	yes	other
CAPEC-608: Cryptanalysis of Cellular Encryption	channel	H	M	none	other
CAPEC-609: Cellular Traffic Intercept	channel	L	M	none	CI
CAPEC-610: Cellular Data Injection	channel	H	H	none	AI, II
CAPEC-611: BitSquatting	device	L	L	none	CI, II, AI
CAPEC-612: WiFi MAC Address Tracking	channel	L	L	none	other
CAPEC-613: WiFi SSID Tracking	channel	L	L	none	other
CAPEC-614: Rooting SIM CardS	device	H	M	yes	AI, II, CI
CAPEC-615: Evil Twin Wi-Fi Attack	channel	L	-	none	CI
CAPEC-617: Cellular Rogue Base Station	device	L	L	none	CI
CAPEC-618: Cellular Broadcast Message Request	device	L	L	yes	other
CAPEC-619: Signal Strength Tracking	channel	L	L	-	other
CAPEC-621: Analysis of Packet Timing and Sizes	channel	L	H	yes	CI
CAPEC-622: Electromagnetic Side-Channel Attack	device	L	M	yes	CI
CAPEC-623: Compromising Emanations Attack	device	L	H	yes	CI
CAPEC-625: Mobile Device Fault Injection	device	-	H	-	CI
CAPEC-626: Smudge Attack	device	-	M	yes	GP
CAPEC-627: Counterfeit GPS Signals	device	-	H	none	other
CAPEC-628: Carry-Off GPS Attack	device	-	H	none	other
CAPEC-629: Unauthorized Use of Device Resources	device	-	H	-	other

nodes of attack graph. Attacks that lead to consequences "get privileges" allow to bypass authentication and to proceed attack on the graph nodes corresponding to the network hosts available to the mobile device user. Other groups correspond to the threats of different types.

The attack graph for the wireless network (Fig. 1(a)) is provided in Fig. 1(b). Wi-Fi router is equipped with Cisco WAP4410N wireless AP firmware 2.0.3.3, Wi-Fi bridge is equipped with Dap-1320 D-Link Wireless Repeater. Attack objects are represented with rectangles or appropriate icons. Attack actions (CAPEC attack patterns or CVE exploitation) are grouped according to their consequences and are represented with circles. Dashed lines link sequential attack actions. Attacks that lead to consequences "GP" (CAPEC-626) allow to proceed attack on the next nodes of the graph.

To *assess network security* it is necessary to define security risks for the network components. Risk is defined as product of the attack probability and the attack impact [11]. The attack probability for the graph nodes that represent attack actions against wireless APs is defined with the same equation as attack probability for the other attack graph nodes on the basis of CVSS indexes to show the complexity of the vulnerability exploitation and by using Bayesian equations for the conditional and unconditional probabilities [14].

But the graph nodes that represent attack actions against connection channels and mobile devices stay not covered. To define attack probabilities for these nodes we take into account several aspects: a probability that attacker will initialize an attack against a mobile device or a wireless channel, and the attack likelihood. To define the probability that attacker will initialize an attack we suggest to use the next scale: Low (L) – the limited number of the known devices (devices that are registered and stored in the organization, the owner and firmware are known) can connect to the wireless AP of the network (appropriate quantitative value – 0.3); Medium (M) – the limited number of the unknown devices (any employee can bring his/her own laptop or smartphone and connect to the network) can connect to the wireless AP of the network (appropriate quantitative value – 0.5); High (H) – unlimited number of the unknown devices can connect to the wireless AP of the network (appropriate quantitative value – 0.7). To define attack likelihood we use fields "Attacker skills" and "Attack prerequisites" of the CAPEC attack patterns [4]. To get quantitative values we define scales for these fields in analogy to CVSS [15]. Scale for the "Attacker skills": H – 0.35; M – 0.61; L – 0.71. If field is not filled then the value is L. Scale for the "Attack prerequisites": yes – 0.45; none – 0.704. If field is not filled, the value is "none". Attack likelihood for the graph node is calculated as multiplication of "Attacker skills" and "Attack prerequisites": $AttackLikelihood = AttackerSkills \times AttackPrerequisites$, where $AttackerSkills$ – attack complexity according to the "Attacker skills" field; $AttackPrerequisites$ – attack prerequisites according to the "Attack prerequisites" field. Final attack probability for the graph node is defined as: $Probability = AttackInit \times AttackLikelihood$, where $AttackInit$ – probability that attacker will initialize an attack against the mobile device or channel; $AttackLikelihood$ – likelihood that attacker can successfully implement an attack. Maximum value of the $Probability$ is 0.35, minimum – 0.05.

We define attack impact as multiplication of the criticality of the targeted asset ($Criticality$) and the impact on the security properties of the asset ($PropImpact$): $Impact = Criticality \times PropImpact$.

Criticality and impact for the wireless AP is defined in the same way as for the other attack graph nodes [14] on the scale from 0 to 10: [criticality_of_confidentiality criticality_of_integrity criticality_of_availability]. Impact on the security properties of the wireless AP is defined on the base of the CVSS indexes C, I and A [15].

For attacks against mobile devices or channels an asset is data on the mobile device. Thus, the asset criticality is defined as criticality of confidentiality, integrity and availability of these data on the scale from 0 to 10 as vector. Impact on the security properties of the asset is defined on the base of the fields "Typical severity" (impact level) and "Attack consequences" (damaged security property). For the "Typical severity" we define the next scale: H – 0.66; M – 0.275; L – 0. If the field is not filled the maximum value is assigned (H). Impact on the security properties is defined as vector: [AI II CI] depending on the "Attack consequences" field. "Get privileges" value leads to impact on all three properties. If value of the "Attack consequences" field is "other" or not filled, it is defined as null impact.

Finally, the risk $Risk$ for the attack graph node is defined as vector of three values – risk of confidentiality violation, risk of integrity violation, and risk of availability violation. Risk for each security property is defined as follows (if node contains few attack patterns, the maximum risk value is selected): *Risk = Probability × Impact*. Minimum risk value for the single security property is 0, maximum − 6.6. For the security assessment three values of risk are summed. Risk for the node is considered as low if it takes value from 0 to 2, medium − 2 to 5 and high if it is >5. Risk for the network component (host, wireless device, etc.) is defined by the maximum risk of the attack graph nodes of this network component for each security property.

4   Case Study and Discussion

In Fig. 2 a simple computer network that includes wireless subnet is represented. Network incorporates the assets: web application (*host* "Web server", *criticality* [10 10 10] in terms of confidentiality, integrity and availability on the scale from 0 to 10); windows server 2008 operation system (OS) (*host* "Web server", *criticality* [10 10 10]); ApacheStruts2 application (*host* "Web server", *criticality* [7 10 10]); Microsoft.NET Framework 4.6.1 (*host* "Application server", *criticality* [7 10 10]); Squid application (*host* "Proxy server", *criticality* [10 10 10]); authentication service (*host* "Authentication server", *criticality* [10 10 10]); slapd service (*host* "Authentication server", *criticality* [10 10 10]); linux OS (*host* "DB server", *criticality* [10 10 10]); mysql (*host* "DB server", *criticality* [10 10 10]); Citrix (*host* "Firewall", *criticality* [10 10 10]); Cisco WAP4410 N wireless AP firmware 2.0.3.3 (*host* "Access Point", *criticality* [10 10 10]); mobile devices (*criticality* [7 7 7]), etc. Attacker from the notebook attempts to attack mobile devices, channels and AP from the external network.

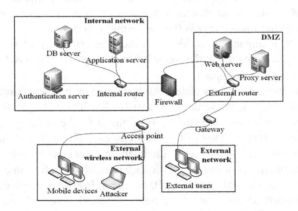

Fig. 2. Topology of the test network

The suggested technique was implemented by the modified tool for security assessment of computer networks [12–14]. The tool was extended to consider mobile components. Simplified version of the generated attack graph for the test network is outlined in Fig. 3. The graph contains possible attack sequences for the external attacker with mobile device. Darkened rectangles are used to represent attack actions. Attack actions for the same host are grouped in the colorless rectangles. Arrows link sequential attack actions (consequences of the parent attack action allow to perform child attack action). C, I and A note confidentiality, integrity and availability, accordingly. Nodes of the attack graph in the user interface of the developed prototype are highlighted with green color for the low risk (light grey in Fig. 3), yellow color - for the medium risk (medium grey in Fig. 3) and red color - for the high risk (dark grey in Fig. 3).

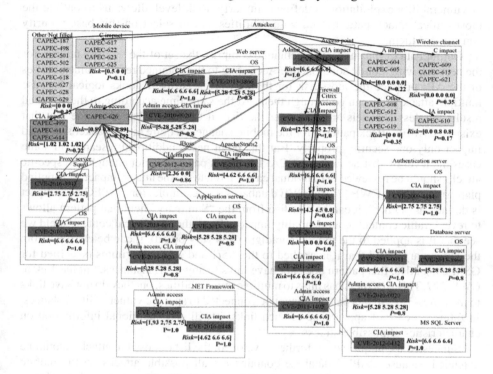

Fig. 3. Attack graph for the test network

Process of the risk calculation for the mobile device, wireless channel and wireless router (access point node in Fig. 3) on the base of the suggested technique is presented below. We consider that unlimited number of unknown devices can connect to the wireless AP of the test network, so *AttackInit* = 0.7.

We will show risk calculation process on the example of CAPEC-626 ("Admin access" group of the mobile device). "Attacker skills" value is Medium, so *AttackerSkills* = 0.61; "Attack prerequisites" exist, so *AttackPrerequisites* = 0.45. *Probability = AttackInit × AttackLikelihood* = 0.7 × 0.61 × 0.45 = 0.192. "Typical severity" for the CAPEC-626 is not filled, so the maximum value (High) is assigned: *PropImpact* = 0.66. Considering asset criticality [7 7 7]: *Impact = Criticality × PropImpact* = 7 × 0.66 = 4.62 for all three security properties (because value of the "Attack consequences" field is "get privileges" that leads to impact on all security properties). *Risk* for this pattern is [0.192 × 4.620.192 × 4.620.192 × 4.62]=[0.890.890.89].. This group comprises only one attack pattern, so *Risk* of this group is [0.890.890.89], total *Risk* is 2.67 (medium). For the wireless router the risk is defined on the base of the CVE-2014-0659. In this case attack probability is determined on the base of the CVSS Exploitability: *Probability* = 1; *PropImpact* is calculated on the base of CVSS impact: *PropImpact* = [0.66 0.66 0.66]. *Risk* = [6.6 6.6 6.6]. Risk for the other nodes that represent attack patterns or vulnerability exploitation is defined similarly. Risk level allows us to outline the most critical attack patterns and vulnerabilities and to select on this base security controls for them.

Output data of the suggested technique comprise the set of the security metrics for the network with mobile components. According to the obtained results vulnerabilities of the APs produce the most risk for the network security. It looks logical because multiple attack paths can go through them. At the same time according to the obtained results wireless channels are not under the risk. It can be explained by the fact that existing CAPEC attack patterns for the mobile channels require high attacker skills and impact only one security property. But this point needs additional research: in some cases the level of abstraction of the CAPEC attack patterns is not enough and specific attacks should be reviewed in individual cases. It relates to the attack impact and applied platforms, links to CWE [7] and CVE databases. For example, for CAPEC-608 impact is defined as "Other", it can be clarified from the "Summary" field that pattern allows to reveal traffic content (confidentiality impact). From the "Technical context" field we see that it is applied to the mobile paradigm (it is very broad), it can be clarified from the "Summary" field that it is applied to the A5/1 and A5/2 algorithms (specified for GSM use). Also, this pattern does not have links to any CVE instances, but has link to CWE-327. This weakness has links to multiple vulnerabilities, but they do not have links to the CWE-327. So this pattern cannot be connected to specific vulnerability instances. In future, in case of appearance of such links, it will give additional information on characteristics of possible attacks.

Suggested technique can be further developed: the list of possible attacks should be extended because CAPEC database contains not all possible attacks on the mobile devices; attack patterns should be processed more carefully; suggested metrics and their scales should be additionally tested. Nevertheless the approach allows to detect possible attack paths in the wireless network and to get quantitative risk values that allow to outline weak places of mobile networks and to select on this base the security controls for them. Compared to the other works in this area the suggested approach is automated, unified and it is more general and applicable to any networks with mobile components.

5   Conclusion

The paper suggests the extension of the approach to the automated risk assessment on the base of the attack graphs to the mobile networks. Distinctive features of the mobile networks are considered, including mobile software, mobility, and weaknesses of the connection channels. CAPEC, CVE and CVSS standards are analyzed if they are applicable to the mobile networks. CAPEC attack patterns for the mobile networks are reviewed. Their fields are analyzed and classified according to their possible values. The technique for consideration of mobile subnets in the process of the attack graph generation is suggested. It is based on the CAPEC attack patterns and vulnerabilities of mobile devices. Also the technique of risk assessment for mobile subnets is suggested. It is based on the values of fields of CAPEC attack patterns and CVSS. The approach will be further extended. In the future work it is planned to review in details the attacks against different mobile devices and connection channels to expand the list of the considered attacks. It can be done on the base of the OWASP mobile checklist [17] and CWE list [7]. Nevertheless the approach allows to get quantitative risk values for the network objects considering attacks against mobile devices. This allow to outline the most critical attack patterns and vulnerabilities and further to select on this base security controls. Application of the suggested approach was shown on the example of calculations for the test network with a mobile subnet.

Acknowledgements. This research is being supported by the grants of the Russian Foundation of Basic Research (15-07-07451, 16-37-00338, 16-29-09482), partial support of budgetary subjects 0073-2015-0004 and 0073-2015-0007, and Grant 074-U01.

References

1. CAPEC-512: Communications. https://capec.mitre.org/data/definitions/512.html
2. CAPEC-553: Mobile Device Patterns. https://capec.mitre.org/data/definitions/553.html
3. Check Point Software Technologies Ltd.: Check Point – 2016 Security Report. https://www.checkpoint.com/resources/security-report/
4. Common Attack Pattern Enumeration and Classification (CAPEC). https://capec.mitre.org
5. Common Configuration Enumeration (CCE). http://cce.mitre.org/
6. Common Vulnerabilities and Exposures (CVE). http://cve.mitre.org/
7. Common Weakness Enumeration (CWE). https://cwe.mitre.org/data/index.html
8. Doynikova, E., Kotenko, I.: Security assessment based on attack graphs and open standards for computer networks with mobile components. Res. Brief. Inf. Commun. Technol. Evol. **2**, 5:1–5:11 (2016)
9. Frei, D.: Conducting a risk assessment for mobile devices. In: Central-VA-ISSA-May-2012-Meeting (2012)
10. Frigault, M., Wang, L., Singhal A., Jajodia, S.: Measuring network security using dynamic bayesian network. In: 2008 ACM Workshop on Quality of Protection (2008)
11. ISO/IEC 27005:2011: Information technology—Security techniques—Information security risk management, 2nd edn. (2011)
12. Kotenko, I., Chechulin, A.: A cyber attack modeling and impact assessment framework. In: 5th International Conference on Cyber Conflict 2013 (CyCon 2013), pp. 119–142. IEEE and NATO COE Publications, Tallinn (2013)
13. Kotenko, I., Doynikova, E.: Evaluation of computer network security based on attack graphs and security event processing. J. Wirel. Mob. Netw. Ubiquitous Comput. Dependable Appl. (JoWUA) **5**(3), 14–29 (2014)
14. Kotenko, I., Doynikova, E.: Security assessment of computer networks based on attack graphs and security events. In: Linawati, Mahendra, M.S., Neuhold, E.J., Tjoa, A.M., You, I. (eds.) ICT-EurAsia 2014. LNCS, vol. 8407, pp. 462–471. Springer, Heidelberg (2014). https://doi.org/10.1007/978-3-642-55032-4_47
15. Mell, P.: A Complete Guide to the Common Vulnerability Scoring System (2007)

16. NVD website. https://nvd.nist.gov/
17. OWASP Mobile Checklist Final 2016. https://drive.google.com/file/d/0BxOPagp1j PHWYmg3Y3BfLVhMcmc/view
18. Platform Enumeration (CPE). http://cpe.mitre.org/
19. Jing, Y., Ahn, G.-J., Zhao, Z., Hu, H.: RiskMon: continuous and automated risk assessment of mobile applications. In: The 4th ACM Conference on Data and Application Security and Privacy, pp. 99–110 (2014)
20. Theoharidou, M., Mylonas, A., Gritzalis, D.: A risk assessment method for smartphones. In: Gritzalis, D., Furnell, S., Theoharidou, M. (eds.) SEC 2012. IAICT, vol. 376, pp. 443–456. Springer, Heidelberg (2012). https://doi.org/10.1007/978-3-642-30436-1_36
21. Schneider, P. (ed.): Threat and Risk Analysis for Mobile Communication Networks and Mobile Terminals. Deliverable 5. Attack analysis and Security concepts for MObile Network infrastructures, supported by collaborative Information exchAnge project (2012)
22. Pandita, R., Xiao, X., Yang, W., Enck, W., Xie, T.: WHYPER: towards automating risk assessment of mobile applications. In: 22nd USENIX Conference on Security (SEC 2013), pp. 527–542 (2013)

Assessment of Computer Network Resilience Under Impact of Cyber Attacks on the Basis of Stochastic Networks Conversion

Igor Kotenko[1,3(✉)], Igor Saenko[1,3], Oleg Lauta[2], and Mikhail Kocinyak[2]

[1] St. Petersburg Institute for Informatics and Automation of Russian Academy of Sciences (SPIIRAS), St. Petersburg, Russia
{ivkote,ibsaen}@comsec.spb.ru
[2] St. Petersburg Signal Academy, St. Petersburg, Russia
{laos-82,koc-1942}@yandex.ru
[3] St. Petersburg National Research University of Information Technologies, Mechanics and Optics, St. Petersburg, Russia

Abstract. The paper suggests an approach to computer network resilience assessment under exposure of cyber attacks, based on analytical attack modeling using the method of stochastic networks transformations. The network resilience assessment methodology and main stages of the proposed method for analytical modeling of cyber attacks are studied. It is shown how the proposed method can be used to generate the reference analytical model of the computer attack. Experimental evaluation of the proposed method for analytical modeling of attacks and developed methodology for assessing resilience of the network under exposure of cyber attacks showed high adequacy of the obtained results and high efficiency of their calculation.

Keywords: Cyber security · Attack modeling · Computer network resilience
Stochastic networks · Laplace transformation

1 Introduction

Efficient and reliable protection of computer networks is impossible without preliminary analysis of possible threats to their security, among which the most powerful are cyber attacks. The possible effects of cyber attacks on computer networks are blocking of management information, introduction of false information, violation of established regulations for collection, processing and transmission of information in automated control systems, failures and malfunctions in computer networks, and compromise of transmitted or received information [1]. For this reason, cyber attacks and the ability to counteract their implementation are the key factors that determine of the *resilience* of computer networks.

The resilience of a computer network will be understood as the network's ability to resist various types of attacks and keep its functioning under impact of these attacks. Assessment of the resilience of computer networks is a complicated problem. We need to solve this problem often enough both at designing computer networks and at their

© Springer Nature Singapore Pte Ltd. 2018
I. You et al. (Eds.): MobiSec 2016, CCIS 797, pp. 107–117, 2018.
https://doi.org/10.1007/978-981-10-7850-7_10

administration. Analytical modeling of cyber attacks largely helps to efficiently solve this problem.

There are many known approaches to the construction of analytical models of cyber attacks. Recently, however, the approach based on *the transformation of stochastic networks* get the growing popularity [2]. It is proved to be good for modeling of multi-stage stochastic processes of different nature. This paper is an extended version of the paper presented on MobiSec 2016 [3]. Contrary to [3], this paper proposes to apply this method for analytical modeling of various types of cyber attacks and use the simulation results to assess the resilience of computer networks.

The further structure of the paper is as follows. Section 2 provides an overview of relevant works. Section 3 examines the content of the methodology for assessing the resilience of computer networks under exposure of cyber attacks based on the transformation of stochastic networks. Section 4 contains the results of the analytical attack modeling for the attack "Scanning of network and its vulnerabilities". The results of experimental evaluation of the computer network resilience is given in Sect. 5. Section 6 contains the main conclusions and directions for further research.

2   Related Work

Functioning of many systems for simulation of discrete events is based on the stochastic processes analysis methods, for example, OPNET [4] and COMNET [5]. These systems use event-driven models of queuing networks. However, due to the fact that implementation of such models leads to significant computational cost, use of stochastic simulation systems to ensure the security of computer networks is of limited use. Another tool used for modeling and analysis of attacks is software tool CAMIAC (Cyber Attack Modeling and Impact Assessment Component) [6, 7]. However, this tool lacks the opportunity to obtain the distribution function of the attack realization time.

The approach for development of stochastic attack models, suggested in [8], takes into account the spread of attacks across parallel links. However, only basic theorems of probability theory are applied. A stochastic security framework, that takes into account the vulnerabilities and calculates security metrics values, is proposed in [9]. It takes into account the temporal aspect of vulnerabilities and examines the life-cycle model of vulnerabilities. However, in our opinion, use of this tool to assess the resilience of computer networks will require considerable computational costs.

Stochastic and statistical models for a set of scenarios in computer science domain were considered in [10]. However, the scenarios, associated with cyber attacks, were not analyzed in this paper.

A stochastic attack simulator based on the use of the situation calculus and the goal-directed procedure invocations was proposed in [11]. However, the drawback of this approach is the need to build attack scenarios on the special situation calculus language.

In a number of computer security papers the interesting results using generative stochastic networks have been obtained. For example, the paper [12] discusses an approach for classifying security threats, which is based on this kind of stochastic networks. The paper [13] describes a method for learning of generative stochastic networks based on back-propagation. The results obtained in this paper confirm the fact that semantic networks can be sufficiently powerful modeling tool. However, the methods for analytical attack modeling were not considered in these papers.

Thus, from the analysis of relevant works we can draw the following conclusions. First, stochastic analytical modeling is of great importance for the development of countermeasures in modern cybersecurity systems. Second, the stochastic models used to simulate attacks, must be able to compute the distribution functions of random variables we are interested in (e.g., time for realization of the attack and its separate stages) with minimal computational cost. Thirdly, the stochastic models should provide high flexibility and to be applicable for modeling of any type attacks. The approaches discussed above do not fully meet these requirements. The method of stochastic network conversion, forming the base for the described below methodology, intended to assess the resilience of computer networks, allows to eliminate this disadvantage.

3 Technique for Computer Network Resilience Assessment

3.1 Resilience Assessment

As the main indicator of the resilience of a computer network operating under the influence of cyber attacks, a *coefficient of correct action* is proposed (K_{ca}). It shows what percentage of the total accounted time the computer network is functioning properly.

To determine the coefficient of correct action for the network, first the coefficients of correct action for each route and the probabilities of affecting these routes are calculated. To perform it, it is necessary to consider the process of functioning of the computer network under impact of attacks, presented in Fig. 1.

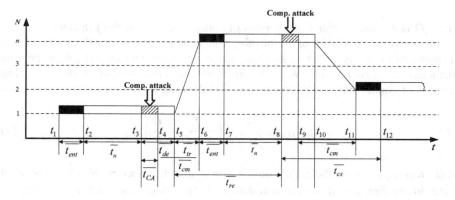

Fig. 1. The process of functioning of computer networks under impact of attacks

In the generalized form, the process of functioning of the computer network under the impact of the attacks is as follows. To perform a transfer of operative information (at moments of time t_2, t_7, t_{12}, etc.) the network operators first enter into the connection

(t_1), for which the average time $\overline{t_{ent}}$ is spent. Then (at time points t_3, t_8, etc.) an information impact system implements a cyber attack in the average time $\overline{t_{CA}}$, which the network operator can detect (at the moments of time t_4, t_9, etc.) in the average time $\overline{t_{de}}$. On discovering the impact of the attack, the network operator will take measures to restore the connection (at the moments of time t_5, t_{10}, etc.) in the mean time $\overline{t_{tr}}$. After this, the network operators enter the connection (at the moments of time t_6, t_{11}, etc.), for which average time $\overline{t_{ent}}$ is spent, and transmitting of operative information is resumed.

Average time $\overline{t_{CS}}$, spent for protection means ($\overline{t_{cm}}$) and the entry into the connection ($\overline{t_{ent}}$), describes the reaction of the control system to the impact of attacks, i.e., is determined by the following sum: $\overline{t_{CS}} = \overline{t_{cm}} + \overline{t_{ent}} = \overline{t_{tr}} + \overline{t_{de}} + \overline{t_{ent}}$.

Coefficient of correct action of the j-th route $K_{ca,j}$ is calculated as follows:

$$K_{ca,j} = \frac{\overline{t_{n,j}}}{\overline{t_{n,j}} + \overline{t_{CA,j}}}. \tag{1}$$

The average time from the moment of acceptance of measures on restoration of connection till the moment of affect of attacks are called *reaction time* $\overline{t_{re}}$. Then the probability $P_{act,j}$ of the attack impact is equal to

$$P_{act,j} = 1 - \frac{\left(\overline{t_{re,j}}\right)^2}{\left(\overline{t_{re,j}} + \overline{t_{ent,j}}\right) \cdot \left(\overline{t_{re,j}} + \overline{t_{cm,j}}\right)}. \tag{2}$$

As the route of information transmission consists of several intervals of communication, the coefficient of correct action of the j-th composite route $K_{ca\_CM,j}$ is equal to

$$K_{ca\_CM,j} = \prod_{j=1}^{O} K_{ca,j}, \tag{3}$$

where O is the total number of intervals of communication on the j-th route.

To assess the possibility of establishing connections and messages' transfer in case of failure of elements or whole sections, let us introduce into consideration the new characteristic – *connectivity* K_{rel} of directions and communication channels. The measure of connectivity is determined by the following formula:

$$K_{rel\_D,i} = \sum_{j=1}^{N} \alpha_j \cdot \left(\frac{H_j}{N+O} + \frac{O}{N}\right), \tag{4}$$

where $K_{rel\_D,i}$ is the coefficient of connectivity of the i-th direction; N is the number of routes in the direction of the communication; H_j is rank of j-th route; $\alpha_{ij} = \gamma^j / \gamma^j_{sum}$ is the weight of j-th route in the information exchange of the i-th direction; γ^j is the intensity of j-th route; γ^j_{sum} is the total load of all the routes.

The set of routes forms *the direction of the communication*, and the set of directions of communications and computer hardware forms the computer network. Coefficient of correct action of the i-th direction of communication is characterized by the probability of functioning in this area of at least one route. It is determined by the following formula:

$$K_{ca\_D,i} = K_{rel\_D,i} \cdot \left(1 - \prod_{j=1}^{N} \left(1 - K_{ca\_CM,j} \right) \cdot P_{act,j} \right), \tag{5}$$

where $K_{ca\_D,i}$ is the coefficient of correct action of the i-th direction.

Given that the computer network consists of M communication directions, the coefficient of correct action of the computer system in conditions of cyber attacks is determined according the following expressions:

$$K_{ca} = K_{rel} \cdot \left(1 - \prod_{i=1}^{M} \left(1 - K_{ca\_D,i} \right) \right), \tag{6}$$

$$K_{rel} = \sum_{i=1}^{M} \alpha_i \cdot \left(\frac{G_i}{M+N} + \frac{N}{M} \right), \tag{7}$$

where K_{ca} is the coefficient of correct action of the computer network; K_{rel} – is the coefficient of the connectivity of the network; G is the rank of the i-th direction; M is the number of directions of communication in the computer network.

Thus, to determine the coefficient of correct action for a computer network it is initially required to determine the average time of impact of attacks. It is proposed to use the reference models of attacks and the method that we will call *the method of transformation of the stochastic network*. The *reference model* of an attack is a sequence (algorithm) of actions of the attacker during the attack implementation.

Let us first consider the main points of the proposed method.

3.2   Method of Stochastic Network Conversion

Under *the stochastic network* we understand a set of interconnected nodes (vertices) and links, the connection of which corresponds to the algorithm of functioning of the system under study. The network is the model of the process that is implemented by this system [14]. A complex process is decomposed into elementary processes, each of which is characterized by the distribution function, average time and its variance. The logic and sequence of processes' execution is determined by a two-pole network, consisting of input, intermediate and output nodes (vertices). The edges correspond to the set of elementary processes, and the vertices (nodes) – to the conditions of their implementation. For each edge the transfer function is determined. This function plays the role of conditional characteristic functions. It is a Laplace transform for the function of density of probability for time of fulfillment of elementary process [15].

Stochastic network contains a set of loops. A *loop* is a connected closed sequence of oriented links of stochastic network, each vertex of which is common to exactly two links or a link that connects a vertex to itself.

The result of the conversion of the stochastic network is *equivalent function* that retain in its structure the distribution parameters and the logic of interaction of elementary random processes. Equivalent function allows to define the first moments of the random time of execution of the target process. If the distribution function of the time phase of the attack is denoted by $G(t)$, then the equivalent function $g(s)$ is calculated as follows:

$$g(s) = \int_0^\infty \exp(-st)d[G(t)]. \tag{8}$$

If we apply the inverse Laplace transform to the equivalent function of process, the result is a function of density of probabilities of the time of execution of this process.

The essence of the proposed method is to replace many elementary links of the network by single equivalent one and in subsequent determination of the equivalent function of the network of the initial moments and the function of distribution of the random time of implementation of the process.

The equivalent function of loop of k-th order is defined as

$$Q_k(s) = \prod_{j=1}^{k} Q_i(s), \tag{9}$$

where $Q_i(s)$ is the equivalent function of the i-th loop of the first order, defined as the product of the equivalent functions of the links within this loop.

Let us connect conditionally the network's output to the input. Then for the desired equivalent function $h(s)$ the expression $h(s) = 1/Q_a(s)$ is just, where $Q_a(s)$ is equivalent function of input for the entire network. After the closure of the output to the input, it is possible use the Mason's equation for closed graphs to determine equivalent function of the original network [16]:

$$H = 1 + \sum_{k=1}^{K} (-1)^k Q_k(s) = 0, \tag{10}$$

where K is the maximum order of the loops included in the stochastic network.

4   Example of Making Reference Models of Cyber Attacks

As an example of making reference models of cyber attacks, let us choose the attack "Scanning of network and its vulnerabilities".

The implementation of this attack has the following steps:

- launch of a hardware-software complex (a network scanner) for the average time $\overline{t_{start}}$ with the time distribution function $W(t)$;
- identification of active elements of the attacked network with probability P_n for the average time $\overline{t_{elem}}$ with the time distribution function $Q(t)$;

- identification of the types of operating systems on active network elements with probability P_n for the average time $\overline{t_{OS}}$ with the time distribution function $D(t)$;
- identification of services on the network elements with probability P_n for the average time $\overline{t_{ser}}$ with the time distribution function $L(t)$;
- identification of vulnerabilities in the average time $\overline{t_{vul}}$ with the distribution function of time $O(t)$.

Meanwhile, if the active elements of the network, types of operating systems and services on them are not determined, then with probability $(1 - P_n)$ the network scanner will be launched again in the average time $\overline{t_{rep}}$ with the function of distribution of time $Z(t)$.

The equivalent function is calculated by formula (8) and allows to define the first moments of the random time of execution of the attack.

Stochastic network reflecting the above stages of the attack is presented in Fig. 2.

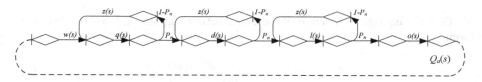

Fig. 2. Stochastic network of the cyber attack "Scanning of the network and its vulnerabilities"

The functions $w(s)$, $l(s)$, $q(s)$, $d(s)$, $o(s)$ and $z(s)$, located at the output nodes of the stochastic network, are *equivalent functions* and are obtained by applying the Laplace transformation to the functions of time distribution $W(t)$, $L(t)$, $Q(t)$, $D(t)$, $O(t)$, and $Z(t)$, respectively.

The stochastic network is closed by connection of its output to its input.

The values of the equivalent functions and the functions of time distribution for each stage of the attack are presented in Table 1.

The first order loops are the loops that contain no other loops and allowing to access each vertex of the loop from any other. The loop of k-th order is the set of k not linked loops of the first order.

Let us determine all the loops in the stochastic network shown in Fig. 2.

First order loops: (1) $w(s) \cdot q(s) \cdot d(s) \cdot P_n^3 \cdot l(s) \cdot o(s)$; (2) $(1 - P_n) \cdot z(s) \cdot q(s)$; (3) $(1 - P_n) \cdot z(s) \cdot d(s)$; (4) $(1 - P_n) \cdot z(s) \cdot l(s)$.

Second order loops: (1) $(1 - P_n)^2 \cdot z^2(s) \cdot q(s) \cdot d(s)$; (2) $(1 - P_n)^2 \cdot z^2(s) \cdot d(s) \cdot l(s)$; (3) $(1 - P_n)^2 \cdot z^2(s) \cdot q(s) \cdot l(s)$.

Third order loop: $(1 - P_n)^3 \cdot z^3(s) \cdot q(s) \cdot d(s) \cdot l(s)$.

Table 1. Functions for estimation of duration of stages of the cyber attack "scanning of the network and its vulnerabilities"

Stage #	Stage content	Equivalent function	Time distribution functions
1	Launch of the hardware-software complex (the network scanner)	$w(s) = \frac{w}{w+s}$	$W(t) = 1 - \exp[-wt]$
2	Identification of services on network elements	$l(s) = \frac{l}{l+s}$	$L(t) = 1 - \exp[-lt]$
3	Identification of active elements of the attacked network	$q(s) = \frac{q}{q+s}$	$Q(t) = 1 - \exp[-qt]$
4	Identification of types of operating systems on active network's elements	$d(s) = \frac{d}{d+s}$	$D(t) = 1 - \exp[-dt]$
5	Identification of network vulnerabilities	$o(s) = \frac{o}{o+s}$	$O(t) = 1 - \exp[-ot]$
6	Restart of the network scanner by attacker	$z(s) = \frac{z}{z+s}$	$Z(t) = 1 - \exp[-zt]$

Then the equivalent function of the entire network in this case has the following form:

$$h(s) = \frac{w(s) \cdot q(s) \cdot d(s) \cdot P_n^3 \cdot l(s) \cdot o(s)}{R(s)}, \qquad (11)$$

where

$$\begin{aligned} R(s) = 1 &- (1 - P_n) \cdot z(s) \cdot q(s) - (1 - P_n) \cdot z(s) \cdot d(s) - (1 - P_n) \cdot z(s) \cdot l(s) \\ &+ (1 - P_n)^2 \cdot z^2(s) \cdot q(s) \cdot d(s) + (1 - P_n)^2 \cdot z^2(s) \cdot d(s) \cdot l(s) + (1 - P_n)^2 \cdot z^2(s) \cdot q(s) \cdot l(s) \quad (12) \\ &- (1 - P_n)^3 \cdot z^3(s) \cdot q(s) \cdot d(s) \cdot l(s). \end{aligned}$$

Using Laplace transformation and Heaviside expansion theorem [17], the function of distribution of probability of time of the attack implementation can be defined as follows:

$$F(t) = \sum_{k=1}^{8} \frac{w \cdot q \cdot d \cdot P_n^3 \cdot l \cdot o \cdot (z + s_k)^3}{\varphi(s_k)} \cdot \frac{1 - \exp[s_k t]}{-s_k}, \qquad (13)$$

where $\varphi(s_k)$ is the conditional denotation of polynomial in denominator; s_k – decomposition poles; $w = 1/\overline{t_{start}}$; $l = 1/\overline{t_{elem}}$; $q = 1/\overline{t_{OS}}$; $d = 1/\overline{t_{ser}}$; $o = 1/\overline{t_{vul}}$; $z = 1/\overline{t_{rep}}$. Polynomial $\varphi(s_k)$ is as follows:

$$\begin{aligned} \varphi(s_k) = (w + s_k) \cdot &[(1 - P_n) \cdot z \cdot [(1 - P_n)^2 \cdot z^2 \cdot q \cdot d \cdot l - [q \cdot (z+s)^2 \cdot (d+s) \cdot (l+s) \\ &- d \cdot (z+s)^2 \cdot (q+s) \cdot (l+s) - l \cdot (z+s)^2 \cdot (q+s) \cdot (d+s) + (1 - P_n) \cdot z \cdot q \cdot d \cdot (z+s) \cdot (l+s) \quad (14) \\ &+ (1 - P_n) \cdot z \cdot l \cdot d \cdot (z+s) \cdot (q+s) + (1 - P_n) \cdot z \cdot q \cdot l \cdot (z+s) \cdot (d+s) - (1 - P_n)^2 \cdot z^2 \cdot q \cdot d \cdot l]]] \end{aligned}$$

Average time $\overline{T}$ spent for the attack implementation is defined as follows:

$$\overline{T} = \sum_{k=1}^{8} \frac{w \cdot q \cdot d \cdot P_n^3 \cdot l \cdot o \cdot (z + s_k)^3}{\varphi(s_k)} \cdot \frac{1}{(-s_k)^2}. \qquad (15)$$

5 Experimental Results

Experimental assessment of resilience of the computer network in conditions of cyber attacks exposure was carried out on the example of the extensive computer network that includes 1,000 personal computers, 20 servers, 50 switches and 15 routers. For this purpose the simulation test bed was developed. It was composed of the following modules: (1) source data input, (2) generation of the duration of the attack stages, (3) control. Module for source data input generated values for the average times of the attack stages and P_n. The generation module formed at random the times for implementation of the attack stages. The control module formed the random value for time of the attack's implementation. We used the values obtained at the output of the generation module, and the probability P_n. The received experimental results are presented in Table 2. For each value of P_n there were carried out 100 experiments. Averages of times for implementation of individual stages of the attack "Scanning of the network and its vulnerabilities" were generated (Table 2).

Table 2. Experimental results for the average attack implementation times

P_n	Analytical model average time, min	Simulation bench average time, min	Error, %
0,2	140	146,1	4,4
0,3	90	89,4	0,7
0,4	70	72,9	4,2
0,5	60	62,4	4,1
0,6	50	50,7	1,3
0,7	45	45,7	1,5
0,8	40	41,3	3,3
0,9	35	35,6	1,8

As it can be seen from Table 2, the error of estimation of the time for the attack realization does not exceed 5%. Therefore, the analytical model is quite adequate. The dependences of the coefficient of correct action from the number of routes are shown in Fig. 3.

As input data we used the following values: $\alpha_i = 1$; $\overline{t_{ent}} = 3\,\text{min}$; $\overline{t_{tr}} = 1\,\text{min}$; $\overline{t_{de}} = 2\,\text{min}$; $\overline{t_{re}} = 10\,\text{min}$; $\overline{t_{CA}} = 13\,\text{min}$. The obtained dependences of the ratio of correct action of the number of routes allow to determine the rational range of the number of required routes when system is exposed to cyber attacks.

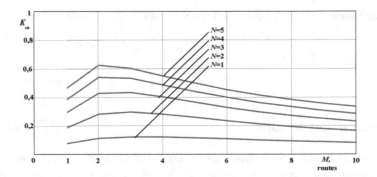

Fig. 3. The dependence of the coefficient of correct action from the number of routes

6 Conclusion

This paper offers the new approach to analytical modeling of cyber attacks, based on the stochastic networks transformations method. The essence of this method is to replace many elementary links of the stochastic network by one equivalent link and subsequent determination of the equivalent network function, as well as the initial moments and the distribution function of the random time implementation of cyber attacks. Validation of the proposed approach was performed to generate the reference patterns of the attack "Scanning of the network and its vulnerabilities". The experimental assessment of the method showed its sufficiently high efficiency.

The developed method for analytical simulation of attacks is put into the basis of the proposed methodology for assessing the resilience of computer networks in terms of cyber attacks. The methodology allows to determine parameters characterizing the operation of the network and justify its structure. The application of reference models of attacks and method of conversion of stochastic networks in the methodology allows to define the probabilistic-temporal characteristics of most known attacks, which are the initial data for the method. Experimental assessment of the developed method for assessing the resilience of the network in conditions of the impact of the attacks showed high adequacy of the results received with its help and high efficiency of computing. Thus, the developed method allows, on the one hand, to determine reference models of typical attacks on computer networks, and on another – to justify the requirements for the network topology and to the selection of tools and ways of its protection. Further research is associated with use of the method of stochastic networks conversion and the methodology of computer network resilience assessment for evaluation of different variants of countermeasures against cyber attacks and decision making to ensure the required resilience of the network.

Acknowledgements. This research is being supported by the grants of the Russian Foundation of Basic Research (15-07-07451, 16-37-00338, 16-29-09482), partial support of budgetary subjects 0073-2015-0004 and 0073-2015-0007, and Grant 074-U01.

References

1. Luvanda, A., Kimani, S., Kimwele, M.: Identifying threats associated with man-in-the middle attacks during communications between a mobile device and the back end server in mobile banking applications. IOSR J. Comput. Eng. (IOSR-JCI) **12**(2), 35–42 (2014)
2. Kelly, F., Yudovina, E.: Stochastic Networks, p. 230. Cambridge University Press, Cambridge (2014)
3. Saenko, I., Lauta, O., Kotenko, I.: Analytical modeling of mobile banking attacks based on a stochastic network conversion technique. IT Converg. Pract. **4**(4), 1–10 (2016)
4. OPNET Technologies. http://www.opnet.com/
5. Ahuja, S.P.: COMNET III: a network simulation laboratory environment for a course in communications networks. In: Proceedings of the 28th Annual Frontiers in Education Conference (FIE 1998), vol. 3, pp. 1085–1088 (1998)
6. Kotenko, I., Chechulin, A.: A cyber attack modeling and impact assessment framework. In: Proceedings of the 5th IEEE International Conference on Cyber Conflict (CyCon), pp. 1–24 (2013)
7. Kotenko, I., Doynikova, E.: Evaluation of computer network security based on attack graphs and security event processing. J. Wirel. Mob. Netw. Ubiquitous Comput. Dependable Appl. (JoWUA) **5**(3), 14–29 (2014)
8. Dudorov, D., Stupples, D., Newby, M.: Probability analysis of cyber attack paths against business and commercial enterprise systems. In: Proceedings of the 2013 European Intelligence and Security Informatics Conference, pp. 38–44 (2013)
9. Abraham, S., Nair, S.: A predictive framework for cyber security analytics using attack graphs. Int. J. Comput. Netw. Commun. (IJCNC) **7**(1), 1–17 (2015)
10. Matlof, N.: From Algorithms to Z-Scores: Probabilistic and Statistical Modeling in Computer Science. http://heather.cs.ucdavis.edu/probstatbook
11. Goldman, R.P.: A stochastic model for intrusions. In: Wespi, A., Vigna, G., Deri, L. (eds.) RAID 2002. LNCS, vol. 2516, pp. 199–218. Springer, Heidelberg (2002). https://doi.org/10.1007/3-540-36084-0_11
12. Zöhrer, M., Pernkopf, F.: General stochastic networks for classification. Adv. Neural. Inf. Process. Syst. **27**, 2015–2023 (2014)
13. Bengio, Y., Thibodeau-Laufer, E., Alain, G., Yosinski, J.: Deep Generative Stochastic Networks Trainable by Backprop (2014). http://arxiv.org/abs/1306.1091
14. Serfozo, R.F.: Introduction to Stochastic Networks. Applications of Mathematics, vol. 44. Springer, New York (1999). https://doi.org/10.1007/978-1-4612-1482-3
15. Williams, J.: Laplace Transforms, Problem Solvers. George Allen & Unwin, London (1973)
16. Phillips, D.T., Garsia-Diaz, A.: Fundamentals of Network Analysis. Prentice-Hall, Englewood Cliffs (1981)
17. Petrova, S.S.: Heaviside and the development of the symbolic calculus. Arch. Hist. Exact Sci. **37**(1), 1–23 (1987)

The Cryptanalysis of WPA & WPA2
Using the Parallel-Computing with GPUs

TienHo Chang[1(✉)], Chiamei Chen[2], Hanwei Hsiao[2], and GuHsin Lai[3]

[1] Department of Management Information, National Sun Yat-sen University, Kaohsiung, Taiwan
D024020001@student.nsysu.edu.tw
[2] Department of Management Information, University of Kaohsiung, Kaohsiung, Taiwan
[3] Department of Technology Crime Investigation, Taiwan Police College, Taipei, Taiwan

Abstract. The encryption of WPA & WPA2 is the present and security protection for the wireless LAN. With the vigorous development of parallel computing (GPU), the speed of cryptanalysis is rising up and getting more popular which causes the great threat to the Wi-Fi security. It is time-consuming for the wireless passwords analysis for the huge total combinations of 95^{63} max. Now, it is the turning point that the leap progress of GPU makes the Wi-Fi cryptanalysis much more efficient than before. In this research, we proposed a much faster speed (270,000 PMKs/s) compared to those in years, and the speed of computing PMKs/s is the major crucial factor and base for the mainstream of wireless passwords attacks, such as brute force, dictionary, time-memory trade-off (rainbow attack), and the generations of dictionary files.

Keywords: Cryptanalysis · GPU · Parallel-computing · WPA & WPA2
Wireless security

1 Introduction

In recent days, as the use of mobile devices (e.g. smartphones and smart watches) increases [1], and it became ubiquitous in the last years [2]. According to the statistics of Wigle.net cumulated from 2002 to 2016, there are 253,075,273 unique Wi-Fi networks [3] at the date of April 30th, 2016 which shows the prosperous vision of wireless LAN and the speedup of wireless products is in the nonlinear trend.

It's deeply worried that the radio waves of wireless LAN directly expose to the air. Many organizations today are faced with all kinds of challenges related to security and privacy of their wireless network [4]. The current mainstream protection of wireless LAN is the protocol of WPA & WPA2 with the digits from 8 to 63, and its characteristics of the algorithm of WPA & WPA2 encryptions using the PBKDF2 method is irreversible and will last for years with the calculation of 4096 times per encryption as simply depicted on the Fig. 1 [5].

The cryptanalysis of WPA & WPA2 using GPU is comparing the hashed value-PMK (Pairwise Master Key) of passwords, and PMK = PBKDF2 (PSK, SSID, SsidLength, 4096, 256) [6]. Though WPA & WPA2 are robust than WEP, it only protectes the data frames, and network information technology makes the world wide range of information

© Springer Nature Singapore Pte Ltd. 2018
I. You et al. (Eds.): MobiSec 2016, CCIS 797, pp. 118–127, 2018.
https://doi.org/10.1007/978-981-10-7850-7_11

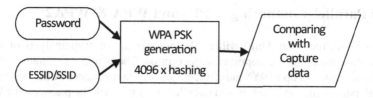

Fig. 1. WPA PSK hash key cracking using password and SSID and multiply hashing function [5].

exchanges convenient increasingly and fast [7]. The management and control frames remained un-encrypted [8]. In brief, the main elements of WPA & WPA2 encryption is the SSID and password of the target AP, as mentioned above, the data frames are unencrypted, so could obtain the messages of the connections between the target AP and its clients by the means of deauthentication. Under that circumstances, the encrypted packets would be collected for cryptanalysis, and just put them in the environment of computing by brute force or dictionary attack. That is, it has to be certain degree of weak password under the basis of specific computing ability. Without the high speed in cryptanalysis, it would be endless waiting which makes the decryption dull, in contrast, we could reach not only the wider range of WPA & WPA2 passwords from 8 to 11 or more digits in numbers but also the lower, upper case letters and even the symbols. Mostly, the recent studies focus on the 8 digits in number only, and run the cryptanalysis in the controlled environment. For the limit in current speed, it is quite difficult to reach the field of real world in the wireless encryption security. Now, the excellence of GPU parallel computing could lead us to see the real situations of the WPA & WPA2 encryption, and can do the analysis of the usage of password for the wireless security. No matter how complicated it is, the WPA & WPA2 is merely the protection of password. The WPA & WPA2 provided more secure mechanisms at the cost of requiring more complicated configuration tasks [9]. Therefore, the security of wireless LAN will be greatly decreased with the deficiency of passwords strength.

For the range of wireless cryptanalysis, it is not mentioned that what the definition of complicated password is in literature. The passwords range of WPA & WPA2 is based on the social engineering attributes which contains the personal messages and characters for the convenience, memorizing, and frequency [10]. This is the entry point for the attack of WPA & WPA2 which is called weak passwords. The single most important aspect of information security is strong passwords. Likewise, the single greatest security failure is weak passwords [11]. By the complication of WPA & WPA2 protocol, each password candidate would be 4096 times of calculations per decryption and the 100 million combinations in number for 8 digits is 4096 * 100 million in cryptanalysis which exhausted the computing ability and time consuming, and that's why the progress of WPA & WPA2 passwords analysis got stuck. Now, the GPU based parallel computing got the evolutionary developing, and be the critical and fundamental solution for cryptanalysis because of its excellent speedup of parallel computing which is the key point under the typical kinds of attack, such as brute force, dictionary, time-memory trade-off (rainbow attack) [12], and the generation of dictionary files.

2   The Parallel-Computing (GPU) and WPA & WPA2

GPU (Graphics Processing Unit) will be the mainstream of cryptanalysis of WPA & WPA2 for the sake of mass computing in decryption. The whole combinations of WPA & WPA2 encryption is up to 95^{63} max, of course, the main concern of the cryptanalysis is the weak passwords, and the key and excellent way to crack the password of WPA & WPA2 is comparing the encrypted values (PMKs) by the computing ability of the machine we implemented. It is impractical to handle the decryption computing with the large scale supercomputer, so the parallel computing of PC is the appropriate and optimal choice for the factors of economic, convenience, and speed. The encrypted packets of WPA & WPA2 could be captured by deauthentication which means DOS (Denial of Service), and this is one of the major weaknesses which is highly challenged by the leap development of wireless LAN technology. Owing to the improvement of parallel computing in practicality and feasibility, the cryptanalysis of WPA & WPA2 is getting more convenient, and the most of all is its upgrading of speed in recent years. The GPU is the applicable and economic in parallel computing, it is because that the cryptanalysis is based on the comparison computing, no matter in what the analytical ways are. The specific cryptanalysis of WPA & WPA2 in parallel computing are:

2.1   The Development and Standing of Parallel-Computing (GPU) in WPA & WPA2

A Graphics Processing Units (GPUs) with a few thousands of extremely simple processors represent a paradigm shift for highly parallel computations [13]. From the lower to the higher level GPU, there are with independent stream cores and RAM, and usually the computing performances of mid or higher level GPUs are more than the PC it attached to. According to Flynn's taxonomy, the implementation of MIMD (multiple

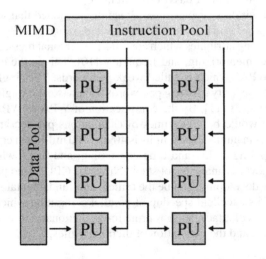

Fig. 2. The architecture of MIMD parallelism [14].

instruction, multiple data) which can be executed with different instructions on different data [14] is fulfilled in GPU in recently years illustrated in Fig. 2, as the GPU-AMD Radeon™ HD 7970 (the GCN-Graphic Core Next architecture) [15] we took in this research.

What the astonishing is the stream cores, the independent tiny cores, and each GPU contains hundreds to thousands of stream cores which is equipped with various frequencies. In parallel computing, FLOPS (FLoating point Operations Per Second) is a measure of computer performance, useful in fields of scientific calculations that make heavy use of floating-point calculations [16]. It presents a comparison between the rate at which compute power has been scaling in successive generations of CPUs and GPUs Fig. 3 [17].

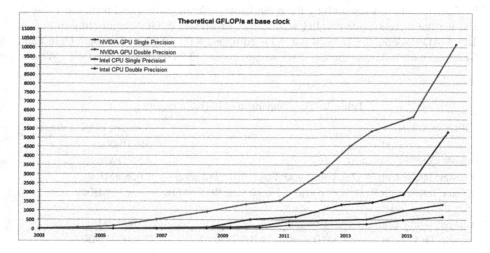

Fig. 3. Floating-point operations per second for the CPU and GPU [17].

What is implemented in this research is the GPU of AMD Radeon™ HD 7970 (GCN) with 4.3 TFLOPS and 2048 stream cores, and we took 2 GPUs-AMD Radeon™ HD 7970 (GCN) for cryptanalysis of WPA & WPA2 by the excellent parallel computing ability. According to the complicated algorithm of WPA & WPA2 protocol, our two GPUs got the excellent power of 8.6 TFLOPS and its real parallel computing speed of WPA & WPA2 cryptanalysis is around 268–270 k PMKs/s. With that speed, it does a challenge for the security of wireless LAN presently. To show the excellence of GPU computing, we compared the AMD Radeon™ HD 7970 (GCN) with the high performance computing system (HPCS) of university as depicted in Table 1. We can see that the two GPUs we took in FLOPS are highly outperformed the high-performance computing system, and it is because that the HPCS is the CPUs computing, not the GPUs which contains great ability for the parallel computing of cryptanalysis.

Table 1. The comparison of FLOPS.

GPUs vs. CPUs	Items	
	FLOPS	Cores
AMD Radeon™ HD 7970 (GCN)*2	8.6 TFLOPS	GPUs *2-4096 stream cores
High-performance computing system	0.7351 TFLOPS	2.3 GHz CPUs *64 + 4.7 GHz CPUs *16

2.2 Cluster Computing and WPA & WPA2

We can see that the comparison of CPUs and GPUs-AMD Radeon™ HD 7970 (GCN) implemented in this research by the remarkable differences in speed from the Table 2, and get the insight of its parallel architecture of MIMD & GCN computing in Fig. 4. The AMD Radeon™ HD 7970 (GCN) is equipped with 32 CUs (Compute Units) and 64 cores in each CU, so there is 2048 stream cores (32 * 64) in each one GPU. We can

Table 2. The comparison of PMK/s computing.

GPUs vs. CPUs	Speed of PMK computing
Intel® Core™ i7 (1 core)	550 PMKs/s
Intel® Core™ i7 (8 cores)	4,500 PMKs/s
Cluster: Intel® Core™ i7 (6 cores) + GeForce 210 *2 (2 cores)	5,056 PMKs/s
Custer: Intel® Core™ i7 *1 (8 cores) + Intel® Core™ i5 *4 (16 cores)	11,167 PMKs/s
Cluster: Intel® Core™ i7 *5 (40 cores)	20,000 PMKs/s
Parallel GPU: (4096 cores) AMD Radeon™ HD 7970 *2	270,000 PMKs/s

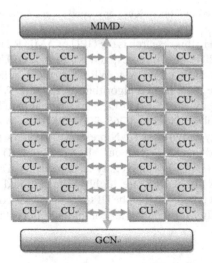

Fig. 4. The parallel architecture of MIMD & GCN computing in AMD Radeon™ HD 7970 (GCN).

get the huge speedup of 49010% from the 550 PMKs/s to 270,000 PMKs/s which shows the excellent parallel computing ability in the GPU we took. With the limit described above, the cryptanalysis is by far the Lab experiment under the self-defined environment, and it could not reach to the real situations of WPA & WPA2 because the current speed is not suitable for the higher digits or complicated combinations of passwords except the speed of 270,000 PMKs/s we proposed.

2.3   The Convenience and Effectiveness of Parallel-Computing (GPU)

There are chain reactions in handling with kinds of researches involved in the high speed computing by the high performance and popularity in parallel computing of GPUs. Now, we could reach to the zones that restricted by the computing speed, such as WPA & WPA2 in real environment, big data, high level of medical image processing, and so forth. From the Table 3, we can see the speed in cryptanalysis of WPA & WPA2 research in literature and the folds of speedup it improved with the GPU employed in this research under the base of 100 million number password combinations.

Table 3. The comparison of PMK/s max in time. 34,800 PMKs/s [18]

The combination of passwords	270,000 PMKs/s	34,800 PMKs/s [15]	Folds
10 million	37 s	287 s	7.7

3   High Speed Cryptanalysis of WPA & WPA2

3.1   The Progress of Parallel-Computing in WPA & WPA2

By the appropriate speedup by GPU in handling the complication of WPA & WPA2 encryption, we could reach to the extent ever had before, and this is the important foundation for wireless cryptanalysis. Basically, the most common digits of WPA & WPA2 cryptanalysis is 8 in the controlled Lab environment [5, 10, 11, 18] and some reaches to the digits of 11–12 under the limited range of dictionary file, of course, that's also the controlled experiment [5]. We can see the great step forward in decryption time from 833.3 min (2,000 PMKs/s) to 6.16 min (270,000 PMKs/s) under the base of 100 million number password combinations which shows the speedup of 13500% from the Table 4, and it dramatically promotes us to expand the possibility of wider digits from 8 to 11. As for 10 billion number password combinations, it would take the 79.2 h max of waiting for cryptanalysis under the speed of 34,800 PMKs/s [18] which makes the analysis time-consuming and impractical. With our speedup of 270,000 PMKs/s, the time would be decreased to the 10.1 h max and the efficiency would be much better if we take the strategy of exclusion of certain impossible password combinations.

Table 4. The comparison of parallel computing in PMK/s.

GPUs vs. CPUs	Speed	Folds
CPU [5]	2,000 PMKs/s	135
CPU + GPU [11]	3,875 PMKs/s	69
CPU: Intel® Core™ i7 *1	4,500 PMKs/s	60
Cluster: CPU-Intel® Core™ i7 *1 + GPU-GeForce 210 *2	5,056 PMKs/s	53.4
GPU [10]	7,783 PMKs/s	39
Cluster: CPU-Intel® Core™ i7 *1 + CPU-Intel® Core™ i5 *4	11,167 PMKs/s	24.2
Cluster: CPU-Intel® Core™ i7 *5	20,000 PMKs/s	13.5
GPU [18]	34,800 PMKs/s	7.7
Parallel GPU: GPU AMD Radeon™-HD 7970 (GCN)*2	270,000 PMKs/s	–

3.2   High Speed Attack of WPA & WPA2 Encryption

With the speed we proposed, we extended the cryptanalysis of WPA & WPA2 outside the lab experiment, and we got 30 real samples of 4 way handshake packets using the deauthentication (Dos Attack) to testify how efficient the speed we proposed-270,000 PMKs/s in the real wireless LAN. For those 30 samples, there are all in the encryption of WPA & WPA2, and we gained the excellent cracking rate of 76.6% within few seconds to minutes. We do the comparisons of the speed in 34,800 PMKs/s [18] in literature and the speed in 270,000 PMKs/s we proposed to see how much time improved in Table 4 which is an important step of WPA & WPA2 cryptanalysis. Basically, we save the 7.7 times energy in the waiting of the cryptanalysis process. This is probably the first time taking the real samples of WPA & WPA2 encryption, and we got the 76.6% of cracking rate from these real samples from the streets. From Fig. 5, we can see the GPUs (AMD Radeon™ HD 7970*2) doing the excellent speed in cracking the packets of 4 ways handshake captured in the real wireless LAN environment. And we

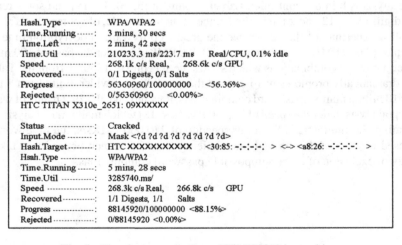

Fig. 5. The cluster computing of HD 7970*2 in cracking.

successfully logged in the target's Wi-Fi networks in the real environment with the cracked password under the academic regulations in Fig. 6.

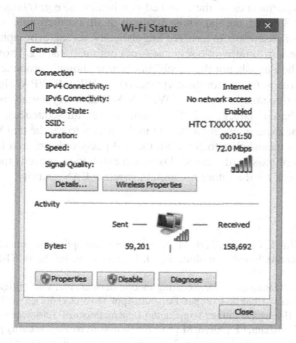

Fig. 6. Login the Wi-Fi with the cracked password.

4 Conclusion

Speed is the crucial factor in the cryptanalysis of WPA & WPA2 because it would take much time more than imaged, no matter in what way based on the foundation of comparing calculations. With the development of technology, the advantage of WPA & WPA2 encryption protocol is no longer maintained because of the constant upgrading and popularity of high parallel computing. The sensitive information can be protected from malicious users by means of access control [19]. But, the weak passwords and the high parallel computing are the powerful currents that break down the present secure WPA & WPA2 encryption because the folks would like to keep the passwords as short as it can be, easy to memory, and have no the idea of setting the secure types of passwords like this-"%5;wU0ck6@A$cdKXji0vQl" for the sake of convenience.

Speed is one of the most important factors in the cryptanalysis of WPA & WPA2 protocol, and the advantages of parallel computing in GPU provide us the chance of insight into the secrets of wireless LAN password protection. By the progress of technology development, the trend will succeed the Moore's law with the non-linear leap, and the dominant standing of WPA & WPA2 protocol will be deeply challenged as the weak passwords kept in mind.

From the cracked passwords, we learned that the efficiency would be much better if we take the rule-based mode of attack using GPU, that is, implement the cracking not computing every sequences of the assigned combinations, e.g. 09xxxxxxxx, we just calculate the last 8 digits, not the whole 10 digits at all. Furthermore, we can focus on the components of passwords in terms of linguistically, social, geographically different which exclude certain "impossible sequences of combinations, e.g. "xqwcd" is not the phonotactics of the English, nor the "qcpb" in Chinese phonetic pronunciation, and that does one of the crucial factors for the cryptanalysis of WPA & WPA2. In the future, we can combine the three major factors of WPA & WPA2 in cryptanalysis which are the "Speed", "Rule-based" attack, and "Exclusion" of certain sequences. And more, we should expand the experiment environment to the streets to get the real WPA & WPA2 encrypted 4 ways handshakes to see what the real passwords are in a large scale, and analyze its types of passwords and SSIDs which mentioned above is the key elements of the TMTO attack for the future research in wireless LAN security.

References

1. Kim, N.Y., Shim, J., Cho, S.J., Park, M., Han, S.: Android application protection against static reverse engineering based on multidexing. J. Internet Serv. Inf. Secur. (JISIS) 6(4), 54–64 (2016)
2. Skovoroda, A., Gamayunov, D.: Securing mobile devices: malware mitigation methods. J. Wirel. Mob. Netw. Ubiquit. Comput. Depend. Appl. (JoWUA) 6(2), 78–97 (2015)
3. General Stats Homepage. https://wigle.net/gps/gps/main/stats/. Last accessed 30 April 2016
4. Fatani, H.A., Zamzami, I.F., Aliyu, M.: Awareness toward wireless security policy: case study of International Islamic University Malaysia. In: Proceedings of the 5th International Conference on Information and Communication Technology for the Muslim World (ICT4M), pp. 1–5. IEEE, Morocco (2013)
5. Krekan, J., Pleva, M., Dobos, L.: Statistical models based password candidates generation for specified language used in wireless LAN security audit. In: Proceedings of the 20th International Conference on Systems, Signals and Image Processing (IWSSIP), pp. 95–98. IEEE, Romania (2013)
6. Ahmed, S., Belali, M.H., Mahmud, I., Rahman, S., Sakib, N.: WPA 2 (Wi-Fi Protected Access 2) security enhancement: analysis and improvement. Global J. Comput. Sci. Tech. 12(6), 83–89 (2012)
7. Chen, C., Anada, H., Kawamoto, J., Sakurai, K.: A hybrid encryption scheme with key-cloning protection: user/terminal double authentication via attributes and fingerprints. J. Internet Serv. Inf. Secur. (JISIS) 6(2), 23–36 (2016)
8. Agarwal, M., Biswas, S., Nandi, S.: Detection of de-authentication denial of service attack in 802.11 networks. In: Proceedings of the Annual IEEE India Conference (INDICON), pp. 1–6. IEEE, India (2013)
9. Petiz, I., Rocha, E., Salvador, P., Nogueira, A.: Using multiscale traffic analysis to detect WPS attacks. In: Proceedings of the IEEE International Conference on Communications Workshops (ICC), pp. 1020–1025. IEEE, Budapest (2013)
10. Zhang, L., Yu, J., Deng, Z., Zhang, R.: The security analysis of WPA encryption in wireless network. In: Proceedings of the 2nd International Conference Consumer Electronics on Communications and Networks (CECNet), pp. 1563–1567. IEEE, China (2012)
11. Tran, K.: GPU - accelerated WPA PSK cracking solutions. Minnesota State University (2010)

12. Oechslin, P.: Making a faster cryptanalytic time-memory trade-off. In: Boneh, D. (ed.) CRYPTO 2003. LNCS, vol. 2729, pp. 617–630. Springer, Heidelberg (2003). https://doi.org/10.1007/978-3-540-45146-4_36

13. Bollapalli, K., Wu, Y., Gulati, K., Khatri, S., Calderbank, A.R.: Highly parallel decoding of space-time codes on graphics processing units. In: Proceedings of the 47th Annual Allerton Conference on Communication, Control, and Computing (Allerton), pp. 1262–1269. IEEE, USA (2009)

14. MIMD Homepage, http://en.wikipedia.org/wiki/MIMD. Last accessed 30 April 2016

15. Nishikawa, N., Iwai, K., Tanaka, H., Kurokawa, T.: Throughput and power efficiency evaluations of block ciphers on kepler and GCN GPUs. In: Proceedings of the First International Symposium on Computing and Networking, pp. 366–372. IEEE, Japan (2013)

16. FLOPS Homepage, http://en.wikipedia.org/wiki/FLOPS. Last accessed 30 April 2016

17. CUDA Preprogramming Guide Homepage. http://docs.nvidia.com/cuda/cuda-c-programming-guide/#axzz3F5ky7blr. Last accessed 30 April 2016

18. Zhang, L., Yu, J., Zong, R., Chang, J., Xue, J.: Prevention research of cracking WPA-PSK key based on GPU. In: Proceedings of the 2nd International Conference on Consumer Electronics, Communications and Networks (CECNet), pp. 1965–1969. IEEE, China (2012)

19. Renugadevi, N., Mala, C.: Improved group key agreement for emergency cognitive radio mobile ad hoc networks. J. Wirel. Mob. Netw. Ubiquit. Comput. Depend. Appl. (JoWUA) 6(3), 73–86 (2015)

A Policy Management System Based on Multi-dimensional Attribution Label

Bosong Liu, Jianfeng Guan[✉], and Zhongbai Jiang

State Key Laboratory of Networking and Switching Technology,
Beijing University of Posts and Telecommunications, Beijing 100876, China
{liubaisong,jfguan,zbjiang}@bupt.edu.cn

Abstract. Due to complex and diverse attributes and dimension information of users, the existing policy system cannot control the multi-dimensional users in fine-grained manner, which results in rigid, coarse-grained management configuration and other issues. Therefore, it is extremely urgent to design a new policy system to meet the requirement for controlling multi-dimensional users. This paper proposes a unified naming mechanism of multidimensional attribute label and designs an efficient policy matching algorithm called Improved Sunday with Map mapping container (ISMM). The ISMM algorithm can deal with repeat pattern string by virtue of the idea of Map container, whose structure is orderly called key-value. ISMM firstly preprocesses and transforms the policies stored in policy server, and then matches the transformed information with the attribution information carried by client. If matching succeeds, we use a policy server to return the matching result as well as value information stored in Map container to client in advance, otherwise policy server would return failure information and submits errors to client. The matching result of ISMM algorithm is 13626 items per second in a given testing environment, comparing to 9764 of Sunday algorithm, 8967 of BM algorithm, 6698 of KMP algorithm, 5880 of BF algorithm, 5933 of regular matching algorithm. The experimental results show that efficiency of ISMM is significantly better than the classic policy matching algorithms (BM, KMP, BF, etc.). Moreover, the designed system can not only solve the problems but also control the multi-dimensional attribute information of user and ensuring the integrity, confidentiality and uniqueness. *abstract* environment.

Keywords: Multi-dimensional attribution label · Efficient matching
Policy management system · ISMM algorithm

1 Introduction

With the rapid development of information network technology and application software, more and more information technologies and automation facilities have been integrated into daily lives, bringing unprecedented convenience. However, these new information carriers have also raised a number of complex security

© Springer Nature Singapore Pte Ltd. 2018
I. You et al. (Eds.): MobiSec 2016, CCIS 797, pp. 128–142, 2018.
https://doi.org/10.1007/978-981-10-7850-7_12

issues while bringing convenience. Security issues of data transmission in the network have gradually become the focus of attention, especially important data files related to confidential, internal information and sensitive information has become the focus of the focus. At the same time, with the increase of users' roles and dimensions, the attribute and dimension information added to the users grow exponentially, and the user attribute and dimension information itself is diversified and isomerized. The complexity of the existing security system cannot achieve fine-grained control of multi-dimensional users. The user's control will be more and more complex. The existing security system cannot control the multi-dimensional users in fine-grained manner. Therefore, it is imminent to overcome and solve the drawbacks of traditional access control system. Controlling the multi-dimensional attribute information of user and ensuring the integrity, confidentiality, uniqueness and non-repudiation of the internal information are the fundamental of solving the problem.

In recent years, policy management has been a research hotspot. In [1], a mathematical model is proposed to motivate employees to comply with Information Systems Security (ISS) policy. The authors also adopt a scenario-based questionnaire to survey employees of Chinese SMEs for model testing. In [2], a method is designed to provide flexible rights management regardless of the access control model in Enterprise Document Management Systems (EDMS) based on policy algebra for logic management using security policies. Reference [3] considers the formal hierarchical model of (cyber) security policy for Instrumentation and Control system by the use of an example of digital Upper Unit Level I&C System of a nuclear power plant. Reference [4] proposes a novel shared LLC management policy for CPU-GPGPU heterogeneous systems called Buffer Filter which takes advantage of memory latency tolerance of GPGPUs. The proposed management policy also has the ability to restrict streaming requests of GPGPU by adding a buffer to memory system and vacate LLC space for cache-sensitive CPU applications to manage those various on-chip resources shared between CPUs and GPGPUs. Reference [5] proposes a new emergency vehicle preemption policy to ensure that emergency vehicles can pass through intersections with no or less delay through identifying its urgent spectacles. Reference [6] provides an overview of security and reliability problems of Vehicular-to-Vehicular Networks. Reference [7] proposes a mathematical model of attacks to implementations. Reference [8] proposes a framework with fine-grained access control mechanism that protects personal health record against service providers and malicious users, which provides cryptographic schemes offering a more suitable solution for enforcing access policies based on user attributes, enhancing security and privacy of the system, as well as enabling access revocation in a hierarchical scheme. Reference [9] proposes to use core-based model engineering to refine diverse access control systems by adding typical semantic abstractions of contemporary policy-controlled operating systems. The authors also apply the method to SELinux system and practically demonstrate how to map policy semantics to an instance of the model. Reference [10] aims to provide an empirical study on the applicability of action research method in information systems.

Specifically, by assessing the adoption of an ISS policy in six small and medium sized enterprises, the authors identify the critical success factors in adopting an ISS policy. Based on an innovative type of model and software analyzer, which is able to compare two different views of the target system, reference [11] analyzes the correct implementation of access policies in a medium-sized real-world system and describes different abstraction levels to prevent the introduction of policies enforcement mechanisms at a global system level.

Although existing policy systems has solved the issues of accessing control to a certain degree, they are helpless to multi-dimensional users. Therefore, in this paper, we propose a new policy management system for users with multi-dimensional attribute information. This system designs a unified naming mechanism of multidimensional attribute labels to control complex attributes and designs an efficient policy matching algorithm called ISMM to improve policy matching speed.

The rest of paper is organized as follows. In Sect. 2, we describe the background of related algorithms, including the researches of several classical policy matching algorithms and the advantages of Map container. In Sect. 3, we describe the function module of the system and describe the unified naming mechanism of multidimensional attribute label. In Sect. 4, we describe the model of ISMM algorithm, including policy matching model, execution and implementation process of ISMM. In Sect. 5, we compares the matching result of ISMM with several classical algorithms. Finally, we conclude this paper and proposes several unresolved problems in Sect. 6.

2   Related Work

2.1   Classical Matching Algorithms

Classic policy matching algorithms include BF algorithm [12], KMP algorithm [13–17], Boyer-Moore (BM) algorithm [18,19], Sunday algorithm [20] and regular expression [21–26]. Specifically, BF algorithm is a basic matching algorithm. It is easily implemented without extra storage space and preprocessing. However, due to the frequent recalling, the matching speed is low. The optimal time complexity of BF algorithm can be $O\ (n - m + 1)$ (n is the length of main string and m is the length of pattern string) and the worst can be $O\ (n + m)$. KMP algorithm adopts the forward prefix matching method. It effectively avoids the recalling of pointer and the meaningless matching to some extent. The time complexity of KMP algorithm is $O\ (n + m)$. BM algorithm is jumping matching algorithm. In the worst case, the time complexity is $O\ (n \times m)$ and depends on the character string and pattern. The average time complexity is sub-linear. The optimal time complexity is $O\ (n/m)$. The time and space complexity of preprocessing are linear which is $O\ (n)$. After the transformation from Regex to finite automation [27,28], the time needed to match a character only depends on the length of character string. The characters in the string are only examined once at most. Daniel M. Sunday proposes Sunday algorithm in 1990s [20]. This algorithm is much better and simpler than the original BM algorithm. Similar to BM, its time complexity is $O\,(n \times m)$ in the worst case. However, it jumps as much as possible characters to perform the match, which is more efficient.

The aforementioned algorithms are classic policy matching algorithms, which have their own superiority in terms of time and space complexity. However, when the computing resource is limited, the efficiency of these algorithms are impaired. In order to illustrate the problem, this paper summarizes the principles and shortcomings of each algorithm and shows in Table 1.

All the existing classical matching algorithms have little difference between each other except Sunday. Sunday has broken the sequence of string and skipped as many as characters. Therefore, the efficiency of Sunday has been greatly improved. However, Sunday cannot overcome the defect of repeated first character. To solve this problem, we propose an improved Map container and apply it to the matching algorithm of resource-limited environment.

2.2   Advantages of Map Container

Map container is a kind of associated container with key-value structure. It builds a red-black tree to sort data. Therefore, each key can only appear once in Map with order. And Map is widely used to deal with one-to-one data.

Table 1. Principles and shortcomings of each algorithm

Algorithm name	Principle	Shortcomings
Brute Force (BF)	$txt[i]$ ($i \in [0, n-m]$) is first set as starting bit. Then, strings are compared with pattern string from front to back. If every character is the same with pattern string, then the string is matched. Otherwise, the comparison will start from next bit with $i + +$. Repeated this process until i reaches $(n - m)$ position	It costs a lot of computing time and memory
Boyer Moore (BM)	A function is first preset for each case. When a mismatch occurs, BM determines moving step according to comparing the functions. When getting maximum safe moving step, pattern string will go to next matching	It cannot meet different demands for policies with different lengths and fields

(continued)

Table 1. (*continued*)

Algorithm name	Principle	Shortcomings
KMP	Several bits are moved forward not bit by bit. Unnecessary comparisons can be avoided and matching efficiency is improved	It costs much CPU resource, not suitable for limited memory
Sunday	Moving step is pre-calculated, and the position in pattern string of right character outside the scope of text string is focused on. If character does not appear in text string, skips and sets moving step as length of pattern string +1, otherwise, moving step is rightmost character to the end of the distance +1	When dealing with repeated first character, efficiency of Sunday will be significantly reduced
Regular Expression	A search pattern is defined through a sequence of characters, which is mainly for pattern matching with strings [26]	Computing ability is limited

3   System Design

3.1   Function Module

The system combines C/S(Client/Server) and B/S(Browser/Server). C/S mainly deals with user access request, label detection and verification, policy matching, file encryption and other operations. B/S is mainly responsible for user configuration management of multi-dimensional attribute information, definition and update of policy. The structure of system is shown in Fig. 1.

When a user accesses the system services, the client software will first detects the multi-dimensional attribute label of user and sends the label to the label server. The label server will request the policy server to distribute the access policy according to current network environment, user label, and service label requested by the user. Label server matches user label with service label and returns the corresponding matching result to user according to the policy rule. If match succeeds, the user is allowed to access the service. Otherwise, the user has no access to the requested service.

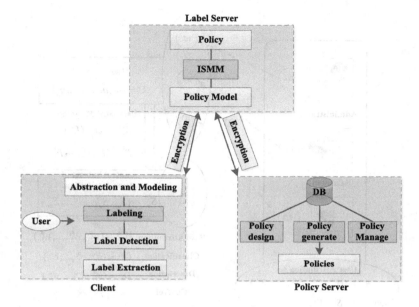

Fig. 1. Structure design of system

3.2 Unified Naming Mechanism of Multidimensional Attribute Label

In order to deal with the complex and multi-dimensional attributions of user, we propose a unified user label to identify each user with different dimensional attributes. The mechanism and related definition in Fig. 2 can be described as follows.

In the collection of users, U is the set of users to be managed, and each element represents a user.

The dimensional sub-set of user attributes can be defined in Eq. 1.

$$S_u^{c_i} = \varphi_{p^i}(U) \tag{1}$$

In the collection, the user label can be generated by filtering different types of user collections and policies. And the user filtering collection can be defined in p^i. The main function of the collection is to construct a user attribute vector as a filtering criterion, through which the user set is filtered.

The dimension attribute of the user can be defined in A^{U_i}. The user label can be defined in Eq. 2. Γ is the function mapping.

$$S_i = \Gamma(A^{U_i}) \tag{2}$$

The multi-dimensional attributes can be defined in Eq. 3.

$$A^{U_i} = \{W^{U_i}, C^{U_i}, D^{U_i}, F^{U_i}, B^{U_i}\} \tag{3}$$

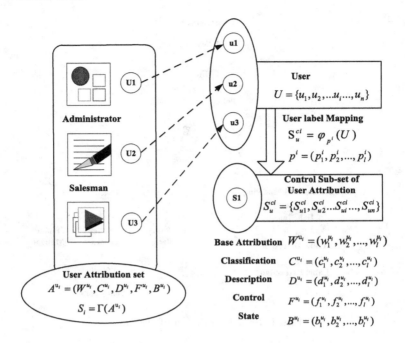

Fig. 2. Label mapping of multidimensional user attribution

In the collection, W^{U_i} is the base attributes of user, and each element is a base attribution of user. C^{U_i} is the classification of user U_i and provides corresponding criteria in different aspects. D^{U_i} is the attribute description set of user U_i, and each element is the attribute description of user to provide an interface for user interworking. F^{U_i} is the set of operations that can be performed on the user U_i, where each element represents what control and operation can be performed on the user. B^{U_i} is a set of state attributes of user, where each element represents the attribute state of the user, and can be controlled according to the current state.

The classification mode of user identifies each dimension attribute and establishes the corresponding mapping relation. Describing and limiting user attributes in multiple dimensions can safely control the basic attributes and behavioral properties of user. Based on the unified naming mechanism, mapping model and policy selection, the system can match user label with service label and control the user more fine-grained.

4   System Model

4.1   Matching Model of Policy

Based on attribution, the domestic management system of policies is mainly responsible for querying the policy in policy server to match attributions sent from client and returning matching result to client. The policy server has stored three Attribution-Mapping tables and one Policy-Mapping tables. The Attribution-Mapping tables are respectively defined as "User Attribution-Rank", "Terminal Attribution-Rank", "Environment Attribution-Rank". The Policy-Mapping table is composed of user attributions, terminal attributions, environment attributions and service rank. When policy server receives the request information from client, which includes user attribution, terminal attribution, environment attribution and service rank, policy server will firstly generate the corresponding ranks through querying the three Attribution-Mapping tables. The generated ranks are rank of user attribution, rank of terminal and rank of environment. In addition, the three generated ranks are the access permission, and service rank is the permission of service with which client applies for accessing. Secondly, policy server will match the three generated ranks with service rank in Policy-Mapping table through ISMM matching algorithm. And then, policy server returns the access policy to client according to the matching result.

As shown in Fig. 3, the information carried by a user can be defined in Eq. 4.

$$R(t) = \{U(t), F(t), B(t), S(t), \cdots\} \tag{4}$$

In Eq. 4, $R(t)$ is the collection of user attribution. In the collection, $U(t)$ is the collection of user. $F(t)$ is collection of service. $B(t)$ is the attribution of user. $S(t)$ is the attribution of service.

In the collection, $U(t)$ can be defined in Eq. 5.

$$U(t) = \{u_1, u_2, \cdots, u_m\} \tag{5}$$

In the Eq. 5, $u_1, u_2, \cdots, u_m$ represent different user. For a single user, such as u_i, the attribution can be defined in Eq. 6.

$$S^{u_i}(t) = \{s_1^{u_i}, s_2^{u_i}, \cdots, s_l^{u_i}\} \tag{6}$$

In the Eq, $s_1^{u_i}, s_2^{u_i}, \cdots, s_l^{u_i}$ are the attributions of u_i. $\varphi_{u_i}(*)$ is the mapping function to generate the rank of user attribution. $\varphi_{u_i}(S^{u_i}(t))$ is the rank of user attribution.

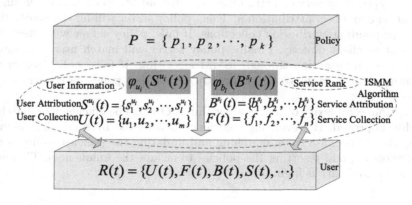

Fig. 3. Matching theoretical model of ISMM algorithm

In the collection, $F(t)$ can be defined in Eq. 7.

$$F(t) = \{f_1, f_2, \cdots, f_n\} \tag{7}$$

In the Eq, $f_1, f_2, \cdots, f_n$ are different services. For a single service, such as f_j, the attribution of service can be defined in Eq. 8.

$$B^{s_i}(t) = \{b_1^{s_i}, b_2^{s_i}, \cdots, b_l^{s_i}\} \tag{8}$$

In the Eq. 8, $b_1^{s_i}, b_2^{s_i}, \cdots, b_l^{s_i}$ are the attributions of s^i. $\varphi_{b_l}(*)$ is the mapping function to generate the rank of service attribution. $\varphi_{b_l}(B^{s_i}(t))$ is the rank of service attribution.

In addition, the policy can be defined in Eq. 9.

$$P = \{p_1, p_2, \cdots, p_k\} \tag{9}$$

In the Eq, $p_1, p_2, \cdots, p_k$ are different policies.

4.2   Principle of ISMM Algorithm

The process of matching is mainly handled on the policy server. Policy server matches user attribution, terminal attribution, environment attribution and service attribution $L(u, t, e, f)$ through ISMM algorithm. When a policy $L(u, t, e, f)$ matches with $L(u, t, e, f)$ in policy server, the match is successful and the user can get the grant to operate application software. Otherwise, the match fails.

As shown in Fig. 4, when policy server receives the matching request from client, it will extract user information and map the information to a corresponding policy. Firstly, ISMM will automatically sort the policies in policy server through the red-black tree of MAP and load the policy information into memory. If fails, policy server will return failure result to client directly. Secondly, policy server will transform the policy information into new information and extract respectively service attribution f, terminal attribution t, environment attribution e and user attribution u. Then, policy server will fill the attributions into corresponding attribution collections. If fails, policy server will return failure result to client directly. Finally, policy server will match user information with policies information through ISMM algorithm. If fails, policy server will also return failure result to client directly. Otherwise, policy server will return success to client.

The time complexity of ISMM algorithm is $O(1)$. The efficiency of matching is highly improved. However, high-efficiency is achieved by sacrificing memory space. That is because when matching and updating the policies, policy server needs reloading and resorting the policies to ensure the uniqueness. Therefore, the space complexity is high.

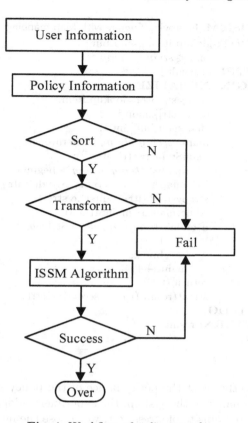

Fig. 4. Workflow of policy match

4.3   Execution Process of ISMM Algorithm

According to the policy matching model and principle of ISMM algorithm above, the execution process of ISMM algorithm can be described as follows.

In the fourth line of description, $map<string, string>$ is a map container to store policies. The container firstly loads the policies and corresponding result through key-value structure of MAP. Then, the container will sort the policies stored in policy server through the structure. In the fifth line, ISMM will preprocess the policies and transform them into text strings. In the sixth line, ISMM will match the policies one by one from front to back. In the twelfth line, ISMM will return the matching and defined results stored in policy server to client.

5   Analysis and Simulation

Compared with the existing policy management system, it is found that the decisive factor of system performance is the policy matching algorithm. The SWOT (Strengths, Weaknesses, Opportunities, and Threats) of policy matching

---

Algorithm ISMM. Improving Sunday with Map mapping

       INPUT: lookup_item[],send_buf[],
               map< *string, string* > ;
       OUTPUT: result[]
       BEGIN INITIALIZE
               char *subStr1=lookup_item,
               char *str[],main_i,
               char send_buf[],int t;
               map< *string, string* >::iterator itr,
               mainStrLen=strlen(str[]);
       DO   itr=map< *string, string* >.begin();
               itr!=map< *string, string* >.end(); itr++
               strcpy(text,(itr− >first).c_str());
               while(main_i<mainStrLen)
               if(mainStr[*main_i*]== subStr[*sub_j*])
                    t=1;
                  break;
                main_i++;
               return (t-1);
               strcat(result,(itr− >second).c_str());
       END DO
       RETURN: result
       END

---

algorithm will directly affect the performance of the policy system. In order to evaluate the performance of the system, the experiment adopts to stress testing. According to the prerequisite of stress test, we choose the number of concurrent access requests and the number of system policy entries as the two important factors of stress test, and changes the factor to compare the label matching rate of server. To highlight the performances of ISMM algorithm, this paper selects several classic policy matching algorithms and makes corresponding simulation experiments among them. The results and analyses are as follows.

5.1 Experimental Results

In order to prove the efficiency of ISMM algorithm, we have tested the policy matching result. The experiment test is finished in label server with resource-limited scenarios. In addition, CPU of Policy-Server is Linux Advanced Server. The processor is FPU V0.1. The memory is 4 GB. In order to verify differences of performance, the test compares the different rate between ISMM and several classic matching algorithms. In addition, the performance is usually effected by the number of concurrent access requests and the number of policies stored in server. Therefore, this paper respectively verifies the two factors and compares the rate between ISMM and several classical algorithms. The parameter settings are shown as in Table 2.

Table 2. Principles and shortcomings of each algorithm

Parameter	Value
CPU of Policy-Server	Linux Advanced Server
Processor	FPU V0.1
Memory	4 GB

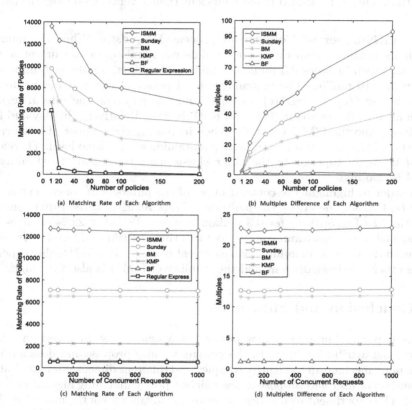

(a) Matching Rate of Each Algorithm

(b) Multiples Difference of Each Algorithm

(c) Matching Rate of Each Algorithm

(d) Multiples Difference of Each Algorithm

Fig. 5. The simulation results

5.2   Analysis of Experimental Results

Effect in Number of Policies Stored in Policy Server. When the number of concurrent access requests is 1000, we have respectively selected different number of policies, which includes 1, 20, 40, 60, 80, 100 and 200. The matching rate of policy of different algorithms are shown in Fig. 5(a). In Fig. 5(a), as for one policy, all the algorithms have little difference. When increasing the number of policies, the matching rates of regex and BF algorithm are almost zero. Similarly, the rates of BM, KMP and Sunday also decrease greatly. However, the rate of ISMM is slowly a big number.

In order to highlight the contrast effect of the number of policies, Fig. 5(b) describes the multiples of rate relative to the rate of regular algorithm. In Fig. 5(b), as for one policy, ISMM is 2.4069 times the regular matching algorithm, and KMP, BM and Sunday are about 1.5 times. All the algorithms have little difference. However, with the increase in number of policies, ISMM, increases greatly, which is several times or even a hundred times the regular matching algorithm. Therefore, ISMM is more efficient than several classic algorithms.

Effect in Number of Concurrent Access Requests. When the number of policies is 20, we respectively select different numbers of concurrent access requests, which includes 0.5 million, 1 million, 2 million, 3 million, 5 million, 8 million and 10 million. The matching rate of policy of different algorithm are shown in Fig. 5(c). In Fig. 5(c), as for 0.5 million requests, the rate of regular matching and BF are about 1000, and KMP is 2000. Relatively, Sunday and BM are 5000, while the ISMM is 13000. When increasing the number of concurrent requests, all the algorithms are almost maintaining at the same level. Therefore, ISMM is highly superior to the other classic algorithms and the stability of ISMM is also high.

In order to highlight the contrast effect of the numbers of concurrent access requests, Fig. 5(d) describes the multiples of rate relative to the rate of regular algorithm. In Fig. 5(d), as for 0.5 million requests, ISMM is 22.7454 times the regular matching algorithm, comparing to 13 times of BM and Sunday. In addition, with the increase in number of concurrent requests, ISMM is highly superior to the other classic algorithms and the stability of ISMM is also very high.

6   Conclusion and Future Work

In this paper, we propose a new policy management system based on multidimensional attribution label. In the system, we also propose and design a unified naming mechanism to identify complex and different dimensional attribution information of user and propose a new efficient policy matching algorithm called ISMM. The experiment results demonstrate the advantages of the matching algorithm. Comparing to the classical algorithms, including BF, KMP, BM, Sunday and regular expression matching algorithms, ISMM does not need to traverse the policies stored in policy server. As for low hardware configuration and limited computing of policy server, although the complexity of algorithm can be linear, the efficiency of all classical algorithms is far less than ISMM. Especially for large numbers of concurrent requests. ISMM algorithm has ameliorated these problems to a certain extent and greatly improved the efficiency. In conclusion, the policy system proposed and designed in this paper has remarkable superiority and innovation compared with the existing policy system. In addition, the system can be more granularly and flexibly in terms of controlling the access of user with multi-dimensional attribution information.

Although ISMM has improved the efficiency significantly, the algorithm also needs optimizing, especially on space complexity.

Acknowledgments. This work was partially supported by the National Basic Research Program of China (973 Program) under Grant No. 2013CB329102, in part by the National Natural Science Foundation of China (NSFC) under Grant No. 61232017, 61372112 and 61003283.

References

1. Shih, H., Guo, X., Lai, K., Cheng, T.C.E.: Taking promotion and prevention mechanisms matter for information systems security policy in Chinese SMEs. In: 2016 2nd International Conference on Information Management (ICIM), pp. 110–115. IEEE Press (2016)
2. Tarkhanov, T.: Policy algebra for access control in enterprise document management systems. In: 2015 9th International Conference on Application of Information and Communication Technologies (AICT), pp. 225–228. IEEE Press (2015)
3. Promyslov, V.G.: Tool for I&C system security policy verification. In: 2015 9th International Conference on Application of Information and Communication Technologies (AICT), pp. 221–224. IEEE Press (2015)
4. Li, S., Meng, J., Yu, L.: Buffer filter: a Last-level cache management policy for CPU-GPGPU heterogeneous system. In: 2015 IEEE 17th International Conference on Embedded Software and Systems (ICESS), pp. 266–271. IEEE Press (2015)
5. Huang, Y., Weng, Y., Zhou, M.: Design of traffic safety control systems for emergency vehicle preemption using timed petri nets. IEEE Trans. Intell. Transp. Syst. **16**(4), 2113–2120 (2015). IEEE Press
6. Desnitsky, V., Levshun, D., Chechulin, A., Kotenko, I.V.: Design technique for secure embedded devices: application for creation of integrated cyber-physical security system. J. Wirel. Mob. Netw. Ubiquitous Comput. Dependable Appl. (JoWUA), **7**(2), 60–80 (2016). IEEE Press
7. Baiardi, F., Tonelli, F., Isoni, L.: Application Vulnerabilities in Risk Assessment and Management. J. Wirel. Mob. Netw. Ubiquitous Comput. Dependable Appl. (JoWUA), **7**(2), 41–59 (2016). IEEE Press
8. Debnath, M.K., Samet, S., Vidyasankar, K.: A secure revocable personal health record system with policy-based fine-grained access control. In: 2015 13th Annual Conference on Privacy, Security and Trust (PST), pp. 109–116. IEEE Press (2015)
9. Amthor P.: A uniform modeling pattern for operating systems access control policies with an application to SELinux. In: 2015 12th International Joint Conference on e-Business and Telecommunications (ICETE), pp. 88–99. IEEE Press (2015)
10. Lopes, I.M., Oliveira, P.: Evaluation of the adoption of an information systems security policy. In: 2015 10th Iberian Conference on Information Systems and Technologies (CISTI), pp. 1–6. IEEE Press (2015)
11. Cheminod, M., Durante, L., Seno, L., Valenzano, A.: Analysis of access control policies in networked embedded systems: a case study. In: 2015 10th IEEE International Symposium on Industrial Embedded Systems (SIES), pp. 1–10. IEEE Press (2015)
12. Enqvist, O., Jiang, F., Kahl, F.: A Brute-Force algorithm for reconstructing a scene from two projections. In: IEEE Conference on Computer Vision and Pattern Recognition (CVPR), pp. 2961–2968. IEEE Press (2011)
13. An, D., Shao, M., Yuan, Z., Shi, H. Pan, Q.: Speaker recognition method based on CPSO clustering and KMP algorithm. In: Seventh International Symposium on Computational Intelligence and Design (ISCID), pp. 556–559. IEEE Press (2014)

14. Kurniawan, D.H., Munir, R.: A new string matching algorithm based on logical indexing. In: IEEE 26th International Conference on Data Engineering (ICDE 2010), pp. 394–399. IEEE Press (2010)
15. Hong, I., Bong, K., Shin, D., Park, S., Lee, K.J., Kim, Y., Yoo, H.J.: A 2.71 nJ/Pixel Gaze-activated object recognition system for low-power mobile Dmart glasses. J. Solid-State Circuits, **51**(1), 45–55 (2016)
16. Ou, Z.: Data structuring and effective retrieval in the mining of web sequential characteristic. In: International Conference on Electronic and Mechanical Engineering and Information Technology (EMEIT), pp. 3551–3554. IEEE Press (2011)
17. Hou, X., Yan, Y., Lu, X.: Hybrid pattern-matching algorithm based on BM-KMP algorithm. In: 3rd International Conference on Advanced Computer Theory and Engineering (ICACTE), pp. 310–313. IEEE Press (2010)
18. Zhu, Y.: Two enhanced BM Algorithm in pattern matching. In: Workshop on Digital Media and Digital Content Management (DMDCM), pp. 341–346. IEEE Press (2011)
19. Qiao, J., Zhang, H.: Improvement of BM algorithm in Intrusion detection system. In: 6th IEEE International Conference on Software Engineering and Service Science (ICSESS), pp. 652–655. IEEE Press (2015)
20. Sunday, D.M.: A very fast substring search algorithm. Commun. ACM **33**(8), 132–142 (1990)
21. Yin, C.: A deterministic finite automata based on improved BM algorithm. In: International Conference on Computer Design and Applications (ICCDA), pp. 389–391. IEEE Press (2010)
22. Lu, H., Zheng, K., Liu, B., Zhang, X., Liu, Y.: A memory-efficient parallel string matching architecture for high-speed intrusion detection. IEEE J. Sel. Areas Commun. **24**(10), 1793–1804 (2006). IEEE Press
23. Krishnamurthy, R., Li, Y., Raghavan, S.: SystemT: a system for declarative information extraction. Newsletter **37**(4), 7–13 (2008)
24. Lenka, R.K., Ranjan, P.: A comparative study on DFA-based pattern matching for deep packet inspection. In: Third International Conference on Computer and Communication Technology (ICCCT), pp. 255–260. IEEE Press (2012)
25. Peng, K., Tang, S., Chen, M., Dong, Q.: Chain-based DFA deflation for fast and scalable regular expression matching using TCAM. In: Seventh ACM/IEEE Symposium on Architectures for Networking and Communications Systems (ANCS), pp. 24–35. IEEE Press (2011)
26. Wang, X., Xu, Y., Jiang, J., Ormond, O., Liu, B., Wang, X.: StriFA: Stride Finite Automata for high speed regular expression matching in network intrusion detection systems. IEEE J. Sel. Areas Commun. **7**(3), 374–384 (2013). IEEE Press
27. Sun, Y., Valgenti, V.C., Kim, M.S.: NFA-based pattern matching for deep packet inspection. In: Proceedings of 20th International Conference on Computer Communications and Networks (ICCCN), pp. 1–6 (2011)
28. Jiang, J., Xu, Y., Pan, T., Tang, Y., Liu, B.: Pattern-based DFA for memory-efficient and scalable multiple regular expression matching. In: IEEE International Conference on Communications (ICC), pp. 1–5. IEEE Press (2010)

Access Control for Cross-Border Transfer of Sensor Data

Seira Hidano[1]([✉]), Shinsaku Kiyomoto[1], Abdur Rahim Biswas[2],
Toshihiro Uchibayashi[3], and Takuo Suganuma[3]

[1] KDDI Research, Inc.,
2-1-15 Ohara, Fujimino-shi, Saitama 356-8502, Japan
se-hidano@kddi-research.jp
[2] CREATE-NET, Trento, Italy
[3] Tohoku University, Sendai, Japan

Abstract. The iKaaS (intelligent Knowledge-as-a-Service) platform unitarily manages the data on existing cloud systems, which allows applications to access their desired data scattered all over the world transparently. Hidano et al. have proposed an access control mechanism suitable for the iKaaS platform to resolve privacy issues on the transfer of personal data to the applications in different countries. They introduced the concept of a privacy certificate authority (CA) to provide support for confirming the validity of the application. The privacy CA is established for each country as the executive agency responsible for the national regulations governing the handling of personal data. In this paper, we design a hierarchical model of multiple privacy CAs responsible for regulations where the areas governed by these regulations are different. The data transfer can be thereby controlled not only for different countries, but also for different economic or political blocs (e.g., European Union) or cities. In addition, focusing on a town management application as a use case of the iKaaS platform, we present how our access control mechanism works.

Keywords: Access control · Security policy · Certificate authority
Data transfer · Town management application

1 Introduction

The Internet of Things (IoT) technologies are play a central role in modern wireless telecommunications, with the development of smart devices, such as environmental sensors and wearable devices for health monitoring, which are called IoT devices. The vast amount of data generated by IoT devices have been used for the prediction of the state of an individual and her surrounding conditions, and moreover the organic integration of heterogeneous data is expected to unlock the potential for more beneficial analysis [7]. Thus, decentralized multi-cloud environments draw increasing attention [4,12,14–16].

© Springer Nature Singapore Pte Ltd. 2018
I. You et al. (Eds.): MobiSec 2016, CCIS 797, pp. 143–153, 2018.
https://doi.org/10.1007/978-981-10-7850-7_13

The iKaaS (intelligent Knowledge-as-a-Service) platforms is one of such environments [6], where a global cloud and existing cloud systems called local clouds are hierarchically arranged. The data on the local clouds are unitarily managed by the global cloud as knowledge, which allows applications to access data all over the world transparently. However, when transferring personal data to applications in different countries, the iKaaS platform must comply with the regulations governing data usage in the country or countries in question. These regulations give different definitions regarding personal data, and the rules for data transfer are different between countries as well [1,3,11]. While early technical studies [5,8,12] on security for decentralized environments have not addressed this kind of privacy issues, Hidano et al. have proposed an access control mechanism capable of flexibly controlling the access permissions of cross-border applications while observing relevant regulations [10]. In this model, a privacy certificate authority (CA) is established for each country as the executive agency responsible for the national regulations governing the handling of personal data. The security gateway refers the privacy certificate issued by the privacy CA in the country where the application exists, and the security policy configured by the privacy CA in the country where the local cloud is set up, in order to interpret the regulations in both countries. However, Hidano et al. did not provide a way to configure access permissions for the applications in a union, a city, or other area. Since the regulations for a union already exist, such as the EU directive [1,3], and it is quite possible that, in the future, the regulations will be established in a city or another area because of growing recent concerns about privacy, the access control mechanism proposed by Hidano et al. would become less applicable in real world situations.

The main contribution of this paper is to apply a new access control mechanism based on a hierarchical model of multiple privacy CAs in [9] to an actual application on the iKaaS platform. The rest of the paper is organized as follows: Sect. 2 overviews the functional capabilities of the iKaaS platform and our contributions. Section 3 provides an architecture of hierarchical privacy CAs on the iKaaS platform and explains the cooperating functions. Section 4 describes a use case of our access control mechanism while focusing on a town management application as an application on the iKaaS platform. Section 5 concludes this paper.

2   iKaaS Platform

Intelligent Knowledge-as-a-Service (iKaaS) aims to unitarily manage the data on the existing cloud systems to provide them as knowledge to the various types of applications with sufficient consideration for security and privacy. In this section, we present an overview of the iKaaS platform and access control for cross-border applications on the iKaaS platform, followed by the contributions made by our work.

2.1   Overview

The iKaaS platform is designed according to the architecture shown in Fig. 1, which is characterized by a hierarchical structure of a global cloud and local clouds. The local clouds are existing cloud systems scratched all over the world, and each local cloud manages various types of data obtained from IoT devices in its own databases called local cloud DBs. A local cloud DB may contain the data from existing databases constructed for other services as well. The query function is introduced to absorb the difference of formats of queries and data. The global cloud has two functions: *resource management* and *data processing*. The resource manager supports the application find out the location of its desired data. In order to realize this function, the global cloud has a catalog on the correspondence relationship between available data and the addresses of local cloud DBs where the data are stored. In addition, the global cloud provides the statistically processed data to the application depending on its request. The iKaaS platform can produce more useful knowledge by analysis using massive-scale and heterogeneous data [2]. Meanwhile, it has a kind of privacy issues. IoT data containing sensitive information of an individual must be dealt with in accordance with the national regulations governing the handling of personal data. In particular, there is the case when data transfer to other countries is legally prohibited. Each local cloud is thus required to install a security gateway at the touch point with the global cloud. The security gateway controls access by the application while observing relevant regulations.

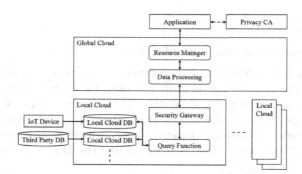

Fig. 1. iKaaS platform.

2.2   Access Control for Cross-Border Application

Hidano et al. have proposed an access control mechanism using a certification called a privacy certificate and a security policy for the iKaaS platform (see [10] for details). They are utilized to control access by the cross-border application under the regulations related to personal data both for the country where the application exists and the country where the local cloud is set up. In order to realize this function in the model of Hidano et al., the privacy CA is established

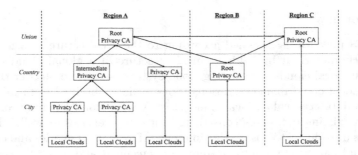

Fig. 2. Architecture of hierarchical privacy CAs.

for each country as the executive agency responsible for the national regulations governing the handling of personal data. The privacy CA on the application side issues the privacy certificate to the application, and the privacy CA on the local cloud side formulates the security policy in the local cloud. When requesting access to a local cloud in a different country, the application presents the privacy certificate to the security gateway. The security gateway uses the privacy certificate to confirm that the application is capable of handling personal data in accordance with the national regulations in the country where the application exists, and refers to the security policy to determine whether to provide the data stored in its local cloud to the application on the basis of the national regulations in the country where the local cloud is set up. After the verification process, the security gateway issues a token to allow the application to access the local cloud.

2.3   Our Contributions

The contributions of our work are as follows:

- We design a hierarchical model consisting of multiple privacy CAs [9]. In this model, the privacy CA is built not only for each country but also for each regulation related to personal data. The privacy certificate is created by multiple privacy CAs in the same region where the application exists while their signatures are added. Thereby the security gateway can confirm the regulations of each area, such as a union like the EU, a country, or a city, simply by referencing a privacy certificate.
- We apply a new access control mechanism using the hierarchical privacy CAs to a use case of iKaaS platform, namely, a town management application. By showing snapshots of the town management application that we developed, we demonstrate access control on the iKaaS platform.

3   Hierarchical Privacy CAs

We propose a hierarchical model of multiple privacy CAs responsible for the different regulations governing the handling of personal data. In this section, we present the architecture of the hierarchical model, and then describe cooperation among the privacy CAs.

3.1 Architecture of Hierarchical Model

Figure 2 shows the architecture for the hierarchical privacy CAs. The privacy CA is built for each area where regulations governing the handling of personal data are effective, such as a union like the EU, country, or city. Our hierarchical model is segmented into regions, and each region consists of three types of privacy CAs: the root privacy CA, intermediate privacy CA, and bottom privacy CA. The root privacy CA is responsible for regulations where the effective area is the largest in the region. If a union establishes regulations that are effective across the entire union, the privacy CA responsible for the regulations is the root privacy CA, like region A or region C in Fig. 2. Each region has a root privacy CA. If there is no union in the region, or the union has no regulations related to personal data, and if the country has regulations, the privacy CA responsible for the national regulation is the root privacy CA, such as region B in Fig. 2. The intermediate privacy CA is responsible for regulations where the effective area is smaller than that for which the root privacy CA is responsible and larger than that for which the bottom privacy CA is responsible. There may be cases when multiple intermediate privacy CAs are built into different layers of the path on a continuum from a root privacy CA to a bottom privacy CA. The bottom privacy CA is the privacy CA where the effective area is the smallest in the path. Each path has a bottom privacy CA. If there is no privacy CA in the lower layers from the root privacy CA, such as regions B and C in Fig. 2, the root privacy CA also plays the role of the bottom privacy CA. The root privacy CA communicates with all root privacy CAs in the other regions and the privacy CAs in the one-level lower layer in the same region. The intermediate privacy CA communicates with the privacy CAs in the one-level upper layer and the one-level lower layer on the same path. The bottom privacy CA communicates with the privacy CA in the one-level upper layer on the same path and the local clouds in the area where its regulations are in effect.

3.2 Cooperation Among Privacy CAs

The privacy CA has two functions: the issuance of the privacy certificate to applications and the configuration of security policies referenced by security gateways:

Issuance of privacy certificate. The privacy certificate is used by the security gateway to confirm that the application is capable of handling personal data in accordance with regulations governing personal data. When receiving a request to access personal data in a different region from the application, privacy CAs of the region where the application exists determine whether the application can handle the personal data on the basis of their regulations, and then issues the privacy certificate to the application. In our model, the requirement is that the application is issued a privacy certificate by privacy CAs before requesting data in local clouds in a different region.

The privacy certificate is created in cooperation with the privacy CAs on the path from the bottom privacy CA that the application requests to the root privacy CA in the same region. After receiving the request from the application, the bottom privacy CA first checks whether the application satisfies the requirements to handle the desired personal data. If there are no problems with the application, an initial privacy certificate is created and passed to the root privacy CA via intermediate privacy CAs. In this process, the intermediate privacy CAs and the root privacy CA check the privacy certificate on the basis of their regulations. The security gateway can then confirm that the application is capable of handling the personal data in compliance with all the relevant regulations on the application side by referencing a privacy certificate.

We present an example of parameters listed on the privacy certificate:

- *CA Names:* The names of the privacy CAs that checked this privacy certificate.
- *Application ID:* The identifier of the application. On the security policy to which the security gateway refers, the access permissions are set for each application ID.
- *Application IP:* The IP address of the application. It may be used by the security gateway to authenticate the application.
- *App. Data Categories:* The types of data that the application deals with, such as location information, environmental information, health information, etc. Multiple values can be specified.
- *Expiry Date:* The expiry date of the privacy certificate.
- *Application PK:* The public key of the application. The key is used to verify the authenticity of the application when the security gateway issues a token to the application. The token is issued after being encrypted with this key and the application is required to decrypt it with the corresponding private key.

However, with just the above parameters, the security gateway cannot confirm that the privacy certificate is created by the correct privacy CAs. In order to resolve this problem, Hidano et al. introduced a method based on the signature of the privacy CA [10]. In this way, before issuing the privacy certificate to the application, the privacy CA generates the signature using its private key and adds it to the privacy certificate. Then, the security gateway verifies the signature using the public key of the privacy CA, which is distributed to the application in advance. We extend the method for our hierarchical model. In our model, all the privacy CAs that verify the privacy certificate add their signatures to the privacy certificate. When passing the privacy certificate to the next privacy CA, the privacy CA sends its public key as well. The next privacy CA generates the signature by encrypting the public key of the previous privacy CA using its private key. This process is repeated until the privacy certificate is passed to the root privacy CA on the application side, and then the privacy certificate is returned to the application. The security gateway can thereby verify the validity of the privacy certificate by using a public key of the root privacy CA. Additionally, we introduce a process whereby the privacy certificate is passed from the application to the root privacy CA in the region of the local

Fig. 3. Data structure of privacy certificate.

cloud which the application wants to access. This is in contrast to the model of Hidano et al., where the privacy CA on the application side did not cooperate with the privacy CA for the local cloud when creating the privacy certificate. The signature of the root privacy CA on the local cloud side is also added to the privacy certificate. This is because the method of distributing the public key to the security gateway directly by the privacy CA on the application side is not efficient, as the privacy CA is required to manage all the security gateways in the different regions. In our method, the privacy CAs on the local cloud side distribute the public key to the security gateway. This key distribution process is performed at the same time as the configuration of the security policy (see the next paragraph for details). The public key of the root privacy CA is also distributed to the other root privacy CAs in advance. On the privacy certificate, in addition to the above parameters, the following parameters are listed:

- *Signatures:* The signatures of the bottom privacy CA, intermediate privacy CAs, and root privacy CA on the application side, and the signature of the root privacy CA on the local cloud side.
- *CA PKs:* The public keys of the bottom privacy CA, intermediate privacy CAs, and root privacy CA on the application side.

Figure 3 is the data structure of the privacy certificate. The root privacy CA on the local cloud side also checks the privacy certificate on the basis of the regulations related to the transfer of personal data in its own area when receiving a request for its signature, and determines whether to provide the data that are classified under the categories specified by the parameter *App. Data Categories* listed on the privacy certificate. The only categories that the application can access are extracted from the categories specified by the parameter *App. Data Categories*, and listed on the privacy certificate as the values of the parameter *LC Data Categories*.

Configuration of security policy. The bottom privacy CA manages the local clouds with personal data in its own area. After adding the signature to the privacy certificate, the root privacy CA on the local cloud side informs the bottom privacy CAs of the values of parameters listed on the privacy certificate via the intermediate privacy CAs. Each bottom privacy CA configures the security policies of relevant local clouds on the basis of the information instead of the

Table 1. Security policy.

Application ID	Data category 1	$\cdots$	Data category N
A	7 days	$\cdots$	0
B	2 weeks	$\cdots$	0
$\vdots$	$\vdots$	$\ddots$	$\vdots$

Fig. 4. VR walkthrough for town management.

root privacy CA. Table 1 shows an example of the security policy. The expiry periods of the access permissions are defined in the security policy. The expiry periods are set on the basis of the value of the parameter *Expiry Date* listed on the privacy certificate or from the viewpoint of security. At the same time, the public key of the root privacy CA on the local cloud side is also distributed to the security gateway via the intermediate privacy CAs and the bottom privacy CA. Cooperation among privacy CAs reduces the number of local clouds that a privacy CA manages, achieving the load distribution of the privacy CA.

4   Access Control for Town Management Application

Focusing on a town management application as a use case of the iKaaS platform, we demonstrate our access control mechanism. We first give an explanation of our town management application, and then present a visual representation of how access control works for this use case.

4.1   Town Management Application

Town management applications aim to provide useful support tools for town management organization personnel to help them with their daily activities related to town management tasks [13]. The iKaaS components are utilized to assess the town's conditions by obtaining diverse kinds of sensor data from installed sensors in the town, by storing data in appropriate databases and by retrieving the data sets from the databases based on the queries from the application. The components are also utilized to merge, process statistically, and analyze

Fig. 5. Privacy certificate for the town management application that works in Spain and accesses data in Japan.

the data sets to meet requirements for utilization of the application. The application converts results from the data sets to the context of the town's situation, and provides presentation of the context in a user-friendly and realistic manner, such as virtual reality (VR) or augmented reality (AR) representation. As an example, we developed a town management application having the functionality to confirm environmental conditions in a town by performing a walkthrough in a VR environment. Figure 4 is a snapshot of our application when a certain time is specified. We can monitor the data obtained from environment sensors installed outdoors by using this application. When clicking a cube on a building in Fig. 4, we can also observe the data obtained by the environment sensors installed inside the building.

4.2 Access Control by Security Gateway

Here let us consider that a company in Spain uses the town management application of Fig. 4 to provide town management services to a town in Japan. In this case, the town management application in Spain retrieves the data stored in the local cloud in Japan. We also assume that the transfer of personal data in Japan to any other country is prohibited. In this scenario, the privacy certificate of Fig. 5 is issued to the town management application. Geospatial information, such as CityGML data, is used for the VR representation of the town. The outdoor environment category includes the data obtained from sensors installed on the outside of buildings, and the indoor environment category includes the data obtained from sensors located inside the buildings. Since data such as indoor temperature and indoor humidity can be considered to be personal data, the indoor environment category is not listed in *LC Data Categories* of the privacy certificate. In addition, the security policy is formulated as Table 2. For the same reason, the value zero is set for the indoor environment category of Spain. Figure 6 shows the result from access control on the iKaaS platform. Although the composition of Fig. 6 is the same as that of Fig. 4, there is no cube on the buildings in Fig. 6. This means that the user cannot observe any sensor data obtained from inside the buildings, and Fig. 6 indicates that access control is conducted properly.

Table 2. Security policy for the town management application in Spain.

Application ID	Geospatial information	Outdoor environment	Indoor environment
Town management	7 days	7 days	0

Fig. 6. Effect of security gateway.

5   Conclusion

The Intelligent Knowledge-as-a-Service (iKaaS) platform unitarily manages the data on existing cloud systems, and provides them as knowledge to various types of applications with sufficient consideration for security and privacy. On the iKaaS platform, queries and data are all exchanged through a security gateway installed at the entrance of each cloud system. We introduced a hierarchical model comprising multiple privacy certificate authorities (CAs) to the iKaaS platform. A privacy CA is established for each regulation related to personal data as its executive agency, and issues a privacy certificate to the application in cooperation with other privacy CAs. The privacy certificate is used by the security gateway to confirm that the application is capable of handling personal data in accordance with the regulations. Our hierarchical model allows the security gateway to configure the access permissions of the application for each union (such as the EU), each county, or each city. Additionally, we demonstrated our access control mechanism while focusing on a town management application as a use case of the iKaaS platform.

Acknowledgments. The work is supported by the EUJ-1-2014 Research and Innovation action: iKaaS; EU Grant number 643262, Strategic Information and Communications R&D Promotion Programme (SCOPE), Ministry of Internal Affairs and Communications, Japan.

References

1. Article 29 Data Protection Working Party: Opinion 8/2014 on the on Recent Developments on the Internet of Things (2014)
2. Bantouna, A., Poulios, G., Tsagkaris, K., Demestichas, P.: Network load predictions based on big data and the utilization of self-organizing maps. Springer J. Netw. Syst. Manage. **22**(2), 150–173 (2014)
3. EU: Directive 95/46/EC of the European Parliament and of the Council of 24 October 1995 on the protection of individuals with regard to the processing of personal data and on the free movement of such data (1995)
4. EU FP7/ICT project 287708: iCore: Internet Connected Objects for Reconfigurable Eco-systems, October 2011–September 2014
5. EU FP7/ICT project 609094: RERUM: REliable, Resilient and secUre IoT for sMart city applications, September 2013–August 2016
6. EU HORIZON 2020 project 643262: iKaaS: intelligent Knowledge-as-a-Service, October 2014–September 2017
7. Faye, S., Louveton, N., Gheorghe, G., Engel, T.: A two-level approach to characterizing human activities from wearable sensor data. J. Wirel. Mobile Netw. **7**(3), 102–110 (2016)
8. Hernandez-Ramos, J.L., Jara, A.J., Marin, L., Skarmeta, A.F.: Distributed capability-based access control for the internet of things. J. Internet Serv. Inf. Secur. (JISIS) **3**(34), 1–16 (2013)
9. Hidano, S., Biswas, A.R., Kiyomoto, S.: Hierarchical privacy CAs for cross-border transfer of personal data. Res. Briefs Inf. Commun. Technol. Evol. (ReBICTE) **2**(2), 1–12 (2016)
10. Hidano, S., Kiyomoto, S., Murakami, Y., Vlacheas, P., Moessner, K.: Design of a security gateway for iKaaS platform. In: Zhang, Y., Peng, L., Youn, C.-H. (eds.) CloudComp 2015. LNICST, vol. 167, pp. 323–333. Springer, Cham (2016). https://doi.org/10.1007/978-3-319-38904-2_34
11. Japan: Act on the Protection of Personal Information, Act No. 57, 30 May 2003
12. de Meer, H., Pöhls, H.C., Posegga, J., Samelin, K.: On the relation between redactable and sanitizable signature schemes. In: Jürjens, J., Piessens, F., Bielova, N. (eds.) ESSoS 2014. LNCS, vol. 8364, pp. 113–130. Springer, Cham (2014). https://doi.org/10.1007/978-3-319-04897-0_8
13. Pokric, B., Krco, S., Drajic, D., Pokric, M., Rajs, V., Mihajlovic, Z., Knezevic, P., Jovanovic, D.: Augmented reality enabled IoT services for environmental monitoring utilising serious gaming concept. J. Wirel. Mobile Netw. Ubiquit. Comput. Dependable Appl. (JoWUA) **6**(1), 37–55 (2015)
14. Poncela, J., Vlacheas, P., Giaffreda, R., De, S., Vecchio, M., Nechifor, S., Barco, R., Aguayo-Torres, M.C., Stavroulaki, V., Moessner, K., Demestichas, P.: Smart cities via data aggregation. Springer J. Wirel. Personal Commun. **76**(2), 149–168 (2014)
15. Robles, T., Alcarria, R., Martin, D., Navarro, M., Calero, R., Iglesias, S., Lopez, M.: An IoT based reference architecture for smart water management processes. J. Wirel. Mobile Netw. Ubiquit. Comput. Dependable Appl. (JoWUA) **6**(1), 4–23 (2015)
16. Vlacheas, P., Giaffreda, R., Stavroulaki, V., Kelaidonis, D., Somov, A., Foteinos, V., Poulios, G., Biswas, A.R., Moessner, K., Demestichas, P.: Enabling smart cities through a cognitive management framework for the internet of things. IEEE Commun. Mag. **51**(6), 102–110 (2013)

Security Analysis Oriented Physical Components Modeling in Quantum Key Distribution

Xilong Mao[1], Yan Li[1], Yan Peng[1], and Baokang Zhao[1,2,3(✉)]

[1] College of Computer, National University of Defense Technology, Changsha 410073, China
mxilong@263.net, 9375422@qq.com, {pengyan15,bkzhao}@nudt.edu.cn
[2] Guangxi Colleges and Universities Key Laboratory of Cloud Computing and Complex Systems,
Guilin University of Electronic Technology, Guilin 541004, China
[3] Guangxi Cooperative Innovation Center of Cloud Computing and Big Data,
Guilin University of Electronic Technology, Guilin 541004, China

Abstract. Quantum Key Distribution (QKD), based on fundamental principles of quantum mechanics, plays an irreplaceable role in national defense, financial and government affairs. Security analysis of QKD system is of great importance. However, existing studies on modeling QKD system are theory analysis based. In this paper, we propose a **S**imulation **S**ystem of **P**hysical **C**omponents (SSPC) in QKD system which modeling the three key modules: single photon source, quantum channel and single photon detector, it could generate the simulated key resemble to real QKD physical system and its parameters of the physical components are configurable. Therefore, solution can be deployed in different QKD physical systems.

Keywords: QKD · Security analysis · Physical components · Modeling

1 Introduction

Quantum key distribution (QKD) [1], based on fundamental principles of quantum mechanics, is unconditionally secure while traditional cryptography has some security problems to be solved [2–4]. QKD plays an irreplaceable role in national defense, financial and government affairs. Field-test demonstrations of QKD networks have been conducted [5–13].

QKD is practical in the field of secure mobile communication. Liu et al. integrated QKD and VoIP steganography to build a QPhone [14] which can provide efficient and real-time security protections. Rima et al. proposed an enhanced scheme for deriving a secured encryption key for WLAN using QKD [15]. Morio et al. proposed a simple polarization tracking method enables free-space quantum cryptography between mobile terminals [16]. Michael et al. have evaluated the status of QKD regarding its practical applicability for securing mobile communication networks [17].

Security analysis based modeling of QKD system is of great importance in Quantum Communication. As shown in Fig. 1, the structure of a typical QKD system consists of two sub-system, physical sub-system and post-processing sub-system [18]. The physical subsystem consists of several physical components: single photon source, quantum

© Springer Nature Singapore Pte Ltd. 2018
I. You et al. (Eds.): MobiSec 2016, CCIS 797, pp. 154–163, 2018.
https://doi.org/10.1007/978-981-10-7850-7_14

channel, and a single photon detector. In the physical sub-system, Both of the two parties (always called Alice and Bob) have Quantum Random Number Generator (QRNG) module, synchronization module, control module, and optical module. The QRNG module is used to generate real random number, the synchronization module is used to realize the time synchronization between Alice and Bob, the control module is used to control the single photon source and the single photon detector and the optical module is used to transmit the photon pulse. As a sender, Alice has laser module. As a receiver, Bob has single photon detector module. Alice and Bob is connected with quantum channel. The raw key is generated between the two physical subsystems through QKD protocol such as BB84 [1], and then it will be sent to the post-processing subsystem. In the post-processing subsystem, there are four procedures: authentication, sifting, information reconciliation and privacy amplification. In the authentication procedure, the public key method (such as RSA [19]) is used to verify the identity of the parties. In the sifting procedure, Alice and Bob check the base they used and discard the key bit corresponding to the different base. In the information reconciliation procedure, information reconciliation algorithm (such as BBBSS [20], Cascade [21], Winnow [22] and LDPC [23]) is used to correct the error bits between Alice and Bob. In the privacy amplification procedure, privacy amplification algorithm (such as Toeplitz [24]) is used to improve the security of the final key.

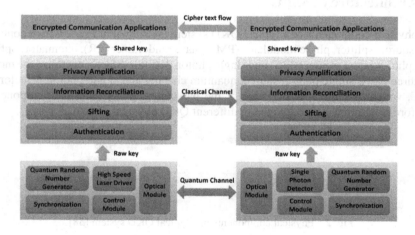

Fig. 1. Structure of a typical QKD system

After the post-processing procedures, the identical secret shared key will be generated for Alice and Bob. Then, Alice and Bob can use the shared key with One Time Pad (OTP) [25] algorithm to encrypt their communication data. Shannon has proved the OTP algorithm is unconditional security in 1949 [26], however, the high cost of the key prevent it from widely used. Now QKD has provide a perfect solution.

The real-world system implementations differ significantly from the ideal theoretical representations. Especially the single photon source and the detector have imperfections.

Therefore, a majority of existing studies on security analysis are not very practical [27–30]. Therefore, quantitatively analysis upon the real QKD system is very critical, especially to generate the data from the physical components.

Existing studies on modeling QKD systems are theory analysis based. Ryan et al. have proposed a framework based on OMNeT++ to model quantum optical components [31], Mailloux et al. have modeled a decoy state enabled QKD system to study the impact of practical limitations [32–35]. Morris et al. use discrete event system to model QKD system components [36, 37].

However, most of existing models are theoretical based which could not generate the data from the physical components. In this paper, we have developed a Simulation System of Physical Components (SSPC) in QKD. In this simulation system, we could configure the value of the parameters according to different physical system and get the simulated output. Our research is focused on getting the simulated data generated by the physical components, and the data is the simulated raw key. Therefore, we can use SSPC to get the raw key, and then conduct further research.

The structure of the paper is as follows. The architecture of SSPC is presented in Sect. 2. The principle and the output of SSPC is presented in Sect. 3. Conclusions are drawn at the end of the paper.

2   Architecture of SSPC

The physical components of a typical QKD system are shown in Fig. 2 which contains laser source, splitter, phase modulator (PM), phase randomizer (PR), attenuator, optical fiber, photon beam splitter (PBS) and single photon detector. SSPC generalize the model into three parts: single photon source, quantum channel and single photon detector. In SSPC, we can set the specific value of the parameters of the physical components, therefore, solution can be deployed in different QKD physical systems.

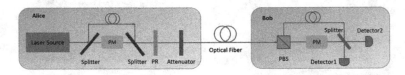

Fig. 2.   Physical components in a typical QKD system [38]

2.1   Mathematical Model of Single Photon Source

Laser is the most common used single photon source at the moment. Most QKD systems based on the BB84 protocol [1] choose the strong attenuated laser to be the single photon source. The output is approximately to be coherent state:

$$\left| \sqrt{\mu}e^{i\theta} \right\rangle \equiv \sqrt{\alpha} = e^{-\mu/2} \sum_{n=0}^{\infty} \frac{\alpha^n}{\sqrt{n!}} \sqrt{n}, \tag{1}$$

and

$$\mu = |\alpha^2| \tag{2}$$

is the average photon number. Suppose that the light emitted from Alice has been randomized in terms of phase, so the quantum state will be transformed into the mixture of the classical photon number:

$$\rho = \int_0^{2\pi} \frac{d\theta}{2\pi} |\alpha\rangle\langle\alpha| = \sum_n P(n|\mu)|n\rangle\langle\mu|, \tag{3}$$

with

$$P(n|\mu) = e^{-\mu}\frac{\mu^n}{n!} \tag{4}$$

2.2   Mathematical Model of Quantum Channel

Most QKD systems are based on the optical fiber, therefore, in this paper we only study the characteristics of fiber channel. Optical fiber loss is mainly described by two parameters: the loss coefficient a, the transmission loss of optical fiber transmission distance L:

$$\eta_{AB} = 10^{-\frac{\alpha L}{10}} \tag{5}$$

In the standard single-mode fiber, the lowest loss factor of the wavelength is 1550 nm, and the loss coefficient is 0.2 dB/km [38], which is the most commonly used fiber network communication wavelength. This wavelength is usually used in optical fiber QKD system.

2.3   Mathematical Model of Single Photon Detector

Discrete-variable protocols use photon-counters as detectors. There are three main characteristics: quantum efficiency h which represents the probability of a detector click when the detector is hit by a photon, and the dark-count rate pd describing the noise of the detector dark counts are events when a detector sends an impulse even if no photon has entered it, and the dead time td of the detector, which means the time it takes to reset the detector after a click.

Avalanche photodiodes (APD) can work at room temperature under the conditions of electric refrigeration, so it is wildly used. There are two kinds of APD, SiAPD and InGaAs-APD. Si-APD is suitable for free-space QKD, whose detection wavelength is between 400 nm to 1000 nm. InGaAs-APD is suitable for optical fiber QKD system, whose detection wavelength is between 950 nm to 1650 nm.

2.4   Quantum Bit Error Rate

Suppose the overall efficiency of the QKD system is η, then:

$$\eta = \eta_d \cdot \eta_{AB} \cdot \eta_B, \tag{6}$$

where η_d is the efficiency of the single photon detector, η_B is the internal transmission efficiency of Bob.

Suppose μ is the average photon number per pulse emitted by Alice, then the probability of a detector click by a signal photon is:

$$p_s = 1 - e^{\eta \mu}. \tag{7}$$

Suppose p_{dark} is the probability the detector click when no photon arrive, then:

$$p_{dark} = 2 \cdot DCR \cdot t_w, \tag{8}$$

Where DCR is the dark count rate of Bob's detector and t_w is the time window of the measurement of detector.

We use e_s to denote the baseline system error and use the e_d to denote the probability of a photon been erroneously detected, then the Quantum Bit Error Rate (QBER) is:

$$QBER = \frac{e_s \cdot p_s + e_d \cdot p_{dark}}{p_s + p_{dark}} \tag{9}$$

3   Software Simulation and Preliminary Results

As shown in Fig. 3, SSPC consists of two part, Alice side and Bob side. Both of them are composed of 3 modules, integrated physical components simulation module, data generation module and data transmission module. The function of the data generation module and the data transmission at Alice side and Bob side are the same. Random number is generated in the data generation module and is used to generate the codewords. The TCP/IP protocol stack is adopted in the module of data transmission to transmit the codewords. At Alice side, the integrated physical components simulation module consists of single photon source simulation sub-module and quantum states production sub-module, which are designed to simulate the preparation of single photon stream. At Bob side, we simulated the single photon detector and quantum channel in the integrated physical components simulation module.

We use the code word to store the information carried by the photon. As shown in Fig. 4, the code word of Alice consists of 8 bits. In the codeword of Alice, the eighth bit means the base used to generate the photon, which has two choices, 0 and 1; the seventh bit means the key to be carried by the photon, which has two choices, 0 and 1; the sixth and fifth bits means the type of state of the photon, which has three choices, 00, 01, 10, standing for vacuum state, signal state and decoy state respectively; the fourth bit to the first bit are padding. Therefore, there are 12 different code words at Alice side.

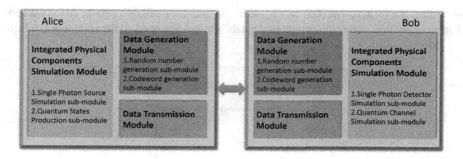

Fig. 3. Software structure of SSPC

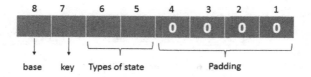

Fig. 4. Format of the codeword of Alice

As shown in Fig. 5, the code word of Bob consists of 8 bits. In the codeword of Bob, the eighth bit to the fourth bit are padding; the third and the second bits stand for the results of the detection of the photon which has three choices, 00, 01, 10; the first bit stands for the base used to detect the photon, which has two choices, 0 and 1. Therefore, there are 6 different code words at Bob side. For example, at Alice side, 10010000 stands for that the type of quantum state is signal, it is made by base 1, and the key it carried is 0.

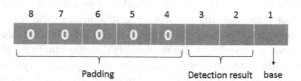

Fig. 5. Format of the codeword of Bob

The procedure of Alice side has four phases: configure phase, photon generation simulation phase, code word generation phase and data transmission phase. In the configure phase, before the program start, the value of the parameters of the physical components have to be set in the GUI (Graphical User Interface) of the server of SSPC which is shown in Fig. 6. We can click the "Reset" button to clear all the values been set. After all the parameters are set, we can click the "Start" button to start the server. In the photon generation simulation phase, first, Alice calculate the probability distribution of the photon type according to the parameters of the physical components. Next, Alice randomly select base and key of each photon according to the probability distribution. In the code word generation phase, Alice generate the code word for each photon according the format specified in Fig. 4. In the data transmission phase, Alice wait for Bob's connection. After the connection established, Alice send all the code word to Bob.

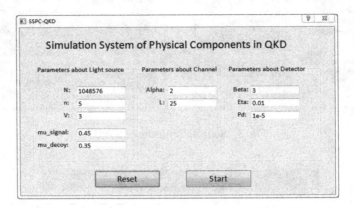

Fig. 6. The server of SSPC

The procedure of Bob side has eight phases: connection phase, data reception phase, pre-sift phase, base sifting phase, base sifting phase, calculation phase, post-sifting phase, photon detection simulation phase and code word generation phase.

In the connection phase and data reception phase, we set the IP address and port of Alice in the Bob side, Bob try to connect Alice and get the code word from Alice. In the pre-sifting phase, after Bob get all the code word, Bob discard the code word corresponding to the vacuum state and the decoy state. In the base sifting phase, Bob randomly choose each base used to measure each photon and discard the code word whose base is different between Alice and Bob. In the calculation phase, Bob calculate the QBER (Quantum Bit Error Rate) and the probability distribution of the measurement result using the parameters. In the post-sifting phase, Bob discard the code word whose measurement result is invalid according to the probability distribution. In the photon detection phase, Bob generate the detection results according to the probability distribution calculated in the calculation phase. In the code word generation phase, Bob generate the code word for each photon according to the format specified in Fig. 5.

The output of SSPC is shown in Fig. 7, the key of Alice is shown in the left and the key of Bob is shown in the right. The results are saved in hexadecimal according to the format in Figs. 4 and 5.

Fig. 7. Output of SSPC

4 Conclusion

In this paper, we propose a method to simulate the physical sub-system of QKD, which simulating the procedure of the production, transformation and detection of quantum states. Using this simulation system, we could get the simulated key ensemble to the data generated by real physical system. We could configure the value of the parameters according to different physical system in our simulating system. Therefore, solution can be deployed in different QKD physical systems.

Acknowledgments. This work was supported in part by National Science Foundation of China under grant No. 61202488, Guangxi Cooperative Innovation Center of cloud computing and Big Data (No. YD16801,YD16505.), and the outstanding young scholar funding of NUDT.

References

1. Bennett, C.H., Brassard, G.: Quantum cryptography: public key distribution and coin tossing. In: Proceedings of the Conference on Computers, Systems and Signal Processing, Bangalore, India, December 1984 (1984)
2. Chen, C., Anada, H., et al.: A hybrid encryption scheme with key-cloning protection: user/ terminal double authentication via attributes and fingerprints. J. Internet Serv. Inf. Secur. 6(2), 23–36 (2016)
3. Kurokawa, T., Nojima, R., Moriai, S.: On the security of CBC mode in SSL3.0 and TLS1.0. J. Internet Serv. Inf. Secur. 6(1), 2–19 (2016)
4. Peng, Y., Wu, C., Zhao, B., Yu, W., Liu, B., Qiao, S.: QKDFlow: QKD based secure communication towards the openflow interface in SDN. In: Yuan, H., Geng, J., Bian, F. (eds.) GRMSE 2016. CCIS, vol. 699, pp. 410–415. Springer, Singapore (2017). https://doi.org/10.1007/978-981-10-3969-0_45

5. Elliott, C., Colvin, A., Pearson, D., et al.: Current status of the DARPA quantum network. In: Proceedings of the Defense and Security. International Society for Optics and Photonics (2005)

6. Peev, M., Pacher, C., Alléaume, R., et al.: The SECOQC quantum key distribution network in Vienna. New J. Phys. **11**(7), 075001 (2009)

7. Chen, T.-Y., Liang, H., Liu, Y., et al.: Field test of a practical secure communication network with decoy-state quantum cryptography. Opt. Express **17**(8), 6540–6549 (2009)

8. Chen, T.-Y., Wang, J., Liang, H., et al.: Metropolitan all-pass and inter-city quantum communication network. Opt. Express **18**(26), 27217–27225 (2010)

9. Wang, S., Chen, W., Yin, Z.-Q., et al.: Field test of wavelength-saving quantum key distribution network. Opt. Lett. **35**(14), 2454–2456 (2010)

10. Sasaki, M., Fujiwara, M., Ishizuka, H., et al.: Field test of quantum key distribution in the Tokyo QKD network. Opt. Express **19**(11), 10387–10409 (2011)

11. Stucki, D., Legre, M., Buntschu, F., et al.: Long-term performance of the SwissQuantum quantum key distribution network in a field environment. New J. Phys. **13**(12), 123001 (2011)

12. Fröhlich, B., Dynes, J.F., Lucamarini, M., et al.: A quantum access network. Nature **501**(7465), 69–72 (2013)

13. Zhao, B., Liu, B., Wu, C., et al.: A novel NTT-based authentication scheme for 10-GHz quantum key distribution systems. IEEE Trans. Ind. Electron. **63**(8), 5101–5108 (2016)

14. Liu, B., Zhao, B., Wei, Z., et al.: Qphone: a quantum security VoIP phone. In: Proceedings of the ACM SIGCOMM Computer Communication Review. ACM (2013)

15. Djellab, R., Benmohammed, M.: Securing encryption key distribution in WLAN via QKD. In: 2012 International Conference on Proceedings of the Cyber-Enabled Distributed Computing and Knowledge Discovery (CyberC). IEEE (2012)

16. Toyoshima, M., Schaefer, C., Shoji, Y., et al.: Mobile quantum cryptography enhances secure communications

17. Marhoefer, M., Wimberger, I., Poppe, A.: Applicability of quantum cryptography for securing Mobile communication networks (2009)

18. Cui, K., Wang, J., Zhang, H.-F., et al.: A real-time design based on FPGA for expeditious error reconciliation in QKD system. Inf. Forensics Secur. IEEE Trans. **8**(1), 184–190 (2013)

19. Rivest, R.L., Shamir, A., Adleman, L.: A method for obtaining digital signatures and public-key cryptosystems. Commun. ACM **21**(2), 120–126 (1978)

20. Bennett, C.H., Bessette, F., Brassard, G., et al.: Experimental quantum cryptography. J. Cryptol. **5**(1), 3–28 (1992)

21. Brassard, G., Salvail, L.: Secret-Key reconciliation by public discussion. In: Helleseth, T. (ed.) EUROCRYPT 1993. LNCS, vol. 765, pp. 410–423. Springer, Heidelberg (1994). https://doi.org/10.1007/3-540-48285-7_35

22. Buttler, W., Lamoreaux, S., Torgerson, J., et al.: Fast, efficient error reconciliation for quantum (2002). 03.67: 2. http://lib-www.lanl.gov/cgi-bin/getfile?00796756.pdf

23. Gallager, R.G.: Low-density parity-check codes. Inf. Theor. IRE Trans. **8**(1), 21–28 (1962)

24. Walenta, N., Burg, A., Caselunghe, D., et al.: A Fast and versatile QKD system with hardware key distillation and wavelength multiplexing (2013). arXiv preprint arXiv:13092583

25. Vernam, G.S.: Cipher printing telegraph systems for secret wire and radio telegraphic communications. Trans. Am. Inst. Electr. Eng. **XLV**(2), 295–301 (1926)

26. Shannon, C.E.: Communication theory of secrecy systems. Bell Syst. Technical J. **28**(4), 656–715 (1949)

27. Koashi, M., Preskill, J.: Secure quantum key distribution with an uncharacterized source. Phys. Rev. Lett. **90**(5), 057902 (2003)

28. Shor, P.W., Preskill, J.: Simple proof of security of the BB84 quantum key distribution protocol. Phys. Rev. Lett. **85**(2), 441 (2000)
29. Baiardi, F., Tonelli, F., Isoni, L.: Application vulnerabilities in risk assessment and management. J. Wirel. Mob. Netw. Ubiquit. Comput. Dependable Appl. (JoWUA) **7**(2), 41–59 (2016)
30. Lim, K., Jeong, Y., Cho, S.-J., et al.: An android application protection scheme against dynamic reverse engineering attacks. J. Wirel. Mob. Netw. Ubiquit. Comput. Dependable Appl. (JoWUA) **7**(3), 40–52 (2016)
31. Engle, R.D., Hodson, D.D., Grimaila, M.R., et al.: Modeling quantum optical components, pulses and fiber channels using OMNeT++. arXiv preprint arXiv:150903091 (2015)
32. Mailloux, L., Engle, R., Grimaila, M., et al.: Modeling decoy state quantum key distribution systems. J. Defense Model. Simul. Appl. Methodol. Technol. **12**(4), 489–506 (2015)
33. Mailloux, L., Grimaila, M., Hodson, D., et al.: A model and simulation framework for studying implementation non-idealities in quantum key distribution systems. IEEE Access **3**, 110–130 (2015)
34. Mailloux, L.O., Grimaila, M.R., Hodson, D.D., et al.: Modeling continuous time optical pulses in a quantum key distribution discrete event simulation. In: Proceedings of the International Conference on Security and Management (SAM). The Steering Committee of The World Congress in Computer Science, Computer Engineering and Applied Computing (WorldComp) (2014)
35. Mailloux, L.O., Morris, J.D., Grimaila, M.R., et al.: A modeling framework for studying quantum key distribution system implementation nonidealities. Access **3**, 110–130 (2015). IEEE
36. Morris, J.D.: Conceptual modeling of a quantum key distribution simulation framework using the discrete event system specification. Air Force Institute of Technology (2014)
37. Morris, J.D., Grimaila, M.R., Hodson, D.D., et al.: Using the discrete event system specification to model quantum key distribution system components. J. Defense Model. Simul. Appl. Methodol. Technol. **12**(4), 457–480 (2015)
38. Xu, B.: The Practical Security of Quantum Key Distribution System. Peking University (2012)

A Novel Hybrid Architecture for High Speed Regular Expression Matching

Chengcheng Xu[1], Baokang Zhao[1(✉)], Shuhui Chen[1], and Jinshu Su[1,2]

[1] College of Computer, National University of Defense Technology,
No. 137, Yanwachi Street, Changsha 410073, Hunan, China
{xuchengcheng,bkzhao,shchen,sjs}@nudt.edu.cn
[2] National Key Laboratory for Parallel and Distributed Processing,
National University of Defense Technology, Changsha 410073, China

Abstract. Mobile devices play an important role in our everyday lives, but they also bring great security threats. Deep packet inspection (DPI) is one of the most efficient methods to detect the malicious information hidden in the mobile traffic, and regular expression matching is widely used in DPI for its powerful expressive ability. However, with the increasing complexity of regular expressions, traditional solutions cannot meet the requirements of both storage and high performance. In this paper, we propose a novel hybrid matching architecture and two-stage memory architecture for the state of the art hybrid FA to solve this problem. Experiment results confirm that our architecture is scalable to complex rule sets, and the matching performance outperforms state of the art memory centric solution by up to 15x.

Keywords: Deep packet inspection · Regular expression matching
Hybrid matching architecture

1 Introduction

Nowadays, mobile devices are an important part of our everyday lives since they provide accesses to ubiquitous services [14, 24–27]. On the other hand, the widely used mobile devices also incur many serious attacks, thus encountering great security challenges. Current mobile network also requires DPI technologies to detect malicious attacks hidden in the traffics. Regular expression matching is widely used in deep packet inspection applications, such as protocol identification, antivirus system, network instruction detection system, etc. The matching process is to inspect the packet payloads to check whether they contain the signatures that predefined by regular expressions.

Traditional method is to convert the signatures to an equivalent nondeterministic finite automata (NFA) or deterministic finite automata (DFA) for automatic processing. NFA is space-efficient with the linear memory complexity of $O(mn)$, where m is the number of regular expressions and n is the average rule length, but the processing complexity for a payload byte maybe up to

© Springer Nature Singapore Pte Ltd. 2018
I. You et al. (Eds.): MobiSec 2016, CCIS 797, pp. 164–174, 2018.
https://doi.org/10.1007/978-981-10-7850-7_15

$O(n^2m)$. On the other hand, DFA has a much better $O(1)$ time processing cost, but the conversion from NFA to DFA may blow up the number of states (state explosion), resulting in a space consumption which can be as large as $O(2^{nm})$. In many practical cases, like NIDS of Snort [5], Bro [2], and Linux application protocol classifier [1] (L7-filter), the integrated DFA can even not be generated under moderate platforms. Hence, both NFA and DFA are not able to provide desirable performance for complex rule sets with moderate platforms. In this paper, we focus on the representative situations where the DFA is not feasible.

As DFA has an excellent matching speed with $O(1)$ time complexity, many researches still focus on DFA based matching. For practical implementation, massive compression algorithms has been proposed to reduce the space requirement of DFA. State transition table is the main data structure of DFA, and it is a two-dimensional matrix, where the rows indicate the DFA states and the columns represent the input characters and each element in the matrix indicates the next transition state for the corresponding DFA state and input character. Resulting from the powerful expressive ability, a lot of redundancy exists in the state transition table. DFA compression is to substitute the state transition table with a more space-saving data structure. According to compression position, the compression algorithms can be divided into state merging algorithms [6], alphabet re-encoding algorithms [8,11] and transition compression algorithms [9,13,15,17,18,23]. Sophisticated algorithms can achieve a compression ratio as high as 95%, but they still can not keep up with the exponential state expansion. In addition, they are not suitable for the situations where state explosion occurs.

In the recent years, researches have concentrated on the DFA state explosion problem, and a series of automatons [7,12,16,19–22] have been proposed to substitute the traditional DFA. However, most of these automatons only provide a simple computation mode, and they even have no comprehensive construction method. The hybrid-FA [7] is a practical automaton lays between NFA and DFA, it terminates the DFA construction algorithm and generates the automaton with a head DFA and a number of tail NFAs. As far as we know, the hybrid-FA is one of the most practical automatons among current representative solutions [7,12,16,19–22]. It achieves a good compromise between memory consumption and matching efficiency, and even the commercial network processors like Cavium's octeon5860 [4] and Broadcom's XLP7XX/9XX [3] also leverage the similar automatons for deep packet inspection.

However, for efficient matching in practice, it still encounters two limitations: (1) Even the DFA part is fast enough, the overall performance is severely limited by the tail NFAs, because the active DFA state and NFA state(s) must be processed synchronously; (2) For efficient processing, the automatons should be deployed on fast on-chip memories. But the head DFA is usually too big for the fast on-chip memories. Thus they can be only deployed on slow off-chip memories like DDR3 SDRAM, which costs hundreds of cycles for each memory access.

In this paper, we proposed a hybrid matching engine architecture and two-stage memory architecture to solve these problems. The hybrid engine architecture can divide the DFA processing and NFA processing into independent stages, thus to omit the limitations from NFA bottleneck. The two-stage memory architecture leverages the access model of DFA states to deploy a few hot states into fast memories, thus to significantly improve the overall DFA processing.

With this mechanism, the hardware engines can focus on the efficient and regular DFA matching and leave the inefficient and irregular NFA matching to software engines. More important, the original integrated process is divided into two independent stages which can be pipelined. Experimental results show that the matching performance of the hybrid architecture outperforms state of the art memory centric solution by up to 15x.

To summarize, our contributions are (1) a novel hybrid regular expression matching architecture with FPGA and multi-core processors, (2) the two-stage memory architecture for hardware engines based on memory centric FPGA, (3) simulation experiments are conducted with three practical rule sets to demonstrate its superiority.

2   Key Findings and Motivations

Hybrid-FA is a practical automaton that suitable for implementation on multi-core platforms with multi-threaded software engines. Each thread processes one packet or flow, and the procedure starts from the initial DFA state. Each time it reads one byte from the input stream, then it inquires the state transition table for the next active state. Once any NFA state is activated, the engine must handle the active NFA state set synchronously with the active DFA state for each input byte. The next input byte can not be processed until both the active DFA state and active NFA state set have been handled. Our first observation is that, the NFA processing is much more time-consuming than DFA, and the thread must wait for the completion of NFA updating before the next input character processing. Thus, even the DFA part can be processed efficiently, the overall throughput is still seriously limited by the tail NFA part. Based on the above analysis, if the tedious NFA processing can be detached from the efficient DFA matching, the overall performance should be significantly improved.

The second observation is that, the matching process is a series of memory accesses in nature. Thus, the matching speed highly depends on the memory access latency. Fast on-chip memories provide preferable access speed, but their space is very limited in moderate platforms, usually not more than 10M byte. The DFA part is usually too large (hundreds of thousands to millions states) to be deployed on these memories in practice. In general, the DFA can only be deployed on large off-chip memories, such as DDR3 SDRAM, but these memories consume as many as hundreds of cycles for each memory access. In addition, the memory accesses must be sequential because the next active state depends on the current active state and input symbol, thus the high-throughput burst access in DDR3 SDRAM is useless.

In fact, there exists some hot states for each automaton, and these hot states occupy most of the memory access during the pattern matching process.

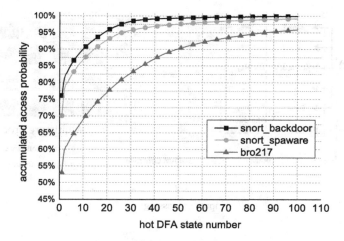

Fig. 1. Access probability for hot DFA states

Figure 1 illustrates the accumulated state access probabilities of hot DFA states for three public rule sets. The abscissa indicates the hot state number, and these states are sorted based on descending order of their memory access probabilities. As we can see, several few hot states occupy the overwhelming majority of DFA accesses. The first 30 hot states of backdoor rule set even occupy 97% of the overall memory accesses. As the bro217 rule set contains much more simple patterns, the concentration degree of hot states is not as good as backdoor and spyware rule set. Even though, it still reaches 90% for the first 50 hot states, and 95% for the first 90 hot states. In addition, this access distribution law is universal for various signature sets and trace files, interested readers may refer to our previous publications [10] for more details. As these tiny part of DFA states account for most memory accesses, if these hot states can be processed efficiently, the overall throughput of DFA matching should be greatly improved.

3   The Hybrid Matching Architecture

Based on the above observations, we propose the hybrid matching architecture and two stage memory architecture as shown in Fig. 2(a) to solve these problems. The whole matching system are composed of two parts: the FPGA part and the multi-core processors part. Parallel hardware matching engines are implemented on the FPGA platform, and parallel software matching threads are instantiated on the multi-core processors platform. The hardware engines and software engines work in parallel, a payload is first processed on a hardware engine, as long as any NFA state is activated, the rest payload bytes are sent to the software engines for the following processing. This hybrid architecture can leverage the pipeline to detach the inefficient NFA matching from the efficient DFA matching, thus providing a desirable performance improvement for hybrid-FA matching.

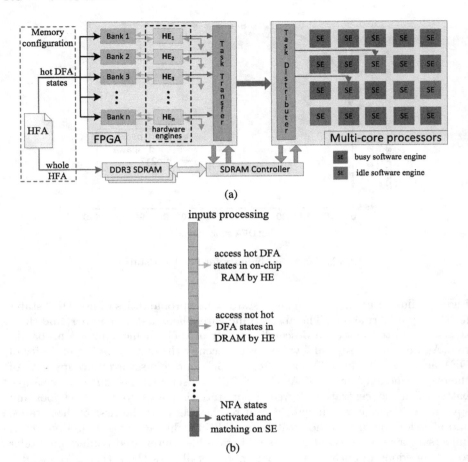

Fig. 2. The hybrid matching architecture and a simple matching example (Color figure online)

In this section, we first introduce the two-stage memory architecture to break the limitation of long memory access latency. Then, we present the hybrid matching architecture to break the bottleneck from the NFA part. The matching process is presented in detail, and the matching performance is also analyzed. Finally, we use real rule sets from L7, Snort and Bro to test the performance of different architectures.

3.1   Two-Stage Memory Architecture

The matching engines are composed of two parts, hardware engines (HE) on FPGA and software engines (SE) on multi-core processors, each hardware and software engine works independently and they shared the same DDR3 SDRAM. In addition, each HE is assigned with an exclusive on-chip RAM bank for fast memory access. The signature sets are compiled to a hybrid-FA according to the space of the DDR3 SDRAM, then the transition tables for some few hot DFA states (usually tens is enough) are deployed on each bank for each hardware engine, and the whole hybrid-FA is deployed on the DDR3 SDRAM. For more details about selection and deployment about hot states, readers may refer to our previous publication [10].

For each payload, first it is distributed to a hardware engine for the DFA part matching. The processing logic for the HE is very simple, it keeps the current active DFA state, each time it reads a payload byte and inquires the DFA state table in on-chip RAM or DDR3 SDRAM for the next state. As we have explained, most DFA state transition table accesses are about hot states which are deployed on the fast on-chip RAM, and each memory access only cost several cycles. Thus the overall matching throughput for the DFA part can achieve tens of Gbps with the two stage memory architecture and tens of hardware engines.

3.2   Hybrid and Asynchronous Matching Architecture

When only employing the hardware engines, once the NFA part is activated for a certain input byte, the engine must process the active DFA state and active NFA state(s) synchronously. However, the NFA processing is very inefficient, because the NFA state table is deployed on the slow DDR3 SDRAM. What's worse, the NFA state accesses are very irregular. Hardware engines must wait for the results returning from the DDR3 SDRAM, which may cost hundreds of cycles for each query. Even we can achieve a considerably high speed for the DFA part, the overall performance is still seriously limited by the NFA part.

To break this bottleneck, we further propose the novel hybrid matching architecture to eliminate the time waiting for NFA processing. This hybrid architecture turns the original synchronous process to a asynchronous process. Anytime when the NFA part is activated, the corresponding hardware engine transfers the rest task to the multi-core processors completely. After that, the hardware engine is ready to process the next stream payload. Then the task distributor thread on the multi-core platform assigns the unfinished task to an idle software engine, and this software engine will be responsible for the matching of rest payload bytes. As only the byte position and current active states need to be passed to software engine, the transmission overhead can be ignored. Figure 2(b) illustrates a general matching example with this architecture, and different colors of input bytes represent the different matching stages and memory accesses as indicated.

3.3   Matching Process of the Hybrid Architecture

Figure 3 represents the hybrid-FA based matching process on the hybrid architecture. For each payload, a hardware engine starts the matching process with the initial DFA state. Each time the engine reads one byte from the input stream, then it acquire the DFA state table for the next active DFA state. The state table maybe on the RAM bank of FPGA or the off-chip DDR3 SDRAM, according to

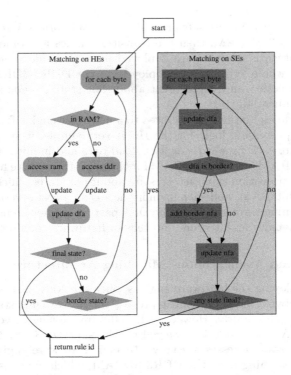

Fig. 3. Hybrid-FA based matching process on the hybrid architecture

whether the acquired DFA state is a hot state. The matching process is terminated if a final DFA state is reached, namely a rule is matched. The NFA part is activated if the current DFA state is a border state. Then the matching process on the hardware engine is finished, the current matching status and the finished position are sent to the multi-core platform, and this hardware engine is ready to process the next stream.

The software engines also work parallelly and independently. The task distributor thread is responsible for the task schedule on the multi-core platform. Each time it fetches a uncompleted task, and allocate it to a idle software matching engine. The software engine starts with the current state and position of the task. Each time it reads one byte from the input stream, and handles the handles the active DFA state and active NFA state synchronously. The process is terminated if any active DFA state or NFA state is a final state, then the corresponding rule ID is returned.

3.4   Analysis of the Matching Performance

With this mechanism, the hardware engines can focus on the efficient and regular DFA matching and leave the inefficient and irregular NFA matching to software engines. More important, the original integrated process is divided into two

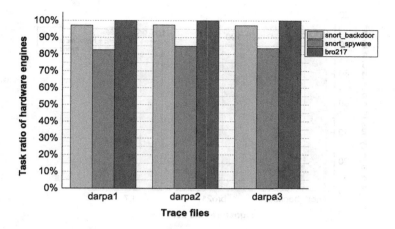

Fig. 4. Task ratio of hardware engines

independent stages which can be pipelined. Now the only problem is how to guarantee that the performance on multi-core processors can keep up with the throughput of hardware engines on FPGA. To make the pipeline work efficiently, we must guarantee that

$$\frac{pay\_len * TaskRatio_{HE}}{Speed_{HE}} \geqslant \frac{pay\_len * TaskRatio_{SE}}{Speed_{SE}} \tag{1}$$

where $TaskRatio_{HE}$ means the payload ratio processed by HEs and $TaskRatio_{SE}$ represents the left payload ratio processed by SEs. One step further, namely

$$\frac{TaskRatio_{HE}}{TaskRatio_{SE}} \geqslant \frac{Speed_{HE}}{Speed_{SE}} \tag{2}$$

Fortunately, the features of hybrid-FA can guarantee that for most streams the NFA activation occurs at the very end of the corresponding payload, or never occurs for some streams. Figure 4 presents the task ratio of hardware engines for different rule sets and trace files. On average, HEs handle 90% packet payloads and SE process the left 10%. In other words, as long as the throughput of software part can reach 1/9 of the hardware part, the overall performance can keep up with the hardware part. It is not difficult to achieve that goal, as multi-core processors have abundant resources and massive threads to handle these tasks concurrently.

3.5   Simulation Results

Figure 5 shows that, for each kind of architecture the cycles cost for processing one payload byte on average. Three rule sets from Snort [5], Bro [2] and L7-filter [1] are tested, each signature set has more than three million states when converting to a pure DFA. We compare the hybrid architecture with the traditional

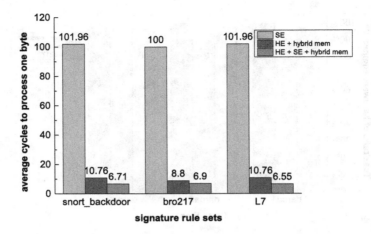

Fig. 5. Simulation results for different architectures

memory centric architecture and the pure hardware engines on memory centric FPGA.

Here we assume the memory access latency is 4 cycles for on-chip RAM and 100 cycles for DDR3 SDRAM, and the hit ratio of on-chip RAM is set as 90%. When only employing software engines, the cost is equal or greater than DDR3 memory access latency, according to the number of NFA activation. When employing the hardware engines with two-stage memory, the cost is highly reduced to tens of cycles, because most memory accesses are captured by on-chip RAM. The actual cost for hardware engines should be much higher, because for hardware engines the processing logic would be much more complex if both DFA part and NFA part are processed together. Finally, when combining them together, the cost is further reduced to a few cycles. In addition to the benefit from two-stage memory architecture of hardware engines, the hybrid architecture can separate the slow NFA part and process them in pipeline, thus to further improve the overall matching speed.

4   Conclusion

Regular expression matching (REM) is the core component of deep packet inspection applications. Due to the ever-increasing scale and complexity of current rule sets, fast REM is facing grate challenges for the state explosion problem. The hybrid-FA is the most practical automaton for REM, but it can not perform well on general memory centric platforms for its inner limitations, including the large memory access latencies and the bottleneck of the NFA part processing.

In this paper, we specially devise a novel hybrid matching architecture for the hybrid-FA. The hybrid architecture is composed of hardware engines on memory centric FPGA and software engines on multi-core processors. Then the DFA part is processed on the fast hardware engines and the NFA part is processed on the slow software engines. In general cases, most of the payload bytes are processed by the DFA part, thus whole matching can be pipelined well even the software engines are much slower than hardware engines. To further reduce the memory access latencies of hardware engines, a two-stage memory architecture is built based on the fast on-chip RAMs of FPGA and large off-chip DDR3 SDRAM. Experiments are conducted on three practical rule sets, and the results show that our hybrid architecture performs 15x faster than the general memory centric platforms for the state of the art hybrid-FA.

Acknowledgments. This work was supported in part by National Science Foundation of China under grant No. 61379148 and No. 61202488, and the outstanding young scholar funding of NUDT.

References

1. Application layer packet classifier for linux (2009). http://l7-filter.sourceforge.net/
2. Bro intrusion detection system (2014). http://www.bro.org/
3. Broadcom, xlp700 series. https://www.broadcom.com/products/enterprise-and-network-processors/processors/xlp700-series
4. Cavium, octeon5860. http://www.cavium.com/OCTEON_MIPS64.html/
5. Snort v2.9 (2014). http://www.snort.org/
6. Becchi, M., Cadambi, S.: Memory-efficient regular expression search using state merging. In: INFOCOM 2007, Proceedings of the 26th IEEE International Conference on Computer Communications, pp. 1064–1072. IEEE (2007)
7. Becchi, M., Crowley, P.: A hybrid finite automaton for practical deep packet inspection. In: Proceedings of the 2007 ACM CoNEXT Conference, p. 1. ACM (2007)
8. Becchi, M., Crowley, P.: Efficient regular expression evaluation: theory to practice. In: Proceedings of the 4th ACM/IEEE Symposium on Architectures for Networking and Communications Systems, pp. 50–59. ACM (2008)
9. Becchi, M., Crowley, P.: A-DFA: a time-and space-efficient DFA compression algorithm for fast regular expression evaluation. ACM Trans. Arch. Code Optim. (TACO) **10**(1), 4 (2013)
10. Chen, S., Lu, R.: A regular expression matching engine with hybrid memories. Comput. Stand. Interfaces **36**(5), 880–888 (2014)
11. Kong, S., Smith, R., Estan, C.: Efficient signature matching with multiple alphabet compression tables. In: Proceedings of the 4th International Conference on Security and Privacy in Communication Networks, p. 1. ACM (2008)
12. Kumar, S., Chandrasekaran, B., Turner, J., Varghese, G.: Curing regular expressions matching algorithms from insomnia, amnesia, and acalculia. In: Proceedings of the 3rd ACM/IEEE Symposium on Architecture for Networking and Communications Systems, pp. 155–164. ACM (2007)
13. Kumar, S., Dharmapurikar, S., Yu, F., Crowley, P., Turner, J.: Algorithms to accelerate multiple regular expressions matching for deep packet inspection. ACM SIGCOMM Comput. Commun. Rev. **36**(4), 339–350 (2006)
14. La Polla, M., Martinelli, F., Sgandurra, D.: A survey on security for mobile devices. IEEE Commun. Surv. Tutor. **15**(1), 446–471 (2013)
15. Liu, A.X., Torng, E.: An overlay automata approach to regular expression matching. In: INFOCOM, 2014 Proceedings IEEE, pp. 952–960. IEEE (2014)

16. Liu, T., Liu, A.X., Shi, J., Sun, Y., Guo, L.: Towards fast and optimal grouping of regular expressions via DFA size estimation. IEEE J. Sel. Areas Commun. **32**(10), 1797–1809 (2014)
17. Patel, J., Liu, A.X., Torng, E.: Bypassing space explosion in high-speed regular expression matching. IEEE/ACM Trans. Netw. (TON) **22**(6), 1701–1714 (2014)
18. Qi, Y., Wang, K., Fong, J., Xue, Y., Li, J., Jiang, W., Prasanna, V.: Feacan: front-end acceleration for content-aware network processing. In: INFOCOM, 2011 Proceedings IEEE, pp. 2114–2122. IEEE (2011)
19. Smith, R., Estan, C., Jha, S.: XFA: faster signature matching with extended automata. In: IEEE Symposium on Security and Privacy, SP 2008, pp. 187–201. IEEE (2008)
20. Wang, K., Fu, Z., Hu, X., Li, J.: Practical regular expression matching free of scalability and performance barriers. Comput. Commun. **54**, 97–119 (2014)
21. Xu, Y., Jiang, J., Wei, R., Song, Y., Chao, H.J.: TFA: a tunable finite automaton for pattern matching in network intrusion detection systems. IEEE J. Sel. Areas Commun. **32**(10), 1810–1821 (2014)
22. Yang, Y., Prasanna, V.K.: Space-time tradeoff in regular expression matching with semi-deterministic finite automata. In: INFOCOM, 2011 Proceedings IEEE, pp. 1853–1861. IEEE (2011)
23. Yu, F., Chen, Z., Diao, Y., Lakshman, T., Katz, R.H.: Fast and memory-efficient regular expression matching for deep packet inspection. In: Proceedings of the 2006 ACM/IEEE Symposium on Architecture for Networking and Communications Systems, pp. 93–102. ACM (2006)
24. Sbeyti, H., Malli, M., Al-Tahat, K., Fadlallah, A., Youssef, M.: Scalable extensible middleware framework for context-aware mobile applications (SCAMMP). J. Wirel. Mob. Netw. Ubiquitous Comput. Dependable Appl. (JoWUA) **7**(3), 77–98 (2016)
25. Carniani, E., Costantino, G., Marino, F., Martinelli, F., Mori, P.: Enhancing video surveillance with usage control and privacy-preserving solutions. J. Wirel. Mob. Netw. Ubiquitous Comput. Dependable Appl. (JoWUA) **7**, 41–64 (2016)
26. Kitana, A., Traore, I., Woungang, I.: Impact study of a mobile botnet over LTE networks. J. Internet Serv. Inf. Secur. (JISIS) **6**(2), 1–22 (2016)
27. Kim, N.Y., Shim, J., Cho, S., Park, M., Han, S.: Android application protection against static reverse engineering based on multidexing. J. Internet Serv. Inf. Secur. (JISIS) **6**(4), 54–64 (2016)

Author Index

Printed in the United States
By Bookmasters

Printed in the United States
By Bookmasters